STYLE IN *HAMLET*

STYLE IN
HAMLET

BY MAURICE CHARNEY

Princeton University Press
Princeton, New Jersey
1969

Printed in the United States of America
by Princeton University Press
Princeton, New Jersey

For
Benjamin and Sadie Charney
les fidèles

Acknowledgments

I AM obliged to Terence Spencer, Director of the Shakespeare Institute, for permitting me to read two short papers to the Shakespeare Conference at Stratford on Avon: *"Hamlet* Without Words" (1964) and "Parody in *Hamlet"* (1966) ; I have gratefully profited from the comments of the audience. The earlier paper was published in an expanded form in *ELH*, XXXII (1965), 457-77, whose editor has given permission to use it, much revised, in the present book. Two chapters of *Style in "Hamlet"* have been presented in the Renaissance Seminar of Columbia University, and its members offered many good suggestions. The Research Council of Rutgers University and its gracious Associate Director, C. F. Main, have given generous support to this project at all stages of its progress.

I wish to thank Bridget Gellert and S. F. Johnson for reading the manuscript and making copious comments. Both James G. McManaway and Donald M. Frame offered valuable observations by letter, and Louise Cason was also notably helpful. Among many books on *Hamlet*, I must record a special debt to Harry Levin's *The Question of Hamlet* (New York, 1961), which makes an eloquent contribution to the study of Shakespeare's style without insisting on that particular word. Finally, my intellectual wife should be remembered for tirelessly and tactfully putting me out of my humor.

Contents

Acknowledgments   vii

Key to References   xi

Introduction   xv

PART ONE: IMAGERY

1. War, Weapons, and Explosives   6
2. Secrecy and Poison   31
3. Corruption   53
   Animals   63
   Disease   75
   Food   89
   Gardens   102
4. Limits   114
   Confinement   115
   Money and Numbers   123
5. Art, Acting, and the Theater   137

PART TWO: STAGING AND STRUCTURE

6. Gesture and Stage Action   161
7. Sound Effects and Music, Costumes, and Stage Properties   177
8. "The Very Cunning of the Scene"   196

PART THREE: DRAMATIC CHARACTER

9. Claudius: "Break not your sleeps for that"   221
10. Polonius: " 'Beautified' is a vile phrase"— " 'Mobled queen' is good"   242
11. Hamlet: "How pregnant sometimes his replies are"   258
    Hamlet as Artist and Critic   258

CONTENTS

The Self-Conscious Style 267

The Witty Style 286

The Passionate Style 295

The Simple Style 305

Conclusion 314

Index 321

Key to References

ALL quotations from *Hamlet* are from the edition by Edward Hubler in the Signet Shakespeare (New York, 1963). This edition, based on Quarto 2, is especially useful for its scrupulous handling of the stage directions. All significant departures from Hubler's text are indicated in the notes, and some proofreading errors of the first edition have been corrected. Other works of Shakespeare are quoted from the one-volume Tudor edition by Peter Alexander (London, 1951), except where otherwise noted. I have also used facsimile editions of the First Folio edited by Helge Kökeritz (New Haven: Yale University Press, 1954); Quarto 2, 1604 (San Marino, Calif.: Huntington Library, 1938); and Quarto 1 (Cambridge, Mass.: Harvard University Press, 1931). Quotations from these texts have been modernized.

Information about the incidence of words is based on *A New and Complete Concordance* to Shakespeare by John Bartlett (London, 1896). Although there are a striking number of words that occur more often in *Hamlet* than in any other play, it is well to keep in mind that this is Shakespeare's longest play. The section on *Hamlet* in Marvin Spevack's new, computer-made concordance (*A Complete and Systematic Concordance to the Works of Shakespeare*, Volume III [Hildesheim, Germany, 1968]) appeared too late for me to use in this study. It is apparent from Spevack's data that Bartlett's entries are extremely incomplete. Dates of Elizabethan plays are given from Alfred Harbage, *Annals of*

English Drama 975-1700 (rev. S. Schoenbaum; London, 1964). Standard dictionaries such as the *Oxford English Dictionary* (abbreviated *OED*), C. T. Onions' *A Shakespeare Glossary*, and Alexander Schmidt's *Shakespeare-Lexicon* (3 edn., rev. Gregor Sarrazin) have been used freely, without quotation marks or footnote references.

The following frequently cited works are indicated in abbreviated form:

1. Kittredge: for *The Tragedy of Hamlet,* ed. George Lyman Kittredge (Boston, 1939).

2. Parrott and Craig: for *The Tragedy of Hamlet: A Critical Edition of the Second Quarto,* ed. Thomas Marc Parrott and Hardin Craig (Princeton: Princeton University Press, 1938).

3. Tilley: for Morris Palmer Tilley, *A Dictionary of the Proverbs in England in the Sixteenth and Seventeenth Centuries* (Ann Arbor: University of Michigan Press, 1950).

4. Travers: for *Shakespeare: Hamlet,* ed. R. Travers (Paris, [1934]). In the Hachette series of Classiques Anglais.

5. *Variorum*: for *A New Variorum Edition of Shakespeare: Hamlet,* ed. Horace Howard Furness (2 vols.; New York: Dover reprint, 1963). First published, 1877.

6. Wilson: for *Hamlet,* ed. John Dover Wilson (Cambridge, Eng.: Cambridge University Press, 1957). New Cambridge edition. First published, 1934; 2nd edn., 1936.

Frequently cited periodicals are abbreviated as follows:

1. *PMLA*: for *Publications of the Modern Language Association of America.*

2. *RES*: for *Review of English Studies.*

3. *SQ*: for *Shakespeare Quarterly.*

4. *SS*: for *Shakespeare Survey.*

Introduction

HAMLET has become a cultural manifestation, a show-case for the historically conditioned madness of critics. When Coleridge says, "I have a smack of Hamlet myself, if I may say so,"[1] and Hazlitt tells us, "It is *we* who are Hamlet,"[2] and Freiligrath exclaims, "Deutschland ist Hamlet!",[3] we know that we have crossed from the secure domain of art into the perilous precincts of life. The word "Hamlet" is defined in most reference books in a way that reflects the cultural tradition of Hamletism. From *Webster's New International Dictionary* (second edition) we learn that "The ghost of the murdered king lays upon Hamlet the duty of avenging him, but Hamlet's habit of mind leads only to repeated postponing of action." Funk and Wagnall's *Standard College Dictionary* (1963) informs us that Hamlet is "a Danish prince whose indecision conflicts with his efforts to avenge the murder of his father." And *The Oxford Companion to English Literature* (fourth edition) offers the most explicit statement of this point of view: "Hamlet vows obedience [to the Ghost]; but his melancholy, introspective, and scrupulous nature makes him irresolute and dilatory in action."

This is not the Hamlet of Shakespeare's play, but

[1] *Coleridge's Writings on Shakespeare*, ed. Terence Hawkes (New York, 1959), p. 140. From *Table Talk*, June 24, 1827.

[2] William Hazlitt, *Characters of Shakespear's Plays* (1817), in *Liber Amoris and Dramatic Criticisms* (London, 1948), p. 247.

[3] Quoted in T.J.B. Spencer, "The Decline of Hamlet," in *Hamlet*, Stratford upon Avon Studies 5 (London, 1963), p. 194.

the more empathic and transcendental hero produced by Romanticism. Conceived on the tragic model of the poet, he is a brooding procrastinator and ineffectual intellectual, whose reflective nature hamstrings his ability to act, and who is constantly affirming how impossible it is for a sensitive and creative spirit to live in this world. According to this version, hesitation about murdering your uncle is the product of a deliciously morbid introspection, so that Laertes is an altogether healthier and more natural young man than Hamlet. I believe, of course, that the Romantic Hamlet is a mythical figure, but myths are different from literary criticism, and cultural manifestations do not depend upon an accurate reading of literary texts.

Style in "Hamlet" is not intended to explode our traditional notions, but only to take another close look at the play. I try to track puns to their most secret hiding places, to revive significances in the language and in the staging that may have long since faded, and to indicate relationships and inner coherences that may not be immediately apparent to reader or spectator. My commitment is strongly historical throughout—it is, in other words, to a *Hamlet* "possible" at the turn of the seventeenth century in England—but I do not tremble at the notion of an anachronistic palimpsest consciously laid on by a modern critic. As much as we may try to work within the meaningful limits of historical truth, there is no way of "fixing" *Hamlet* at one moment of time.

Style has generally been neglected by critics of Shakespeare, as if it could only be studied impressionistically as a branch of belletristics, or objectively as an aspect of linguistic description. I steer a middle course between the schools of admiration and of computation, although I am certainly closer to the former. Brevity may be the soul of wit, but I have knowingly developed *Style in "Hamlet"* as fully as possible in order to present a sample analysis of a Shakespearean play. My secret wish is that this book, through its persistence and comprehensiveness, may suggest an approach suitable to other plays of Shakespeare.

I choose to interpret style in its widest sense, which ⟨...⟩ of expression used by an author ⟨...⟩ this broad meaning it ⟨...⟩ embodiment of a theme ⟨...⟩ e manner. An author's ⟨...⟩ mark, but one that can ⟨...⟩ nt ways over the course of his work. In Shakespeare's career, for example, his style is never self-consistent or homogeneous for very long. Even at the height of his powers, he seems to have had the uncontrollable urge to experiment, perhaps only to emulate his colleagues, as in the social realism of *The Merry Wives of Windsor*—a style in which Jonson and Dekker were then scoring their most notable successes.

We need to take some account of the fact that Shakespeare does not always choose to do things that he is good at, nor does he seem to have the impulse to produce a large number of similar and safe masterpieces. In *Julius Caesar*, for example, he seems to be trying out a special "Roman" style, limited in diction, imagery, and imaginative devices, almost at the very moment that he is composing *Hamlet*, which is certainly his most unlimited, most unconventional, and most stylistically inventive play. As Alfred Hart informs us, *Hamlet* has more than 600 fresh or previously unused words, nearly 400 of which do not recur in any later play. About 170 of these fresh words appear for the first time in English literature, and the 3,882 words of *Hamlet* constitute the "largest and most expressive vocabulary" in Shakespeare.[4]

The sense of infinite variety in Shakespeare's style should suggest that he was much more deliberate about the effects he was trying to achieve than we now generally believe. I would not want to broach the question of whether Shakespeare knowingly created patterns of imagery or developed elaborate contrasts and analogies between characters. Luckily, we don't need to establish Shakespeare's purposiveness before we can speak about his style. It would be more profitable to look at the limiting preconditions within which he worked. In considering *Hamlet*, for example, we must begin with the fact that it is an Elizabethan tragedy, written primarily in blank verse. It is also a revenge play, which has a strong but puzzling relation to the conventions and traditions of other revenge plays.

Style in "Hamlet" is divided into three parts. Imagery is the topic of the long first section, which attempts to fill a need recently noted by Kenneth Muir: "It is curious that no one has made a detailed investigation of the

4 Alfred Hart, "Vocabularies of Shakespeare's Plays," *RES*, XIX (1943), 135.

imagery of *Hamlet* and *Macbeth*."[5] I owe an obvious debt to Heilman's admirable books on *King Lear* and *Othello*.[6] My earlier book, *Shakespeare's Roman Plays* (Harvard University Press, 1961), emphasized the function of imagery in the drama, but *Style in "Hamlet"* is freer from methodological commitment. I now believe that the study of imagery cannot be separated from a larger concern with style.

The first part of the present book explores the symbolism of war, weapons, and explosives, as well as of secrecy and poison, in both their verbal and nonverbal development. Weapons, for example, are the subject of metaphors and nonfigurative references, but they are also stage properties that enter directly into the action. Secrecy may be studied in this same double way, since the eavesdropping scenes on stage support the verbal theme. The longest chapter, on the imagery of corruption, grows out of the familiar order-disorder symbolism of animals, disease, food, and gardens, and tries to suggest some new possibilities. The chapter on limits, dealing with the imagery of confinement, money, and numbers, is itself designed to test the limits of criticism in explicating a play. Part One ends with a speculative chapter on art, acting, and the theater, in which I consider Shakespeare's terms of art and professional allusions.

[5] Kenneth Muir, "Imagery and Symbolism in *Hamlet*," *Etudes Anglaises*, XVII (1964), 352.

[6] Robert Bechtold Heilman, *This Great Stage: Image and Structure in King Lear* (Baton Rouge: Louisiana State University Press, 1948), and *Magic in the Web: Action and Language in Othello* (Lexington: University of Kentucky Press, 1956).

The middle section of the book, on staging and structure, continues the discussion of imagery in nonverbal, presentational terms. Our elusive *"Hamlet* without words" is made up of gesture and stage action, sound effects and music, costumes, stage properties, and the sequences of contrasted scenes. All these topics represent style in its theatrical aspect. The sounds of *Hamlet,* for example, may be as significant a part of the play as the words—they are not in any sense a mere adjunct of the production. To understand Claudius, one must take account of his noisy and flamboyant rouses, when he drinks healths to the accompaniment of drums, trumpets, and the firing of cannon outside the theater. These sound effects work together with verbal themes to establish Claudius as a dominating presence in the play.

Dramatic character is the subject of the final section, and in it I try to resuscitate the valetudinarian topic of character analysis by separating character from psychological motivation. Once the dramatis personae are no longer burdened by the need to be real people, we can look at their typical modes of expression as devices of characterization. We can thus approach the roles in *Hamlet* from the standpoint of the actor in order to see in what ways they have been individualized. Brief chapters on the styles of Claudius and Polonius lead up to a long chapter on Hamlet, who is presented in terms of his self-conscious, witty, passionate, and simple styles. As a character, he represents Shakespeare's most sustained stylistic experiment.

The drama as a form raises difficult questions about style, since many of its effects are a matter of presentation rather than language, and the momentary realization of these effects on stage has an elusive, unverifiable quality very different from that of words on the printed page. Readers and critics alike generally solve this problem by agreeing among themselves to ignore Shakespeare the dramatist in favor of Shakespeare the poet. We applaud, tacitly at least, the judgment of Lamb, with its emphasis on soliloquy:

> Why, nine parts in ten of what Hamlet does, are transactions between himself and his moral sense, they are the effusions of his solitary musings, which he retires to holes and corners and the most sequestered parts of the palace to pour forth; or rather, they are the silent meditations with which his bosom is bursting, reduced to *words* for the sake of the reader, who must else remain ignorant of what is passing there. These profound sorrows, these light-and-noise-abhorring ruminations, which the tongue scarce dares utter to deaf walls and chambers, how can they be represented by a gesticulating actor, who comes and mouths them out before an audience, making four hundred people his confidants at once?[7]

Hazlitt, therefore, is only echoing received opinion when he says: "We do not like to see our author's plays acted, and least of all, *Hamlet*. There is no play that suffers so much in being transferred to the stage."[8]

[7] Charles Lamb, "On the Tragedies of Shakspeare, considered with reference to their fitness for Stage Representation" (1811), in *Shakespeare Criticism: A Selection*, ed. D. Nichol Smith (London: Oxford University Press, 1916), p. 195.

[8] Hazlitt, *Characters of Shakespear's Plays*, p. 254.

This point of view may perhaps be justified by Shakespearean productions of the early nineteenth century, but the divorce between the theater and dramatic literature is also responsible for the worst vagaries of Romantic criticism. We would not today have the audacity to put these arguments in the same form as Lamb and Hazlitt, but our assumptions about Shakespeare and the theater are similar to theirs. This is unfortunate, especially for our understanding of style, since by separating Shakespeare's plays from their natural and life-giving context in the theater, we rob them of their most characteristic excellences.

PART ONE
IMAGERY

BY THIS time, we should have recovered from the sanguine hopes of early students of Shakespeare's imagery to pluck out the heart of his mystery and show "the very age and body of the time his form and pressure" (3.2.24-25). The tables and bar graphs (in color) of Caroline Spurgeon's *Shakespeare's Imagery and What It Tells Us* cannot conceal the fact that everything depends not on the counting of images, but on Miss Spurgeon's intuition. I believe that the statistics in this book are completely erroneous, partly because they are based on a limited notion of what an image is and partly because of overlapping and vaguely defined subject-matter categories. Yet the book retains its enormous value for students of Shakespeare because Miss Spurgeon is such an astute critic. The images do not provide the inductive data from which conclusions may be drawn, as she would like us to believe, but rather serve to support and to illustrate her understanding of the plays.

In her discussion of *Hamlet*, Miss Spurgeon's concern with the imagery of disease and corruption reflects a standard nineteenth-century interpretation, and her preoccupation with Hamlet himself, almost to the exclusion of all other characters, is a part of this approach. It is not from any objective count of the images that Miss Spurgeon reaches the following conclusion:

> To Shakespeare's pictorial imagination, therefore, the problem in *Hamlet* is not predominantly that of will and reason, of a mind too philosophic or a nature

temperamentally unfitted to act quickly; he sees it pictorially *not as the problem of an individual at all,* but as something greater and even more mysterious, as a *condition* for which the individual himself is apparently not responsible, any more than the sick man is to blame for the infection which strikes and devours him, but which, nevertheless, in its course and development, impartially and relentlessly, annihilates him and others, innocent and guilty alike. That is the tragedy of *Hamlet,* as it is perhaps the chief tragic mystery of life.[1]

I do not wish to dispute the truth of this statement, since I believe that the imagery of disease helps to set the tone of *Hamlet,* but I would take issue with the sense of morbid passivity that this paragraph conveys. It seems to have more relevance to the tragic universe of Thomas Hardy than to that of Shakespeare. Even such a careful study as W. H. Clemen's *The Development of Shakespeare's Imagery* shares Miss Spurgeon's narrow emphasis on disease.

It is only recently that Kenneth Muir has ventured to challenge the dominance of disease imagery in *Hamlet.*[2] By studying the images in context, he has shown that they have a meaning different from that supposed

---

[1] Caroline F. E. Spurgeon, *Shakespeare's Imagery and What It Tells Us* (Boston, 1958), pp. 318-19. First published by Cambridge University Press, 1935.

[2] Muir, "Imagery and Symbolism in *Hamlet,*" pp. 352-63. See also Muir's brief volume in the Studies in English Literature series (No. 13): *Shakespeare: Hamlet* (London, 1963), esp. pp. 13-19.

by Spurgeon and Clemen: "It is apparent from this analysis of the sickness imagery in the play that it throws light on Elsinore rather than on Hamlet himself. He is not the diseased figure depicted by a long line of critics —or, at least, the imagery cannot justifiably be used in support of such an interpretation."[3] The theory of a sick Hamlet in a sick world is not an objective, scientific truth arrived at by assembling all the relevant data, but a familiar notion that suggests itself quite independently of any concern for images.

I cannot claim that my interpretation of *Hamlet* is the inevitable product of an inductive study of its imagery. In the discussion that follows I stress certain symbolic themes rather than others partly because of the iterative patterns I find in the play, but also partly because of what I am looking for. Different critics, starting with different preconceptions and different values, are likely to arrive at very different results even in so factual a topic as the subject matter of the images. In short, one cannot separate the image from what it images, the vehicle from the tenor. To claim otherwise would be to give the image a spuriously autonomous status.

[3] Muir, "Imagery and Symbolism in *Hamlet*," p. 356.

1. War, Weapons, and Explosives

IF WE believe that *Hamlet* is a vigorous and active play, an exciting and at times vicious struggle for survival between Hamlet and Claudius and their allies, then we must logically begin our discussion not with disease, but with war, weapons, and explosives. This imagery enters Miss Spurgeon's book only in the appendix,[1] and in Clemen there is no more than a passing mention of "the soldier's trade and strategy."[2] By Kenneth Muir's reckoning, however, the largest group of images in *Hamlet* is derived from war: "The images of war and violence should have the effect of counteracting some interpretations of the play, in which the psychology of the hero is regarded as the centre of interest."[3] I strongly agree with Muir, and I shall try in this chapter to show how the military imagery establishes a point of view. The most important subject matter is weapons and explosives, with emphasis on their ability to destroy. This imagery forces us to see the action of the play as a relation between antagonist and protagonist, "the pass and fell incensèd points/ Of mighty opposites" (5.2.61-62), and not as a dramatized projection of a single character. We are not allowed to forget "that Claudius and

---

[1] Spurgeon, *Shakespeare's Imagery*, p. 369.

[2] W. H. Clemen, *The Development of Shakespeare's Imagery* (London, 1951), p. 108. First published in German in a longer version (Bonn, 1936).

[3] Muir, "Imagery and Symbolism in *Hamlet*," p. 363. See also R. A. Foakes's admirable essay, "*Hamlet* and the Court of Elsinore," *SS*, IX (1956), 35-43, which calls our attention to the "frequent imagery of war" (p. 36).

Hamlet are engaged in a duel to the death, a duel which does ultimately lead to both their deaths."[4]

Let us begin with Hamlet's sword, and it is worth dwelling on this humble property if only to dispel those perfumed clouds that still hang about the "sweet Prince" (5.2.360). We should remember the Hamlet so vividly evoked for us by Ophelia, the "courtier's, soldier's, scholar's, eye, tongue, sword" (3.1.154), and we ought not to be surprised that he acquits himself so well with his weapon. In his first encounter with the Ghost, he breaks away from the grip of Horatio and Marcellus and threatens to draw his sword to support his menacing pun: "Unhand me, gentlemen./ By heaven, I'll make a ghost of him that lets me!" (1.4.84-85). In Elizabethan English there is a quibble on the contradictory meanings of "lets": hinders and allows. Hamlet is saying that he will run through whoever tries to obstruct him, if indeed that person is so foolhardy as to permit himself to be made a ghost. The punning suggests the bravado so strong in Hamlet's murder of Polonius. At the end of the scene with the Ghost, Hamlet insists that his companions swear a formal oath of secrecy on his sword, whose hilt forms a cross, and the Ghost seconds him from *"under the stage"*: "Swear by his sword" (1.5.148 s.d., 161).

In Hamlet's "To be, or not to be" soliloquy, he debates the alternatives of suffering "outrageous fortune," or taking "arms against a sea of troubles" (3.1.58-59). This image has caused undue grief to pictorially minded persons, who want the "sea of troubles" to be an actual

[4] Muir, "Imagery and Symbolism in *Hamlet*," p. 361.

sea and Hamlet a Celtic warrior combating the foamy flood with sword in hand. The unheroic alternative to taking arms is the "bare bodkin" (76), a diminutive weapon, a pocket dagger, a stiletto, or perhaps only a long hairpin or an instrument for piercing holes in cloth. It is a "bare bodkin," a mere bodkin, in the sense that even with a bodkin one "might his quietus make" (75) —one doesn't need a sword. In *Richard II*, Death "with a little pin/ Bores through his castle wall, and farewell, king!" (3.2.169-70). "Bodkin" is also the familiar diminutive of the oath "God's bodkin" (2.2.540) or "bodikin," meaning the dear little body of God.

Hamlet's use of sword imagery follows the dramatic action to a climax after *The Mousetrap*, when he is intent upon his revenge. In a strongly homicidal mood, which begins with the soliloquy at the end of Act III, Scene ii and continues through the soliloquy in Act IV, Scene iv and his departure for England, Hamlet attempts to play the swaggering role of stage revenger. More than a verbal link connects "Now could I drink hot blood" (3.2.398) and "O, from this time forth,/ My thoughts be bloody, or be nothing worth!" (4.4.65-66). At the end of Act III, Scene ii Hamlet is wrestling with the active possibility that he may, like Nero, be tempted to kill his mother. He needs to curb his own murderous impulses by an act of will: "Let me be cruel, not unnatural;/ I will speak daggers to her, but use none" (403-4); and Gertrude then confirms her symbolic stabbing in almost the same image: "These words like daggers enter in my ears" (3.4.96).

Hamlet's soliloquy at the end of Act III, Scene ii is

continued in the soliloquy of the next scene, less than
seventy-five lines away, in which he debates with himself
whether to stab Claudius in the back while he is praying.
Hamlet draws his sword quickly and unthinkingly, and,
as he considers the possibilities of a satisfying revenge,
he keeps the sword poised in his hand to emphasize his
murderous intent. When he sheathes it at line 88—"Up,
sword"—it is not from any tenderness of conscience, but
only to wait for "a more horrid hent," or a more damna-
tion-provoking occasion to seize it again. According to
the accepted canons of the stage revenger, it is not
enough just to kill a man: "Why, this is hire and salary,
not revenge" (3.3.79). One must do it quaintly, ingeniously, artistically, and if possible damn both body
and soul at one stroke, as Laertes hopes to do with Hamlet: "The devil take thy soul!" (5.1.260).

Hamlet imagines scenes that are histrionically and
aesthetically fitting for his "more horrid hent":

> When he is drunk asleep, or in his rage,
> Or in th' incestuous pleasure of his bed,
> At game a-swearing, or about some act
> That has no relish of salvation in't—
> Then trip him, that his heels may kick at heaven,
> And that his soul may be as damned and black
> As hell, whereto it goes.   (3.3.89-95)

In tripping up his enemy from behind at just the moment that will send him headfirst hellwards, Hamlet
puts himself in the company of Gamaliel Ratsey, Black
Will and Shakebag of *Arden of Feversham* (1591), and
the redoubtable Cutwolfe of *The Unfortunate Traveller*

(1594). Samuel Johnson was surely right in principle when he thought that "This speech, in which Hamlet, represented as a virtuous character, is not content with taking blood for blood, but contrives damnation for the man that he would punish, is too horrible to be read or to be uttered."[5]

The upshot of Hamlet's mood comes in the next scene, with the murder of Polonius. By invincible logic, after Gertrude and Claudius have been ruled out, Polonius becomes the obvious victim. This killing appeases for the moment Hamlet's desire to

> . . . drink hot blood
> And do such business as the bitter day[6]
> Would quake to look on. (3.2.398-400)

[5] "Notes to *Hamlet*" in *Johnson's Notes to Shakespeare*, ed. Arthur Sherbo, Augustan Reprint Society, Publication 73 (Los Angeles: 1958), p. 170. See also A. Clutton-Brock, *Shakespeare's "Hamlet"* (London, 1922), pp. 69-70, and Eleanor Prosser, *Hamlet and Revenge* (Stanford: Stanford University Press, 1967), pp. 183-91 and Appendix B.

[6] This is the reading of Quarto 2; Folio reads: "And do such bitter business as the day," which almost all editors except Steevens prefer (see *Variorum*, I, 273). It is curious that even such strong partisans of Quarto 2 as Parrott and Craig, Wilson, and Hubler reject "And do such business as the bitter day" without any comment, or with only the most perfunctory explanation, such as Parrott and Craig's claim that it is "a common printer's error of transposition" (p. 164). If the "bitter day" is Doomsday, then the phrase is particularly appropriate for Hamlet's dire imprecations in this soliloquy. At the "very witching time of night," "churchyards yawn" (3.2.396-97), and graves yield up the spirits of their dead, as they will do on the Day of Judgment. Hamlet means that he could now do such bloody "business" as even Doomsday would quake with fear to look upon.

The fact that it is not the king is only one of those unpredictable ironies that fall between the intent and the deed. Hamlet acts with all the swagger of the professional swordsman. On the first sound behind the arras, he "Whips out his rapier" (as we are told at 4.1.10) and strikes without any reflection, hesitation, or fear. He celebrates the death of his unseen opponent with a gambling image: "How now? A rat? Dead for a ducat, dead!" (3.4.25). We might almost be listening here to "The fiery Tybalt, with his sword prepar'd" (*Romeo and Juliet* 1.1.107).

It is not until the final scene of the play that Hamlet is fully convinced of the justice of his revenge. After a summary indictment of Claudius, he asks Horatio: "is't not perfect conscience/ To quit him with this arm?" (5.2.67-68). Hamlet's "arm" with which he will give Claudius his "quietus" (3.1.75) is both his limb and his sword, and the wordplay recalls the Clown's not-so-innocent pun in the graveyard: "'A was the first that ever bore arms" (5.1.34)—a reference more appropriate to Cain than to Adam. In this same prefiguring passage in Act V, Scene ii, Hamlet's curious assertion that "a man's life's no more than to say 'one'" (74) may refer to "the single thrust of a rapier,"[7] since he indicates his first hit in the fencing match with the exclamation "One" (281). This is the single stroke of justice with sword in hand.

Just before the encounter with Laertes, a sword image draws our attention to an obvious point: that Claudius, and not Laertes, is Hamlet's real antagonist. In Hamlet's

[7] Wilson, p. 243.

icy comment on the fate of Rosencrantz and Guildenstern, he imagines himself engaged in deadly rapier play
with Claudius:

> 'Tis dangerous when the baser nature comes
> Between the pass and fell incensèd points
> Of mighty opposites.   (5.2.60-62)

"Pass" is a technical term from dueling, as in the "dozen
passes" (166-67) of the king's wager and in the lethal
"pass of practice" by which Laertes is to "requite" Hamlet (4.7.138-39). Despite all provocations, Hamlet is
never capable of regarding Laertes as his enemy, even in
the outrageous scene in Ophelia's grave. There is genuine bewilderment in his question: "What is the reason that you use me thus?/ I loved you ever" (5.1.291-
92). This is a good example of the way in which the
dramatic action can move in an opposite direction from
the facts of the plot.

Laertes' sword enters directly into the action during
the fencing match, and his poor showing there has led
some tenderhearted persons to believe him hampered
because he is fighting "almost against my conscience"
(5.2.297). But this supposed sensibility of Laertes runs
counter to his ranting and diabolic tone as stage revenger. To show himself his father's son in deed "More
than in words," he is ready "To cut" Hamlet's "throat
i' th' church" (4.7.126), which completes his declaration
from the rebellion scene: "I dare damnation" (4.5.133).
And Laertes is the one who, not to be outdone by Claudius, suggests anointing his unbated sword with "an
unction of a mountebank,/ So mortal that, but dip a

knife in it," nothing "can save the thing from death/ That is but scratched withal" (4.7.141-42, 145-46). Polonius would have been proud of his son's ingenuity, since it was he who had advised him to

> Beware
> Of entrance to a quarrel; but being in,
> Bear't that th' opposèd may beware of thee.
> (1.3.65-67)

There is something direly prophetic in this, and Laertes' intense preoccupation with keeping his "name ungored" (5.2.251) seems also to stem from his father's precepts. One explanation for Laertes' weak fencing in Act V, Scene ii, then, is that the king has cozened him with flattery of his skill. "Thou know'st we work by wit, and not by witchcraft," says Iago (*Othello* 2.3.360), echoing the "witchcraft" of Claudius' "wits" (1.5.43).

The armed figure of Pyrrhus in the Player's speech[8] offers a striking analogy to Hamlet and Laertes and the sword imagery associated with them. Here, early in the play, in the passionate rhetoric of Aeneas' tale to Dido, is set forth the type figure of the revenger, emotionless and inhuman, intent only on slaughter. It is a non-psychological, flat portrait, but it is meant to provide an extreme by which to measure both Hamlet and Laertes, who at times come dangerously close to Pyrrhus. In Hamlet's opening lines, the "sable arms" of the "rugged Pyrrhus" (2.2.463) suggest the same wordplay

---

[8] See the elaborate explication of this speech in Harry Levin, *The Question of Hamlet* (New York, 1961). First published by Oxford University Press, 1959.

that we have noticed in 5.2.68: arms are both limbs and weapons, although here the former sense predominates. Pyrrhus is heraldically decked out in the "total gules" (2.2.468) of slaughter. His "fell sword" (484) is matched with the "antique sword" of old Priam, which, "Rebellious to his arm, lies where it falls,/ Repugnant to command" (480-82). "Antique" and "antic," two spellings of the same word, play on the related meanings of ancient and grotesque: this is Priam's "antic disposition" (1.5.172). Pyrrhus presses on like an irresistible, inhuman force, so that with the mere "whiff and wind of his fell sword/ Th' unnervèd father falls" (2.2.484-85). There is a momentary histrionic pause when Pyrrhus' sword, "Which was declining on the milky head/ Of reverend Priam, seemed i' th' air to stick" (489-90). The image anticipates the prayer scene, where Hamlet stands over the kneeling Claudius with his sword drawn, "And like a neutral to his will and matter/ Did nothing" (492-93).

Pyrrhus' "rousèd vengeance" (499) as a swordsman is heightened by mythological allusions:

> And never did the Cyclops' hammers fall
> On Mars's armor, forged for proof eterne,
> With less remorse than Pyrrhus' bleeding sword
> Now falls on Priam.   (2.2.500-3)

The rhetoric of this passage is Marlovian, especially the Latinism "bleeding sword" for "bloody sword," and the feeling of invidious comparison about the whole figure ("with less remorse than"). There is a final reflection of Pyrrhus at work as seen through the eyes of the "mobled queen" (513) : "When she saw Pyrrhus make malicious sport/ In mincing with his sword her husband's limbs" (524-25) . The cruelty of this "malicious sport" is much tempered by the formality of the style, although not, of course, for the First Player, whose strong emotions are intensified by the figures of speech.

The violence of swordplay in *Hamlet* is extended in a group of images derived from the sharpening of weapons, especially sword, knife, or ax. In his instructions to Rosencrantz and Guildenstern, Claudius advises them to give Hamlet "a further edge" (3.1.26) , as if he were the blade of a knife. During *The Mousetrap*, Hamlet uses the image of the knife-edge or sword-edge in a specifically phallic way; to Ophelia's "You are keen, my lord, you are keen," he replies provocatively: "It would cost you a groaning to take off mine edge" (3.2.254-56) . The transferred sense of sword is also present in the Ghost's admonition: "This visitation/ Is but to whet thy almost blunted purpose" (3.4.111-12) . Purpose should be a keen sword whetted by the will; the Ghost will not let Hamlet forget that, Shylock-like, he must sharpen his blade. The most amusing image of this sort occurs in Hamlet's report to Horatio of the fate prepared for him in England:

> That on the supervise, no leisure bated,
> No, not to stay the grinding of the ax,
> My head should be struck off.   (5.2.23-25)

Hamlet's revulsion at being killed with a dull ax is an aesthetic detail comparable in quality to his feeling for the lawyer in the graveyard now being knocked "about the sconce with a dirty shovel" (5.1.103).

The battle between the "mighty opposites" (5.2.62), Hamlet and Claudius, generates one of the primary images of *Hamlet*, whose reverberations are felt in most of the other characters, even "The fair Ophelia" (3.1. 89). Her chastity is represented in the Petrarchan conceit of a fortified castle assaulted by amorous knights. This sort of talk endows Act I, Scene iii with a good deal of military imagery. If "Virtue itself scapes not calumnious strokes" (38), what then is poor Ophelia to do? Both Laertes and Polonius think of Hamlet as an invincible ravisher, and Laertes imagines his sister yielding up her virginity in an alarmingly specific image: "or your chaste treasure open/ To his unmastered importunity" (31-32), which suggests the opening of the gates in a besieged town that has just capitulated.

Laertes tries to terrify his sister into retreating from the line of battle:

> Fear it, Ophelia, fear it, my dear sister,
> And keep you in the rear of your affection,
> Out of the shot and danger of desire.
>
> (1.3.33-35)

Desire is the enemy, well armed and aggressive, as Hamlet tells his mother: "Proclaim no shame/ When the compulsive ardor gives the charge" (3.4.86-87). In characteristic fashion, Laertes gives his sister the same sort of prudent and worldly advice that he is soon to receive from Polonius, but his speech is more long-winded and platitudinous than his father's: "Be wary then; best safety lies in fear; / Youth to itself rebels, though none else near" (1.3.43-44). In short, youth is a volatile substance that can explode even without contact.

Hamlet is a conspicuously noisy and active play, with more cannonading than any other work of Shakespeare.[9] The cannonading is particularly associated with the "rouses" (or carouses) of Claudius, his pledging of toasts and drinking of healths. The sound effects which accompany the "rouse" are carefully enumerated by the king just before the fencing match:

> Give me the cups,
> And let the kettle to the trumpet speak,
> The trumpet to the cannoneer without,[10]
> The cannons to the heavens, the heaven to earth,
> "Now the King drinks to Hamlet." (5.2.275-79)

The sequence begins with a roll on the kettledrums, which is followed by a trumpet fanfare, which is followed in turn by a firing of the theater cannon or "chambers." The extra rebounds from cannon to heaven

[9] See Frances Ann Shirley, *Shakespeare's Use of Off-Stage Sounds* (Lincoln: University of Nebraska Press, 1963), p. 83.

[10] The "cannoneer without" seems to indicate that he is not only outside the castle of Elsinore, but also that he is firing his "chambers" from just outside the Globe theater. To fire even a small cannon in the "huts" of the theater would seem to offer, at the least, a serious hazard to the plaster, if not to the building itself. See Shirley, *Shakespeare's Use of Off-Stage Sounds*, pp. 30-31. The Globe theater was burned down on June 29, 1613, when its thatched roof was ignited by "shooting off certain chambers in way of triumph" (E. K. Chambers, *The Elizabethan Stage* [London: Oxford University Press, 1923], II, 419).

and from heaven to earth are meant to show the "hubris" of Claudius, who thinks of himself as Jupiter *tonans*:

> No jocund health that Denmark drinks today,
> But the great cannon to the clouds shall tell,
> And the King's rouse the heaven shall bruit again,
> Respeaking earthly thunder.   (1.2.125-28)

We remember the familiar association of thunder with the wrath of the gods.

It is a significant dramatic irony that we hear the king's rouse offstage just before the Ghost appears in Act I, Scene iv. The Quarto 2 stage direction reads: "*A flourish of trumpets and two pieces goes off*" (1.4.6 s.d.), and there are also kettledrums in Hamlet's description:

> The King doth wake tonight and takes his rouse,
> Keeps wassail, and the swagg'ring upspring reels,
> And as he drains his draughts of Rhenish down
> The kettledrum and trumpet thus bray out
> The triumph of his pledge.   (1.4.8-12)

The drunken braying and brawling of Claudius and his court offstage prepare us for the confrontation with another king, "that was to this/ Hyperion to a satyr" (1.2.139-40). It is a bold study in contrasts, similar in effect to the offstage sounds of Caesar playing to the mob that punctuate Cassius' persuasion of Brutus in Act I, Scene ii of *Julius Caesar*.

The firing of cannon is strongly emphasized in the final scene of *Hamlet*. After the first hit in the fencing match, the Quarto 2 stage direction calls for *"Drum, trumpets, and shot. Flourish; a piece goes off"* (5.2.282 s.d.) . This is part of the formal asseveration, almost like applause, that the king has arranged to mask the realities of the scene:

> If Hamlet give the first or second hit,
> Or quit in answer of the third exchange,
> Let all the battlements their ordnance fire.
>
> (5.2.269-71)

It is a powerful and startling effect, a finely ironic celebration of one who is "Most generous, and free from all contriving" (4.7.135) .

After Hamlet has been mortally wounded by Laertes, the denouement is announced by the offstage sounds of Fortinbras and his army: *"March afar off, and shot[11] within"* (5.2.350 s.d., Folio) , at which Hamlet asks, "What warlike noise is this?" Osric, the factotum of the scene, announces:

> Young Fortinbras, with conquest come from Poland,
> To th' ambassadors of England gives
> This warlike volley. (5.2.351-53)

These martial sounds are almost the last thing that Hamlet hears, and they give him assurance of a new order of truth and justice in Denmark: "I do prophesy th' election lights/ On Fortinbras" (356-57) .

At the end of the play, it is Fortinbras who prepares

---

[11] The Folio reads *"shout,"* which was emended to *"shot"* by Steevens. Most modern editors, on the basis of 5.2.350 and 353, follow Steevens.

Hamlet's military funeral: "Let four captains/ Bear Hamlet like a soldier to the stage" (5.2.396-97). This answers Horatio's request, "give order that these bodies/ High on a stage be placèd to the view" (378-79); a "stage" is a raised platform or dais like the one on which Caesar's body rests during the orations of Brutus and Antony. Hamlet will be accorded all military honors, "all quality,/ Pride, pomp, and circumstance, of glorious war!" (*Othello* 3.3.357-58). As Fortinbras says in his final eulogy:

> For he was likely, had he been put on,
> To have proved most royal; and for his passage
> The soldiers' music and the rite of war
> Speak loudly for him.
> Take up the bodies. Such a sight as this
> Becomes the field, but here shows much amiss.
>
> (5.2.398-403)

Fortinbras, in uniform, returning from the Polish wars, knows what "Becomes the field" and what "shows much amiss" in civil society. To restore reason, morality, and order to Denmark, one must "Take up the bodies" and bury Hamlet "like a soldier" (397).

"The soldiers' music" is presumably the dead march, beat on muffled drums, and "the rite of war" is the military pageantry prescribed for dead heroes, such as full-dress uniform, trailing pikes, and slow-step march. We should also add to these indications the lowered "colors" —those flags and banners that would identify an army moving in procession. In the Folio direction, Fortinbras enters this scene "*with Drum, Colors, and Attendants*"

(5.2.362 s.d.) . There are some useful specifications for staging a soldier's funeral in Aufidius' speech at the end of *Coriolanus*:

> Take him [Coriolanus] up.
> Help, three o' th' chiefest soldiers; I'll be one.
> Beat thou the drum, that it speak mournfully;
> Trail your steel pikes. (5.6.148-51)

The last line of *Hamlet* suggests another possibility for "soldiers' music": "Go, bid the soldiers shoot," followed by the Folio direction *"Exeunt marching; after the which a peal of ordnance are shot off."* In Joseph Papp's open-air production of *Hamlet* during the summer of 1964, these sounds created an awesome effect, as the peals of ordnance echoed and reechoed in the Gothic wildness of Central Park.

The play's aggressive content is embodied in other references to cannon, most notably in Hamlet's anguished cry after his encounter with the new king and queen: "Or that the Everlasting had not fixed/ His canon 'gainst self-slaughter" (1.2.131-32) . The pun is underscored by the spelling "cannon" in Quarto 2 and Folio, but the word "fixed" also suggests stationary guns like those guarding the harbor of Elsinore. God's "canon" is pointed one way, and Claudius' "cannon," just six lines before, is pointed another, calling on the heavens to respeak his "earthly thunder" (128) . Hamlet's soliloquy is almost a direct answer to the rodomontade of his uncle-father's rouse. After Polonius' death, Claudius fears that his reputation may be destroyed by secret artillery:

[So, haply, slander,][12]
Whose whisper o'er the world's diameter,
As level as the cannon to his blank
Transports his poisoned shot, may miss our name
And hit the woundless air.   (4.1.40-44)

If it hits its target or "blank," the "poisoned shot" will explode and reveal Claudius' guilt.

The main emphasis of the imagery of ordnance and explosives is on a shattering destructiveness, as in that haunting passage about Claudius' "sorrows" (4.5.78) just before Laertes and his armed rabble are heard at the door:

O my dear Gertrude, this,
Like to a murd'ring piece, in many places
Gives me superfluous death.   (4.5.94-96)

"This" refers to the reports of Laertes' insurrection, but, more generally, it marks that tragic sense in Claudius that "all occasions do inform against" him (4.4.32) . The "murd'ring piece" or "murderer" was a small cannon filled with shrapnel, which was designed to scatter its shot and inflict maximum casualties. "When sorrows come, they come not single spies,/ But in battalions" (4.5.78-79) , and so death, too, comes superfluously with the "murd'ring piece"—it is the "plurisy" that "Dies in his own too-much" (4.7.117-18) .

Claudius' plot against Hamlet is similarly multiple. As he tells the rapt Laertes:

[12] This is Capell's conjecture to fill a lacuna in the text.

> Therefore this project [the unbated and poisoned
> rapier]
> Should have a back or second, that might hold
> If this did blast in proof.   (4.7.152-54)

The image is probably drawn "from the trying or proving of fire-arms or cannon,"[13] and it is ironic that although Claudius works by poison, his most characteristic
image should be the exploding missile. Hamlet taunts
the king with an ordnance image when he rises to interrupt the play: "What, frighted with false fire?" (3.2.
272). Shakespeare uses the technical term "false fire"
for the blank discharge of weapons, powder without
shot, merely the murder of a Player King—"poison in
jest" (3.2.240). Claudius presumably thinks that Hamlet's "false fire" will be followed by more dangerous
explosives.

As for the king's agents, Rosencrantz and Guildenstern, Hamlet will fight them with all the cunning of
booby-trap warfare:

> For 'tis the sport to have the enginer
> Hoist with his own petar, and 't shall go hard
> But I will delve one yard below their mines
> And blow them at the moon.   (3.4.207-10)

The ordnance words are used in both their technical
and general senses. For example, an "enginer" is not
just a demolition expert, but a contriver, a Machiavel;
"hoist" suggests hanging as well as being blown into

---

[13] *Variorum*, I, 369.

the air by an explosive; "mines" are sapping and under-
mining; and "petar" is "an engine, made like a bell or
mortar, and filled with explosives, used especially for
blowing up gates,"[14] and derived from the French word
péter, meaning to fart. In Hamlet's image, he pictures
himself working, like the Ghost in the cellarage, "A
worthy pioner" (1.5.163), to delve beneath the mines
of his enemies and set off their explosives unawares. He,
too, will be a crafty and unpredictable "old mole," who
can "work i' th' earth so fast" (162).

We may match the imagery of offense (sword, cannon, and explosives) with the imagery of defense, especially armor. We think first of the Ghost, who is "in
arms" (1.2.255), and who, "in complete steel,/ Revisits
thus the glimpses of the moon" (1.4.52-53). "Complete"
suggests not only full armor, but also an ethical sense:
perfect in nature or quality. " 'A was a man, take him
for all in all" (1.2.187), says his son, and in the first act
his "slow and stately" "solemn march" (201-2) and his
"martial stalk" (1.1.66) about the stage show him as the
exemplary soldier, sent untimely to an unquiet grave.
Even Claudius speaks of him as "our most valiant
brother" (1.2.25).

The Ghost's costume is historically identified as "the
very armor he had on/ When he the ambitious Norway
combated" (1.1.60-61). Horatio's report supplies Hamlet with the details so necessary in this sort of narration:
the Ghost was "Armèd at point exactly, cap-a-pe" (1.2.
200), which is explained some lines further as "From
top to toe" and "from head to foot" (228). There is
another definition of "cap-a-pe" in Rosencrantz and

14 Travers, p. 161.

Guildenstern's description of their relations with the goddess Fortuna; they are neither "the very button" "On Fortune's cap," "Nor the soles of her shoe" (2.2. 232-33). The Ghost also carried a truncheon or marshal's baton (1.2.204), and "wore his beaver up" (230); the "beaver" is the movable visor of the headpiece.

Despite all of this descriptive detail, the Ghost's stage armor was probably made of a supple, silvered leather, the traditional "leather pilch" of the Induction to *A Warning for Faire Women* (1599):

> . . . a filthie whining ghost,
> Lapt in some fowle sheete, or a leather pilch,
> Comes skreaming like a pigge halfe stickt,
> And cries Vindicta, reuenge, reuenge. . . .[15]

This may be a reference to the sensational *Ur-Hamlet*, on which Shakespeare's play is thought to be based. Although there was much literal realism of costume on the Elizabethan stage, the Ghost did not wear actual armor because the actor—and there is a tradition that Shakespeare himself played the Ghost[16]—needed to be nimble enough to ascend and descend the stage traps, and to be able, without superfluous clanking, to fade "on the crowing of the cock" (1.1.157).

The martial figure of the Ghost dominates the first act

[15] See William J. Lawrence, " 'Hamlet' as Shakespeare Staged It," *Pre-Restoration Stage Studies* (Cambridge, Mass.: Harvard University Press, 1927), pp. 108-9. *A Warning for Faire Women* is quoted from J. S. Farmer, *Old English Plays, Student's Facsimile Edition* (London, 1909-14), Vol. CLXIII. The text reads "pelch" for "pilch."

[16] See E. K. Chambers, *William Shakespeare: A Study of Facts and Problems* (London: Oxford University Press, 1930), I, 84.

of *Hamlet*. He appears in the midst of a national emergency in Denmark (indicated by soldiers on guard duty), a frantic armaments race, and a general atmosphere of anxiety and foreboding. The workers in the defense industries are now on a twenty-four hour shift, "the night joint-laborer with the day" (1.1.78), and the "sore task" of the impressed shipwrights "Does not divide the Sunday from the week" (75-76). There is a suggestion of forced labor in the presence of the military guard, the "most observant watch," that "So nightly toils [i.e., makes to toil] the subject of the land" (71-72). Into this military context of cold war and national hysteria enters the Ghost, as the recently dead war hero of the Danes who comes not to offer them reassurance, but to insist that "The time is out of joint" (1.5.188) and that "Something is rotten in the state of Denmark" (1.4.90).

It is worth noting that in the closet scene the Ghost does not appear to Hamlet in armor (despite the notorious illustration in Rowe's 1709 edition of Shakespeare), but "in his habit as he lived" (3.4.136). This change in costume marks an important distinction between the Ghost's public and private roles. Quarto 1 has the Ghost enter in its "nightgown," which makes good sense if one remembers that the Elizabethan nightgown was a warm, lined garment, sometimes trimmed with fur, that is the equivalent of our dressing gown (although it could be worn both indoors and out). Julius Caesar and Brutus both appear in nightgowns for drafty scenes in *Julius Caesar* (2.2 and 4.3). In *Hamlet*, Act III, Scene iv takes place in the queen's "closet," or private room,[17] where it would be inappropriate, as well as bad manners, for even her deceased husband to show himself in armor.

In the closet scene, Hamlet uses an extended metaphor of armor for the heart still assailable by sense:

> Peace, sit you down
> And let me wring your heart, for so I shall
> If it be made of penetrable stuff,
> If damnèd custom have not brazed[18] it so
> That it be proof and bulwark against sense.
>
> (3.4.35-39)

[17] The Elizabethan word "closet" means simply a private room or apartment, as distinguished from a public room. Thus the king's private secretary is called the "clerk of the closet" (*Variorum*, I, 125). "Closet" does not mean "bed chamber," and the ponderous marriage bed that usually dominates Act III, Scene iv is entirely out of place.

This lexicographical distinction is significant because it bears directly on the criticism of the closet scene. A. C. Bradley, for example, constructs his sentimental stage picture from the theatrical practice of his time; if Hamlet's "heart ever found relief, it was when those feelings [of horror and loathing for his uncle], mingled with the love that never died out in him, poured themselves forth in a flood as he stood in his mother's chamber beside his father's marriage-bed" (*Shakespearean Tragedy* [2 edn.; London, 1905], p. 119). Significantly, Bradley substitutes "chamber" for "closet," but no marriage bed is needed to reinforce Hamlet's blatantly sexual harangue. In the same tradition, J. Dover Wilson calls Act III, Scene iv the "bedroom scene" and locates it in the "Queen's bedchamber" (*What Happens in Hamlet* [3 edn.; Cambridge, Eng.: Cambridge University Press, 1959], pp. 246, 250—first published, 1935).

[18] The word in Quarto 2 is "brasd," which some modern editors (Wilson, for example) give as "brassed." But "brasd" seems to be only a variant spelling of Folio's "braz'd," rather than a word with a separate meaning.

"Damnèd custom," "That monster custom, who all sense doth eat" (3.4.162), is trying to harden Gertrude's heart, to plate it with brass, so that it will be armed against the onslaughts of feeling and good sense. This is one of the most striking images in the play for the complacency (and complaisance, too) of "Th' imperial jointress to this warlike state" (1.2.9), and its terms are drawn specifically from metalworking. "Proof" is the quality of armor that makes it capable of withstanding blows, as in "Mars's armor, forged for proof eterne" (2.2.501) of the Player's speech, so that, by metonymy, "proof" can refer to the proved, impenetrable armor itself. "Bulwark" is a bastion or fortification, and it completes an Old Testament emblem of sensibility warring against the hardened heart. Later in the scene, Gertrude represents her contrition in an equally emblematic figure: "O Hamlet, thou hast cleft my heart in twain" (3.4.157). The "brazed" heart and the heart cleft in twain are pictorial opposites, and Hamlet continues in this illustrative mode with what is perhaps the most painfully didactic image in the play: "O, throw away the worser part of it,/ And live the purer with the other half" (158-59).

The prominence of the Ghost in the first act is matched by the emergence of Fortinbras at the end of the play as new king of the Danes, so that both the beginning and the end of *Hamlet* have a strong military emphasis. Fortinbras, whose name derives from the knights of medieval romance, shows many traces of his origin, and his Polish expedition raises for Hamlet the question of honor so passionately debated in *Troilus and Cressida*. Hamlet is forced, like Hector, to admit the heroic and romantic truth of Troilus and Paris: "When honor's at the stake," one may find "great argument" even "in a straw" (4.4.54-56), "an eggshell" (53), "a fantasy and trick of fame" (61). It is a point of honor just because it is so unreasonable and so unrelated to worldly standards of profit and loss: "a little patch of ground/ That hath in it no profit but the name" (18-19). "What's aught but as 'tis valued?" asks Troilus in a searing question (*Troilus and Cressida* 2.2.52). And "a delicate and tender prince," "with divine ambition puffed" (4.4.48-49), goes to fight in Poland as an exercise in spirit necessary to all future kings of Denmark. Fortinbras is indeed the "adventurous knight" of Hamlet's stage types, who knows how to "use his foil and target" (2.2.329-30), a chivalric warrior "Of unimprovèd mettle hot and full" (1.1.96). But he is disappointingly undeveloped in the play, and he seems to be created only for his one great moment at the end.

Hamlet never aspires to the military virtue of the Ghost or of Fortinbras, and certainly not to the corrupted mixture of valor and bravado represented by Laertes. He also dissociates himself from the nonheroic, practical, and politic Claudius, who is rigorously excluded from any military attributes at all. Hamlet dies "like a soldier" (5.2.397) without having lived like one, but we are meant to believe Fortinbras when he tells us in the final speech of the play that Hamlet "was likely, had he been put on,/ To have proved most royal" (398-99). In Ophelia's earlier eulogy, he was the perfect combination of courtier, soldier, and scholar, "Th' expectancy and rose of the fair state" (3.1.155) . We should not gloss over these flattering assertions, which indicate a very different Hamlet from the brooding intellectual of Romantic criticism.

The important imagery of war, weapons, and explosives calls attention to the issues of public life, to the state of the nation, to politics, morality, and kingship, and forces us to abandon our unhealthy preoccupation with the psychology of the hero. This imagery also reminds us that *Hamlet* can be assimilated to the dramatic structure of the English history plays, which it follows by only a few years. The feeling of tragedy is heightened by the historical background of Denmark and the court of Elsinore, which makes the "truths" that "are told" in "the swelling act" (*Macbeth* 1.3.127-28) so much more immediate and persuasive.

2. Secrecy and Poison

IN THE recent prolific growth of studies of imagery, there has been an unfortunate turn to subtlety of interpretation. The image patterns have been heard singing their siren "undersongs" in despite of the main composition. I believe this emphasis is unfortunate, especially in the drama, because the leading imagery of a play has to be very obvious in order to accomplish its effects. If repetition is crucial to the idea of a symbolic theme, its workings must necessarily be cumulative and reinforcing rather than self-contained and self-expressive. I am, of course, simplifying the issues, but it would seem to me axiomatic that the imagery of a play must follow the movement of the dramatic action. We can see in *Hamlet* certain primary images or symbols that exert an influence, radiate, reverberate, or echo throughout the play to form a pattern of references to a significant subject matter. The image of Claudius and Hamlet pitted against each other as "mighty opposites" lies at the heart of the previous chapter on war, weapons, and explosives.

The theme of secrecy and poison, which is the subject of the present chapter, develops from Claudius' secret poisoning of Hamlet's father before the play opens. This is the hidden evil that must be brought to light, and *Hamlet* has much in common with the melodramatic structure of Sophocles' *Oedipus*,[1] which also depends

[1] See H.D.F. Kitto, *Form and Meaning in Drama* (London, 1960). First published, 1956. See also Francis Fergusson, *The Idea*

upon the gradual revelation of a guilty secret and its tragic consequences for the kingdom of Thebes. The dramatic action in both plays moves away from secrecy and toward a purgation of those poisons that are destroying the body politic. This does not mean that Creon and Fortinbras are better kings than Oedipus was and Hamlet might have been, but they do represent the possibility of a new beginning.

Secrecy indicates premeditation, deliberateness, artifice, and hypocrisy—all qualities that intensify our sense of the magnitude of evil in tragedy. "That one may smile, and smile, and be a villain" (1.5.108), says Hamlet, and he inscribes it in his tables as the ultimate truth of the Ghost's narration. This is an apt example of how Hamlet is beginning to lose his innocence, as he stands poised on the threshold of new and forbidding insights. Contrary to Eliot's notorious judgment that the emotion of Hamlet is "in *excess* of the facts as they appear,"[2] the crime on which the play is based has "the primal eldest curse upon't,/ A brother's murder" (3.3.37-38).

---

of a Theater (Garden City, N.Y., 1953), esp. pp. 130-32. First published by Princeton University Press, 1949.

[2] T. S. Eliot, "Hamlet and His Problems" (1919), *Selected Essays 1917-1932* (New York, 1932), p. 125. Eliot's dissatisfaction with *Hamlet* may be paralleled in critics of the *Scrutiny* group such as L. C. Knights, *An Approach to "Hamlet"* (London, 1961), and D. A. Traversi, *An Approach to Shakespeare* (2 edn.; Garden City, N.Y., 1956), pp. 81-107. Traversi, for example, says of the closet scene: "we must feel once more that there is something excessive about the emotion conveyed, that its roots lie not in the external facts of Hamlet's situation, but in an intense distortion, imperfectly understood by the speaker himself (and perhaps by his creator) within his own experience" (p. 98).

As Claudius says so lucidly, "it smells to heaven" (36).
We are never allowed to get that stink out of our nos-
trils, and it is disgustingly strengthened by "the rank
sweat of an enseamèd bed" (3.4.93).

Claudius attempts to conceal his murder with regal
and rhetorical unction, and there is a striking resemblance between him and Henry IV, who can never forget his butchery of Richard II at Pomfret. Both could
say equally well, and with the same self-conscious irony,
"Uneasy lies the head that wears a crown" (2 *Henry IV*
3.1.31). While Hamlet is trying to confirm the Ghost's
revelation, Claudius is trying to find out how much
Hamlet knows. There are plotter and victim, hunter
and prey, set against each other and busily exchanging
roles. As Hamlet says so energetically at the end of the
closet scene: "O, 'tis most sweet/ When in one line two
crafts directly meet" (3.4.210-11). The "crafts" are
craftiness, although there may also be a quibble on
naval warfare.

We do not learn the secret of what is "rotten in the
state of Denmark" (1.4.90) until the Ghost's narration
of its murder in Act I, Scene v. "O my prophetic soul"
(40), exclaims Hamlet, and he corroborates the vague
fears and anxieties we have had since the beginning of
the play. The Ghost's account is unusually full and explicit. Its fifty lines (42-91) [3] are, after the "rogue and

---

[3] There is no basis at all, either in Quarto 2 or Folio, for as-
signing line 80—"O, horrible! O, horrible! Most horrible!"—to
Hamlet, as Rann and other editors do. Samuel Johnson confessed
that the transposition "was ingeniously hinted to me by a very
learned lady" (*Johnson's Notes to Shakespeare*, ed. Arthur Sherbo,
p. 161). See Kittredge's textual note, p. 302.

peasant slave" soliloquy (2.2.559-617) of Hamlet, the longest speech in the play, and the formal, oratorical style suggests a link with both the Player's tale of Troy and the Player King.

The elder Hamlet is poisoned with Italianate artfulness as he is taking his customary "after-dinner's sleep" (*Measure for Measure* 3.1.33). He is surprised upon his "secure hour" (1.5.61) by the thief Claudius, who "stole" into his "orchard" or garden. Significantly, Claudius pours his poison into "the porches" (63) of his sleeping brother's ears. This is the symbolic act that lies behind *Hamlet* and provides an archetype of evil, like original sin. In the Ghost's own report, he represents the body politic by the synecdoche of its ear:

> . . . the whole ear of Denmark
> Is by a forgèd process of my death
> Rankly abused.   (1.5.36-38)

A "forgèd process" is a legal deception, a poisoning of public opinion for which Hamlet must provide the antidote.

The Ghost tells us that it was killed "With juice of cursed hebona in a vial" (1.5.62), which is a mysterious poison made from the ebony tree, or more likely from either yew or henbane.[4] The poison Lucianus uses in *The Mousetrap* is more generally described: "Thou mixture rank, of midnight weeds collected" (3.2.263), as

---

[4] See Wilson's notes, pp. 161 and 297, and the note in Parrott and Craig, p. 100. Sir William T. Thiselton-Dyer makes a strong argument for henbane in his essay on plants in *Shakespeare's England* (London: Oxford University Press, 1917), I, 509.

is the mountebank's "unction" (4.7.141) with which Laertes will anoint his sword. As we might expect, Claudius does not inform us what poison he uses for the "chalice" (4.7.160) of wine in the fencing match, although we do learn from the dying Laertes that "It is a poison tempered by himself" (5.2.329) —there is an enormous versatility in this king.

In the Ghost's narration the poison is described primarily in terms of disease. It is "The leperous distillment" (1.5.64), and its physiological effects are precisely rendered:

> . . . swift as quicksilver it courses through
> The natural gates and alleys of the body,
> And with a sudden vigor it doth posset
> And curd, like eager droppings into milk,
> The thin and wholesome blood. So did it mine,
> And a most instant tetter barked about
> Most lazarlike with vile and loathsome crust
> All my smooth body.   (1.5.66-73)

The point of the imagery is that the poison turns something beautiful—"See what a grace was seated on this brow" (3.4.56) —into something vile and loathsome, a leper covered with sores and scabs. The ugliness of the imagery externalizes the repulsiveness of Claudius' crime.

The mingling of the themes of poison and disease (and of food, too, in lines 68-70) presents a typical problem in Shakespeare's imagery. What is the dominant subject matter here, and how shall we classify this passage about the elder Hamlet's murder? In Clemen's discussion, which acknowledges a debt to Caroline Spurgeon, the passage expresses the *"leitmotif"*[5] of the imagery of sickness. It seems to me, however, that what is important in the whole context of the murder is not disease, but the poisonous duplicity of Claudius. "Something is rotten in the state of Denmark" (1.4.90) because this is a secret crime, a hidden evil. If there is indeed a leitmotif of disease imagery stemming from the Ghost's narration, it does not refer merely to disease in general, but to the hidden disease, the disease that is deliberately concealed.

The most striking example of this imagery comes right after the Ghost's exit in the closet scene. Gertrude cannot see or hear the Ghost, "yet all that is I see" (3.4.133), so that she can now conveniently think Hamlet mad and all his frenzied advice only the ravings of a lunatic. But Hamlet refuses to allow his mother any false comfort:

> Lay not that flattering unction to your soul,
> That not your trespass but my madness speaks.
> It will but skin and film the ulcerous place
> Whiles rank corruption, mining all within,
> Infects unseen.   (3.4.146-50)

The "unction" applied to the "ulcerous place" will merely give the illusion of healing, a "skin and film," while the infection itself rages beneath. It is a "flattering" unction because it offers only the deceptive ap-

[5] Clemen, *The Development of Shakespeare's Imagery*, p. 113. See also Muir's comments on Clemen in "Imagery and Symbolism in *Hamlet*," pp. 352-53.

pearance of cure. Claudius' crime is the prototype of the evil that "Infects unseen."

Festering and ulceration dominate the theme of hidden disease, and there is symbolic appropriateness in the idea of a secret, inner corruption. Hamlet's comment on the Fortinbras expedition uses an image very like the "ulcerous place" of the closet scene:

> This is th' imposthume of much wealth and peace,
> That inward breaks, and shows no cause without
> Why the man dies. (4.4.27-29)

Cotgrave's dictionary (1611) defines an "imposthume" as "an inward swelling full of corrupt matter,"[6] to which we may add that it is a purulent abscess or cyst, not visible externally, but which, by suddenly bursting, pours its lethal poison into the body. That the luxury and ease of peace is a disease which only war can cure is a familiar notion, but in this context Hamlet seems to be thinking of Claudius' "peace-rotten Denmark"[7] rather than of Norway or Poland.

The imagery of hidden disease has an interesting reversibility for antagonist and protagonist. Thus, one of the symbolic ways that Claudius counters Hamlet is by thinking of him as the hidden disease that must be cured at any cost, even death. This is almost exactly what Claudius tells the king of England in his "sovereign process" importing "The present death of Hamlet" (4.3.63,65):

[6] *Variorum*, I, 324.

[7] Paul A. Jorgensen, *Shakespeare's Military World* (Berkeley: University of California Press, 1956), p. 205.

> Do it, England,
> For like the hectic in my blood he rages,
> And thou must cure me.   (4.3.65-67)

Hamlet has become Claudius' consumptive fever, which "rages" furiously in his blood and threatens to destroy him. Immediately after the death of Polonius, Hamlet is again to Claudius a secret and almost mortal disease. Instead of restraining "This mad young man,"

> . . . so much was our love
> We would not understand what was most fit,
> But, like the owner of a foul disease,
> To keep it from divulging, let it feed
> Even on the pith of life.   (4.1.19-23)

The identity of the "foul disease" is left deliberately vague, but it is one so abhorrent that it must be kept undivulged even at the risk of death.

There is a similar image in the king's directions to Rosencrantz and Guildenstern. They are to find out from Hamlet "Whether aught to us unknown afflicts him thus,/ That opened lies within our remedy" (2.2.17-18). "Opened" means disclosed or revealed, but in this context it suggests the opening of an ulcer, imposthume, or other festering sore by surgical incision. "Remedy" is also a threatening word, especially when spoken by Claudius, and the curative English voyage that he finally proposes will end with Hamlet's head "struck off" (5.2.25). A reversal of this imagery shows us Hamlet as Claudius' surgeon, with *The Mousetrap* as a therapeutic instrument:

I'll observe his looks,
I'll tent him to the quick. If 'a do blench,
I know my course.   (2.2.608-10)

A "tent" was a roll of lint used to search and cleanse a
wound to keep it from becoming infected. The wound
here is Claudius' guilty secret, which will be brought
to light by the play, and Hamlet takes a cruel pleasure
in probing his uncle's flesh "to the quick."

The hidden disease is only one form of concealment
in a play filled with secrecy, duplicity, and poisonous
deception. The Ghost's narration of its murder in Act
I, Scene v establishes the poison plot as central to the
meaning of the play. After the exposition in Act I, the
poison plot is grotesquely recapitulated in *The Murder
of Gonzago* and its dumb show in Act III, then presented
directly for the first time in the lethal fencing match of
Act V. In their symmetrical control of the beginning,
middle, and end of the play, these three poison plots
shape the structure of *Hamlet*.

When the king asks his nephew-son if there is any
"offense" (3.2.239) in *The Mousetrap*, Hamlet answers
with the same pun as that used in the Ghost scene (1.5.
134-37) : "No, no, they do but jest, poison in jest; no
offense i' th' world" (3.2.240-41) . "Poison in jest" separates the mimic play world from the real world of afternoon naps in the "orchard" and the dangers of a "leperous" distillment. We have already seen the *"poisoner"*
at work in the dumb show (140 s.d.) . He is *"another
man"* in Quarto 2 (but a more sinister *"Fellow"* in
Folio) , who *"takes off"* the Player King's *"crown, kisses*

it, pours poison in the sleeper's ears, and leaves him."
Claudius is seeing his crime exactly reenacted, with
more explicit detail than the Ghost could provide in
its narration. After the murder and the Player Queen's
*"passionate action," "The poisoner, with some three or
four, come in again, seem to condole with her."* When
the dead body is removed, *"The poisoner woos the
Queen with gifts; she seems harsh awhile, but in the end
accepts love."* The Player Queen may find hints for the
acting of her part in Lady Anne of *Richard III*, who is
sardonically wooed by Gloucester at the very coffin of
her father-in-law (Act I, Scene ii).

The character called *"The poisoner"* in the dumb
show becomes in the play Lucianus, who is, significantly,
nephew to Duke Gonzago of Vienna, the Player King.
The setting inevitably reminds us of another "knavish
piece of work" (3.2.246) in process in the Vienna of
Measure for Measure—there is even a Claudio in *Hamlet* (4.7.40). Lucianus is an obvious grotesque, a stage
murderer in the style of the mustache-twirling villain
of Victorian melodrama, and the events of the murder
are consciously distanced and displaced, so that Claudius will not be allowed any easy psychological identification with the character. Hamlet, as stage manager of
the show, must set the mugging Lucianus to his task:
"Leave thy damnable faces and begin" (3.2.259). Lucianus' "Thoughts black, hands apt, drugs fit, and time
agreeing,/ Confederate season, else no creature seeing"
(261-62) will seem absurd to all except the "galled
jade," who may begin to "winch" (248) when the vial
of poison is apostrophized, and be positively startled

when Lucianus *"Pours the poison"* (266 s.d.) into the ears of the Player King. As presenter or chorus, Hamlet continues the role of Lucianus: "'A poisons him i' th' garden for his estate" (267), while the king rises to stop the performance.

He has been touched home by this double reenactment of his secret crime, in dumb show and in play. "It will have blood; they say blood will have blood," says Macbeth, and even "The secret'st man of blood" will be "brought forth" (*Macbeth* 3.4.122, 125-26). It is a primitive notion of justice, yet one that is satisfying in its sense of inevitable retribution. Nothing can ultimately be concealed, "For murder, though it have no tongue, will speak/ With most miraculous organ" (2.2. 605-6). We have the same idea in an early speech of Hamlet: "Foul deeds will rise,/ Though all the earth o'erwhelm them, to men's eyes" (1.2.257-58). "O'erwhelm" indicates something crushing and monumental, but time, although a destroyer (*edax rerum*), also brings all things to light.

This idea is demonstrated in the staging, when the king, rising from the play, calls out: "Give me some light. Away!" (3.2.275), and his cry is echoed by Polonius and his attendants: "Lights, lights, lights!" (276).[8] Claudius entered the scene *"with his Guard carrying torches"* (91 s.d.), a conventional way to represent night in an afternoon performance, and this Guard lights him out after the play. The ability to make

---

[8] Quarto 2 gives this line to Polonius, as does Quarto 1 (under the name of Corambis). Folio's speech prefix is *All*, which seems to me to make for a better stage effect.

metaphors out of the staging, and especially out of its limitations, is one of the characteristic strengths of Elizabethan drama. Here Claudius calls for the light of torches to take away the more lurid light of *The Murder of Gonzago*, and he needs those lights to show him his way in the dark castle of Elsinore. Now that there are no longer any secrets between Hamlet and him, the action of the play can enter a more openly aggressive phase. It is surely one of the most unexpected turns of the plot that Hamlet's triumph in the play scene should be so short-lived, and that, through the murder of Polonius, the initiative should so definitely pass to his enemies.

The king's new plot, devised with amazing swiftness after Hamlet's escape, gives us a fascinating glimpse of Claudius at work. We have the same sort of brilliance and inventiveness in this poison plot as was displayed in the murder of Hamlet's father, and the connection develops that sense of recapitulation so important to tragedy. There is special emphasis on "venom." Laertes' skill in fencing "Did Hamlet so envenom with his envy" (4.7.103), and Claudius reassures Laertes with mention of the poisoned drink, which will serve if Hamlet "by chance escape your venomed stuck" (161). That violent monosyllable "stuck" is characteristic of Claudius' style and very different in sound and connotations from "stoccado," which it abbreviates (compare the equally menacing "push," at 5.1.297). In the match itself, the mortally wounded Laertes reveals that Hamlet is now holding the "treacherous instrument," "Unbated and envenomed" (5.2.317-18). Hamlet is amazed at the

complexity of his uncle's villainy—"The point envenomed too?" (322)—but he will use the instruments provided by an "ordinant" (48) heaven: "Then, venom,
to thy work" (323). Venom is an appropriate image for
a play in which "The serpent that did sting thy father's
life/ Now wears his crown" (1.5.39-40).

The catastrophe in *Hamlet* is precipitated by the
poisoning of Gertrude, which is only one in a series of
ironic misdirections in the perfect plot of Claudius and
Laertes, who, in the words of the Player King, "Their
own enactures with themselves destroy" (3.2.203). "The
Queen carouses to thy fortune, Hamlet" (5.2.290), exclaims Gertrude. When she raises the cup, the king says
knowingly, "Gertrude, do not drink" (291), but he will
go no further than that to save her life. Like Macbeth,
he will "fight the course" "bear-like" to the very end
(*Macbeth* 5.7.2). So Gertrude follows her first husband
to a death by poison, accompanied by Hamlet, Laertes,
and the redoubtable Claudius, impenitent and resourceful to the end. His last line is: "O, yet defend me,
friends. I am but hurt" (5.2.325), as if he had no faith
in the efficacy of Laertes' poison. But Hamlet forces on
him, with a bitter pun, a dose of the "poison tempered
by himself" (329): "Drink off this potion. Is thy union
here?/ Follow my mother" (327-28). Claudius' "union" is the beautiful pearl, presumably hollowed out to
hold poison, that he threw into the cup to pledge Hamlet. Since his union with Gertrude was accomplished
by poisoning her husband and his brother, all that remains of their guilty coupling is "in the cup." The

king's poisoned cup mocks the chalice of wine in the marriage sacrament.

Concealment in *Hamlet* is an important verbal theme, especially in the three poison plots that shape the play, but it also becomes part of the stage action in the eavesdropping scenes of Act III: Scene i, where Ophelia is the decoy, and Scene iv, where Polonius "conveys" himself behind the arras and is stabbed to death for his pains. We may follow the theme of secrecy in the first of these encounters, which is carefully developed out of a series of interlocking events.

When Ophelia tells her father of Hamlet's frightening appearance "as I was sewing in my closet" (2.1.77), Polonius' court mentality springs immediately into action: "Mad for thy love" (85), "This is the very ecstasy of love" (102). The father's first reaction is to proceed publicly and openly:

> Come, go we to the King.
> This must be known, which, being kept close, might move
> More grief to hide than hate to utter love.
>
> (2.1.117-19)

There seems to be no possibility for secrets in Polonius' household, nor for any privacy either. "Close" means hidden or shut up, as in the king's advice to Laertes to "Keep close within your chamber" (4.7.129), or "lie low," until the plot against Hamlet is ripe. The complex syntax of Polonius' couplet should banish any doubts about his subtlety and sophistication; he may be tedious and labyrinthine, but he is no fool.

In the next scene, Polonius' offer to disclose his secret to the king becomes a momentous occasion, celebrated with all the pomp and ceremony of a classical oration. "What might you think," he asks,

> If I had played the desk or table book,
> Or given my heart a winking, mute and dumb,
> Or looked upon this love with idle sight?
>   (2.2.136-38)

He will write no secrets in his "table book," as Hamlet does after seeing the Ghost (1.5.107), nor wink—and the Folio reading gives us an apt word for a politician—to his heart to be "mute and dumb." There is irony in Polonius' vehement insistence on candor and openness, and his Baconian devotion to truth:

> If circumstances lead me, I will find
> Where truth is hid, though it were hid indeed
> Within the center.   (2.2.157-59)

From this passionate search for truth—"Hide fox, and all after" (4.2.30-31)—comes the eavesdropping plot, in which Polonius will "loose" his daughter to Hamlet while he is walking "Here in the lobby" (2.2. 162,161). "Loose" is one of the most offensive words in the play because, by calling up the scene of the cow loosed to the bull, it reminds us of the harsh vulgarities in the Polonian family circle. Ophelia will be the decoy for Hamlet, while Polonius and the king will place themselves "behind an arras" to "Mark the encounter" (163-64)—"encounter" continues the connotations of "loose," which end in the "farm and carters" (167) image. The arras, or tapestry hanging at the back of the stage, suggests an Elizabethan interior, but it also served as a convenient curtain (in a theater that had no front curtains) , by means of which simple discoveries and concealments could be made.

Because of all these preparations, the act of eavesdropping becomes an insidious plot, with not a few theatrical resemblances to a scene within a scene. The king has "closely sent for Hamlet hither" (3.1.29) —and the word "closely" implies deceit—"That he, as 'twere by accident, may here/ Affront Ophelia" (30-31) . "Affront" is used in its etymological sense of "encounter," although it certainly carries a connotation of abuse to Hamlet as well as to Ophelia. The masterstroke of the stage manager is seen in the phrase "as 'twere by accident," whose calculating spontaneity gives us an insight into Claudius' role throughout the play.

Claudius picks up the Polonian word "encounter" (2.2.164) , which suggests combat, and he tries to give the whole affair a studied legality:

> Her father and myself (lawful espials)
> Will so bestow ourselves that, seeing unseen,
> We may of their encounter frankly judge. . . .
>
> (3.1.32-34)

In contrast to other spies in the play, they will be "lawful espials" and "seeing unseen," a brilliant expression for the eavesdropper's position, with an inescapable connotation of one-way mirrors. "Rank corruption," we remember, "Infects unseen" (3.4.149-50) , and Polonius dies as "The unseen good old man" (4.1.12) . Hamlet, however, is "Th' observed of all observers" (3.1. 157), which, in a play with so much spying, must inevitably be meant in "more than one sense," as Foakes indicates.[9]

Hamlet has a large vocabulary of Machiavellian "policy" words that give the play a distinctive atmosphere of anxiety and danger. Most of these "policy" words are not significant in themselves, but we may take as examples two that have some thematic importance: "practice" and "shuffling." The details of the plot against Hamlet, as Claudius explains them to Laertes, have an attractive simplicity:

> . . . with ease,
> Or with a little shuffling, you may choose
> A sword unbated, and, in a pass of practice,
> Requite him for your father.   (4.7.136-39)

Claudius may be using the word "practice" in a general sense, for the sport of fencing, or specifically, for a skillful thrust (a "practiced pass"), but he is probably also thinking of the treachery of the plot itself. The king is so certain of his cunning that even Gertrude "shall uncharge the practice/ And call it accident" (67-68). There is an element of pride in one's work here, in the art that conceals art and convinces us that it is natural. By a familiar tragic turn, the plot against Hamlet depends upon his "being remiss,/ Most generous, and free from all contriving," so that he "Will not peruse the foils" (134-36). Hamlet thinks of Laertes as "A very noble youth" (5.1.226), and in his candor he

[9] Foakes, "*Hamlet* and the Court of Elsinore," p. 38.

shares Othello's fatally "free and open nature/ That thinks men honest that but seem to be so" (*Othello* 1.3.393-94). Magnanimity is the very quality that makes both men so vulnerable to tragedy.

Claudius' disciple, Guildenstern, also plays on the neutral and Machiavellian senses of "practice." He welcomes his task of spying on Hamlet with a riddling enthusiasm: "Heavens make our presence and our practices/ Pleasant and helpful to him!" (2.2.38-39). Hamlet soon sees through the pun, and the pleasant court manners of Guildenstern and Rosencrantz become no more than informers' wiles. In a more literal sense, Laertes acknowledges his fatal duplicity: "The foul practice/ Hath turned itself on me" (5.2.318-19), but we make special allowances for him as the victim of Claudius' superior practice.

Like "miching mallecho," the word "shuffling" also "means mischief" (3.2.142-43), and in relation to Claudius' plot it suggests the mountebank's skill by which one may find, with "ease," an unbated blade on a table of bated foils. This word conjures up for me the Folio staging of the fencing match: *In scuffling they change rapiers* (5.2.303 s.d.), where, by a trick of verbal and moral symmetry, the "*scuffling*" undoes the "shuffling." The word also carries an allusion to card-playing, especially in the sense of deceptive shuffling to produce the right cards in the right places.[10]

---

[10] There may be similar wordplay on Claudius' "royal knavery" (5.2.19): king and servant exist not only in the court, but also in the court cards (the "coat" or "picture" cards), and Hamlet means to say that at Elsinore the king is a jack, or base fellow.

There is a significant example of shuffling in Hamlet's "To be, or not to be" soliloquy:

> For in that sleep of death what dreams may come
> When we have shuffled off this mortal coil,
> Must give us pause.   (3.1.66-68)

"Shuffled off" is not a pleasant image, and a sense of deception is attached to it from its other contexts. Both "this mortal coil" and the "dreams" of the "sleep of death" have their reciprocal unattractiveness, so that neither can possibly outbalance the other, and we are left at the end with a puzzled will. In addition to its obvious sense of turmoil, fuss, and disturbance, "mortal coil" could also mean the round globe of the earth, as symbolized by the concentric coils of a pile of ship's rope. "Shuffled," then, would refer to the evasive motions one makes in taking leave of this earth and this life.[11]

The most unforgettable shuffling is in Claudius' soliloquy:

> In the corrupted currents of this world
> Offense's gilded hand may shove by justice,
> And oft 'tis seen the wicked prize itself
> Buys out the law. But 'tis not so above.
> There is no shuffling. . . .   (3.3.57-61)

Shakespeare defines the word for us by its context. Its root meaning of a shambling or clumsy gait, a dragging of the feet, becomes the symbol for all the evasiveness,

---

[11] See Wilson, p. xxxiv, and M. M. Mahood, *Shakespeare's Wordplay* (London, 1957), p. 122.

trickery, and deceit practiced "In the corrupted currents
of this world," as contrasted with the straightness, openness, honesty, and candor required "above." Claudius
sees himself for what he is, without any mitigation. He
is the shuffler who knows how to "shove by" justice;
he is the giver of bribes who knows how to pay part
of the loot in order to keep the rest. These are the
"uses of this world" (1.2.134), but Claudius makes no
attempt to deceive himself about the uses of the other
world. For all of its chilling lucidity, his soliloquy is
still full of a cynical devotion to shuffling.

Claudius is irresistibly intelligent, as Iago is, and like
Iago he mimics in his plotting Shakespeare's own gift
for setting characters in action and for creating exciting
scenes. It is precisely this feeling that the antagonist is
overwhelming, that the protagonist is in the grip of
forces beyond his powers of resistance, that allows the
element of chance or irony to come into play, as it does
so powerfully in *Hamlet*. How can the hero escape this
inevitable triple plot of unbated rapier, poisoned tip,
and poisoned chalice? He cannot, of course, escape it,
but heaven may show that it is "ordinant" (5.2.48) by
making the evil purposes fall "on th' inventors' heads"
(386). Things turn out differently from what Claudius
and Laertes suppose, and their triumph is cut short at
the very moment when it seems most assured. Ironic reversal[12] is the favorite plot device of poetic justice: the

[12] See Thomas F. Van Laan, "Ironic Reversal in *Hamlet*,"
Studies in English Literature, VI (1966), 247-62, and Warren V.
Shepard, "Hoisting the Enginer with His Own Petar," *SQ*, VII
(1956), 281-85. See also Tilley, W204 and F626.

tables are turned, "the enginer/ Hoist with his own petar" (3.4.207-08), and the "woodcock" caught in his "own springe" (5.2.307). The tragic point of this peripeteia is made most tellingly by the Player King:

> Our wills and fates do so contrary run
> That our devices still are overthrown;
> Our thoughts are ours, their ends none of our own.
> (3.2.217-19)

The element of secrecy in Shakespeare's *Hamlet* reflects an important aspect of the source story, and although Shakespeare makes much less of it than do Saxo Grammaticus or Belleforest, it is still a crucial part of the dramatic action. Hamlet and his few friends are set against Claudius and his many agents. The struggle is obviously one-sided, yet we never have the impression that Hamlet is crushed. At the most unlikely moment, just as he is being shipped under guard to his death in England, he is asserting boldly:

> I do not know
> Why yet I live to say, "This thing's to do,"
> Sith I have cause, and will, and strength, and means
> To do't. (4.4.43-46)

His assessment of his position is wildly illogical, yet forceful asseveration is, in the context of a play, itself a sign of force. Hamlet's secrecy, which he furthers by his "antic disposition" (1.5.172), is one of his most effective weapons against Claudius, who has at his command all the power and policy of the kingdom of Denmark, whereas Hamlet is limited to guerrilla warfare.

If we are sensitive to the realities of Claudius' regime,

we understand why Hamlet needs to go into hiding after his escape from the English voyage. The mystification of Hamlet's letter to Horatio—"These good fellows will bring thee where I am" (4.6.27-28)—suggests a fear that he may be secretly murdered. There is similar mystification in the delivery of Hamlet's oracular letter to the king. In answer to Claudius' question, "Who brought them?" (4.7.38), the anonymous messenger speaks in vague meanderings:

> Sailors, my lord, they say; I saw them not.
> They were given me by Claudio; he received them
> Of him that brought them.   (4.7.39-41)

Who is this cryptic Claudio, whose name is the Italian form of Claudius? The king suspects some "abuse" (50), but the handwriting is unmistakably authentic.

In an earlier scene, Hamlet gives his uncle a start when he says that he sees a "cherub" (4.3.48) that sees all of the king's secret purposes, and he seems to survive his English voyage by the help of this same cherubic intelligence. In his pirate-posted letter, he appears to be writing of a miraculous deliverance, a rebirth: "High and mighty, you shall know I am set naked on your kingdom" (4.7.43-44). The king is stunned and incredulous: " 'Naked'!" (51). We learn later that Hamlet still has his sturdy "sea gown scarfed about" him (5.2.13), so we need not worry about the state of his apparel. But that startling and simple word "naked"—unprovided, bare, unarmed, open, plain, undisguised—seems by itself to negate all of Claudius' plots and poisoned imaginings.

3. Corruption

"HOW WEARY, stale, flat, and unprofitable/ Seem to me all the uses of this world" (1.2.133-34), says Hamlet in an early scene, and later on: "this goodly frame, the earth, seems to me a sterile promontory; this most excellent canopy, the air, look you, this brave o'erhanging firmament, this majestical roof fretted with golden fire: why, it appeareth nothing to me but a foul and pestilent congregation of vapors" (2.2.306-11). Shortly before the catastrophe, he is still troubled by the unresolved war between the bestial and angelic forces in man:

> What is a man,
> If his chief good and market of his time
> Be but to sleep and feed? A beast, no more.
> Sure he that made us with such large discourse,
> Looking before and after, gave us not
> That capability and godlike reason
> To fust in us unused.   (4.4.33-39)

There is no satisfying resolution to this conflict, nor any way to avoid the inevitable "taint" that the revenger acquires in the course of his revenge. The Ghost's admonition, "Taint not thy mind" (1.5.85), is impossible to obey in a world that is already tainted.[1] In the proverbial formula, pitch defileth (Tilley, P358), and one's "nature is subdu'd/ To what it works in, like the dyer's hand" (Sonnet CXI).

Caroline Spurgeon has written perceptively of "the

---

[1] But see Knights, *An Approach to "Hamlet,"* who puts a strong emphasis on Hamlet's "taint."

evil smell of evil deeds"[2] in Shakespeare, and Richard Altick has applied this dictum to *Hamlet*.[3] Like Lear's hand, the play "smells of mortality" (*King Lear* 4.6.133) in much more than a figurative sense. As Foakes tells us, "the imagery of corruption, like much else in the play's language, needs to be seen as closely related to, and in some sense a part of it, a larger thematic structure concerned with seeming and being, with shows and the truths that they conceal, with fair appearance and ugly realities, and with the difficulties of interpreting what is seen."[4] This imagery is part of the extensive order-disorder symbolism in Shakespeare that G. Wilson Knight has made the central concern of his criticism. In its broadest sense, the imagery of food and animals is used to express man's lapse from his rational, divinely endowed condition to the appetitive state of a beast. Disease imagery marks a malfunction in the human organism that may also reflect disorder in the body politic and in the cosmos itself, and the ideal symbolic garden, modeled on the garden of Eden, may become choked with weeds, "her wholesome herbs/ Swarming with caterpillars" (*Richard II* 3.4.46-47). These four themes—animals, disease, food, and gardens—all represent fundamental dualisms of good and evil, which are deeply embedded in the faded metaphors and proverbial wisdom of daily discourse.

[2] Spurgeon, *Shakespeare's Imagery*, p. 162.

[3] Richard D. Altick, "*Hamlet* and the Odor of Mortality," *SQ*, V (1954), 167-76.

[4] R. A. Foakes, "Character and Speech in 'Hamlet,'" in *Hamlet*, Stratford upon Avon Studies 5, pp. 152-53.

The familiarity of these patterns allows Shakespeare to work unexpected and ironic turns, as when Hamlet, refusing to kill Claudius, says, "This physic but prolongs thy sickly days" (3.3.96). "Physic" may mean a cathartic, since Hamlet has just observed Claudius "purging" (85) his soul. But if one keeps to the more general sense of remedy, Hamlet seems to be indulging a cruel impulse to prolong Claudius' "sickly days" rather than cure him. Hamlet will eventually kill him in a more satisfyingly "horrid hent" (88), so that the only effect of the present delay will be to extend Claudius' torment. Thus, with a menacing quibble, the exit line (96) of the melancholy prince asserts the potency of Dr. Hamlet's "physic."

Among general qualities of corruption, the most significant is rankness, and it should come as no surprise that *Hamlet* has more "rank" words than any other play in the canon. The "rank sweat of an enseamèd bed" (3.4.93) is the most startling image here, because it is intended to shock Gertrude out of her lust. "Rank" means noisome, rancid, having an offensively strong smell. In *The Merry Wives of Windsor*, Falstaff in his buck-basket was rammed in "with foul shirts and smocks, socks, foul stockings, greasy napkins, that, Master Brook, there was the rankest compound of villainous smell that ever offended nostril" (3.5.81-83). "Rank" is also a word for an animal in heat, as in Shylock's description: "the ewes, being rank,/ In end of autumn turned to the rams" (*The Merchant of Venice* 1.3.75-76). These sexual implications are present when Hamlet warns his mother against "rank corruption, mining all within" (3.4.149).

Another meaning of "rank" that lends itself to metaphor is excessive vigorousness in growth, over-luxuriance, like that of weeds, a sense that may also be illustrated from the closet scene: "do not spread the compost on the weeds/ To make them ranker" (3.4.152-53). Presumably weeds are already rank enough without any aid from the compost heap, since they do not depend upon the niceties of human attention to flourish. "Most subject is the fattest soil to weeds" (2 *Henry IV* 4.4.54), says King Henry of Prince Hal, offering us a proverbial insight into the workings of the tragic fall (see Tilley, W241). In *Henry VIII*, Cranmer is "a rank weed" (5. 1.52) that must be rooted out, and in *As You Like It* Jaques advises the Duke to "weed your better judgments/ Of all opinion that grows rank in them" (2.7. 45-46).

The garden sense of "rank" is very strong in Hamlet's first soliloquy. The smiling prosperity of Claudius' court belies the decay of the world on which it is based; reality is now

> . . . an unweeded garden
> That grows to seed. Things rank and gross in nature
> Possess it merely.   (1.2.135-37)

Just as "the bloat King" (3.4.183) has Denmark in fee simple, so the garden of this world no longer follows the model of that first happy garden in Eden. At the center of Hamlet's passionate disgust are "Things rank and gross in nature." "Rank and gross" is a familiar Elizabethan linkage. The connotations of "gross"— coarse, sensual, overfed, excessively material, wanting in fineness or delicacy—overlap with those of "rank," and one word helps to define the other. In the Ghost's report,

> . . . the whole ear of Denmark
> Is by a forgèd process of my death
> Rankly abused.   (1.5.36-38)

"Rankly" means grossly in this context, with the added sense of the virulent stink of foul play. We remember that Claudius took Hamlet's father "grossly, full of bread,/ With all his crimes broad blown, as flush as May" (3.3.80-81), and that "Examples gross as earth exhort" (4.4.46) Hamlet to his revenge. There are also the "long purples" of Ophelia's garlands, "That liberal shepherds give a grosser name" (4.7.169-70).[5]

The imagery of rankness is most striking at the beginning of Claudius' soliloquy, when he arraigns himself before the bar of eternal justice:

> O, my offense is rank, it smells to heaven;
> It hath the primal eldest curse upon't,
> A brother's murder.   (3.3.36-38)

"The evil smell of evil deeds" is presented not only by direct statement ("it smells to heaven"), but also by the strong connotations of "rank" and "offense."[6] Claudius' crime offends the senses as well as the spirit; it stinks like Abel's rotting corpse. There is a curious parallel to this passage in Iago's insinuations about Des-

---

[5] See Edward A. Armstrong, *Shakespeare's Imagination* (rev. edn.; Lincoln: University of Nebraska Press, 1963), note 1 on pp. 94-95. This note was written for the revised edition.

[6] See Altick's commentary on "offense" words in *"Hamlet* and the Odor of Mortality," pp. 173-75.

demona's lust for a black man: "Foh! one may smell in such a will most rank,/ Foul disproportion, thoughts unnatural" (*Othello* 3.3.236-37). This is the abuse of the Moor "in the rank garb" (*Othello* 2.1.300), and we may see in Claudius' "rank" will a lust for power similar to Iago's. There is a sensuality of achieved ambition that operates more powerfully than any sensuality for merely physical objects, and therefore the secondary meaning of "rank" as one's official standing or degree of dignity in the world seems to me inescapable in Claudius' confession. His offense *is* rank, both as adjective and noun.

Unlike "rank," "foul" is not a complex word, but its meanings help to support the imagery of corruption. It signifies ugly, dirty, impure, and may be used as a general negative term; in the sense of polluted and filthy it may also suggest stink. Above all, the killing of Hamlet's father is a "foul and most unnatural murder" (1.5.25), a point which the Ghost drives home by repetition: "Murder most foul, as in the best it is,/ But this most foul, strange, and unnatural" (27-28). Hamlet's suspicions of "foul play" (1.2.256) have been justified, and "Foul deeds" (257) have indeed risen from their concealment. When Claudius tries to pray, he sees at once how false his words are: " 'Forgive me my foul murder'?" (3.3.52). Like Macbeth, he has played "most foully for't" (*Macbeth* 3.1.3) and therefore cannot pray.

In the course of his revenge, Hamlet appears to Ophelia with his "stockings fouled" (2.1.79), he sees the firmament as "a foul and pestilent congregation of vapors" (2.2.311), and his imagination may have become "as foul/ As Vulcan's stithy"[7] (3.2.85-86). The image of Vulcan's smoky forge has the same negative reference as Gertrude's "reechy kisses" (3.4.185), which derive their sense of filthy, squalid, and disgusting from the root idea of a smoking fire. In another instance, the "owner of a foul disease" (4.1.21) tries, even at the cost of his life, "To keep it from divulging" (22); there is the same unidentified evil in this "foul" as there is in the "foul crimes" (1.5.12) or sins of the Ghost, which it must now try to purge away in its purgatorial "prison house" (14). At the end of the play, Laertes' "foul practice" (5.2.318) turns against him, and he is caught "as a woodcock" in his "own springe" (307). No single use of "foul" is of special importance, but all the examples together do say something about the world of *Hamlet*.

The imagery of soiling and tainting adds another significant aspect to the idea of corruption in the play. The Ghost warns Hamlet: "Taint not thy mind" (1.5.85), and there is a combined sense of staining, infection, and even putrefaction in that use of the word. It is much less dire in Polonius' instructions to Reynaldo to breathe Laertes' "faults so quaintly/ That they may seem the taints of liberty" (2.1.31-32). Here the sense of the word is closer to that of spot or blemish, through an etymological connection with the Latin *tinctus*. The "black and grainèd spots" in Gertrude's soul that "will not leave

---

[7] Renaissance mythographers interpreted the image of "Vulcan's stithy" or forge as an archetype of the creative imagination, the "quick forge and working-house of thought" (*Henry V* Prol. V, 23).

their tinct" (3.4.91-92) are akin to this meaning. They are indelible, dyed in grain, and they have infallibly tainted her son's mind. Hamlet speaks later of having "a mother stained" (4.4.57), which seems in its sexual connotations to bear some relation to those black soul-spots of the closet scene. Hamlet's "sullied flesh" (1.2.129) would fit well into this imagery if one could prefer this much-debated reading of Quarto 2 to the "solid flesh" of Folio.[8]

Death is the most literal aspect of corruption in *Hamlet*. There is much talk of death in the play, and many dead bodies, too, which must be removed in full view of the audience. Hamlet's slaying of the "unseen good old man" (4.1.12) may be an impulsive act, but the exertion required to "lug the guts into the neighbor room" (3.4.213) provides an objective correlative for death. The effort is indicated by the Folio stage direction: *"Exit Hamlet, tugging in Polonius"* (218 s.d.). The *"tugging"* begins with Hamlet's punning line: "Come, sir, to draw toward an end with you" (217), a matter more difficult to accomplish when the garrulous old counselor was

[8] It is well to keep in mind that "sullied" is an emendation and that it occurs in no authoritative text; Quarto 2 has "sallied" and Folio "solid." Hubler reads "sullied," for which Wilson offers a strong argument in *The Manuscript of Shakespeare's Hamlet* (Cambridge, Eng.: Cambridge University Press, 1934), II, 307-15. See also Sidney Warhaft, "Hamlet's Solid Flesh Resolved," *ELH*, XXVIII (1961), 21-30; Samuel A. Weiss, " 'Solid,' 'Sullied' and Mutability: A Study in Imagery," *SQ*, X (1959), 219-27; and Fredson Bowers, "Hamlet's 'Sullied' or 'Solid' Flesh: A Bibliographical Case-History," *SS*, IX (1956), 44-48. In "This Sullied Solid Flesh," *Studia Neophilologica*, XXX (1958), 3-10, Helge Kökeritz objects strongly to Bowers' thesis.

alive. The body of Polonius is the stage equivalent of the weary weight of mortality.

There is another elaborate pun in Hamlet's prediction that "This man shall set me packing" (3.4.212). The obvious sense of "packing" is preparation for a journey, with a strong connotation of being in a hurry, but the context of the line suggests plotting and conspiracy. Hamlet is packing the deck against his enemies, as Antony suspects that Cleopatra has "Pack'd cards with Caesar, and false-play'd my glory/ Unto an enemy's triumph [=trump and victory procession]" (*Antony and Cleopatra* 4.14.19-20). Hamlet also exerts himself to pack away the body of Polonius in its temporary resting place, "as you go up the stairs into the lobby" (4.3.36-37).

The theme of mortality reaches its climax in the graveyard scene of Act V. This is probably the boldest and most original scene in the play. Its irrelevance, by French neoclassical standards, to the main action prompted Garrick to omit it in his later version of *Hamlet* and to assert in a letter to Sir William Young: "I had sworn I would not leave the stage till I had rescued that noble play from all the rubbish of the fifth act. . . ."[9] It seems to me, however, that the graveyard scene, in its abrupt change from everything that has preceded it, is a triumph in the Elizabethan art of contrast, especially difficult in a play that does not have a multiple plot.

[9] Quoted in George Winchester Stone, Jr., "Garrick's Long Lost Alteration of *Hamlet*," *PMLA*, XLIX (1934), 893. The letter is dated January 10, 1773, and Garrick's altered version of the play was first presented on December 18, 1772, at Drury Lane.

The imagery of mortality may be traced in the stage properties of this scene, beginning with the skull of the lawyer, who was "in's time a great buyer of land" (5. 1.105), but who now in death finds himself scarcely able to cope with his present estate of coffin and tomb: "Will his vouchers vouch him no more of his purchases, and double ones too, than the length and breadth of a pair of indentures? The very conveyances of his lands will scarcely lie in this box, and must th' inheritor himself have no more, ha?" (109-14). "This box" means, of course, the skull itself, about which Wilson has an imaginative note. He points out that Hamlet turns the top of the skull "towards the audience as he speaks, displaying its parchment-like surface and its serrated sutures, strikingly similar to the indented lines which divide 'a pair of indentures' into its parts."[10] Those not close to the stage, however, would surely not be able to distinguish the cranial sutures.

The Clown-gravedigger gives Hamlet the skull of Yorick, a fellow of ironically "infinite jest" (5.1.186-87), for closer inspection. Hamlet's apostrophe demands a skull with at least the lower jaw intact, since the demonstrative "Here" requires a proper object to complete its meaning: "Here hung those lips that I have kissed I know not how oft" (189-91). The skull is further described as "grinning" and "chapfall'n," not "chapless" (90) like that of the imagined courtier. To Hamlet its odor is overpowering: "And smelt so? Pah!" (202). By this common stink, Hamlet equates the skull of Yorick with that of Alexander the Great, who may, like "a king," "go a progress through the guts of a beggar"

[10] Wilson, p. 236.

(4.3.30-31) and wind up, with "Imperious Caesar" (5.1.215), "stopping a bunghole" (206) in a beer barrel or patching "a wall t' expel the winter's flaw" (218).

There is more than curious interest in Hamlet's insistent questioning of the gravedigger: "How long will a man lie i' th' earth ere he rot?" (5.1.165). "Goodman Delver" (14) answers with professional circumspection, as if to give this unknown stranger a "taste" of his "quality" (2.2.441): "Faith, if 'a be not rotten before 'a die (as we have many pocky corses nowadays that will scarce hold the laying in), 'a will last you some eight year or nine year. A tanner will last you nine year" (5.1.166-69). As the guardian of mortality, the gravedigger is exacting in his measurement of time. A tanner's corpse can resist decomposition because "his hide is so tanned with his trade that 'a will keep out water a great while, and your water is a sore decayer of your whoreson dead body" (171-73). With a student's diligence, Hamlet tries to inform himself about the grave he must shortly lie in, and the clown-show and wit-combat in the graveyard teach him something he could never have learned at the University of Wittenberg. Even if " 'Twere to consider too curiously, to consider so" (207-8), Hamlet reaches a new understanding of the nature of mortality in this scene. He has cleared his mind of illusions, and in the next scene he is prepared not only to die well, but also to kill well.

Animals

The animal imagery of *Hamlet* shares the predominantly negative tone of such imagery throughout Shakespeare. Although *Hamlet* has some noble animals such

as the lion or the eagle, and a few gentle creatures such
as the dove, these are overwhelmed by a mass of gross,
predatory, cunning, and filthy beasts which symbolize
man's loss of the godlike faculty of reason and his re-
version to a life of will and appetite. The chief aspects
of animal imagery are hunting, trapping, snaring, net-
ting, and angling, and we have an emphasis on aggression and prey similar to that which characterized the
imagery of war. Both kinds of imagery imply a threat of
attack that "craves wary walking" (*Julius Caesar* 2.1.15).

One of the central facts of the play is that Claudius
and his agents are hunting Hamlet, who taxes Guildenstern and Rosencrantz with their pursuit of him: "why
do you go about to recover the wind of me, as if you
would drive me into a toil?" (3.2.353-55). A "toil" is
a net in which to catch large game such as deer. By getting on their windward side, one may entice them into
the trap. Rosencrantz and Guildenstern are attempting
to "draw" Hamlet "on to pleasures" (2.2.15), to "drive
his purpose into these delights" (3.1.27), and to "pluck
out the heart" of his "mystery" (3.2.373-74). The insistent allusions to hunting convert even such a ceremonial phrase as "We'll wait upon you" (2.2.271) into
a suggestion that Rosencrantz and Guildenstern are ly-
ing in wait in order to snare Hamlet. On his English
voyage Hamlet is "benetted round with villains" (5.2.
29), but, like Laertes, they are the proverbially foolish woodcocks who are caught in their "own springe"
(5.2.307). Laertes' image almost exactly matches his
father's earlier phrase for Hamlet's "holy vows": "Ay,
springes to catch woodcocks" (1.3.114-15). For all their

cunning, the Polonius family does not have a good casualty record.

Polonius hunts "the trail of policy" (2.2.47) most subtly in the pursuit of his own son in Paris, where the sport of "indirections" (2.1.66) has its own pleasures apart from any objective purpose. Both "encompass-ment" (10) and "windlasses" are "assays of bias" (65), circuitous and winding attempts to trap game. The idea of artful pursuit is also expressed in a fishing image: "See you now—/ Your bait of falsehood take this carp of truth" (62-63), a difficult fish to land. We remember that Hamlet accuses Claudius of throwing out his "an-gle," or fishing line, "for my proper life" (5.2.66).

Death is also a hunter, as he is personified by Fortin-bras at the end of the play:

> This quarry cries on havoc. O proud Death,
> What feast is toward in thine eternal cell
> That thou so many princes at a shot
> So bloodily hast struck?   (5.2.365-68)

"Quarry" refers to the heap of deer killed at a single hunting, and "havoc" is a military cry for indiscrimi-nate slaughter, as in Antony's oration: "Cry 'Havoc!' and let slip the dogs of war" (*Julius Caesar* 3.1.274). "Proud Death" is hunting for game to supply its feast, and only princes are suitable. This image is an apt ex-ample of how the hunting and military themes both have a common purpose.

There is a brief counter-imagery in which Hamlet figures as the hunter, especially with his play, *The Mousetrap*. The title is meant "Tropically" (3.2.243), or figuratively, according to the medieval fourfold method of interpretation, and the pun on the title is underscored by the Quarto 1 spelling, "trapically." Hamlet designed his play to "catch the conscience of the King" (2.2.617), who is no woodcock to the springe, but a tough villain who can take an enormous amount of psychological punishment.

The most significant animal imagery in *Hamlet* is that derived from falconry, a form of hunting that parallels the art of war. There is a riddling hawk image in Hamlet's explanation of his madness to Rosencrantz and Guildenstern: "I am but mad north-northwest: when the wind is southerly I know a hawk from a handsaw" (2.2.387-88). The phrase is proverbial, and "handsaw" (in both Quarto 2 and Folio) has been considered a corruption of "hernshaw" or heron, although both "hawk" and "handsaw" are also terms for familiar tools. Despite these distracting meanings, I think we are supposed to understand that Hamlet is not so mad but that he can distinguish preying hawks (Rosencrantz and Guildenstern) from one of their favorite quarries, the heron (Hamlet himself), and the mention of specific winds supports the idea of hunting.

Earlier in the play, Marcellus and Hamlet exchange a bantering set of falconer's cries to bring the bird back to the lure or fist:

Marcellus. Illo, ho, ho, my lord!
Hamlet. Hillo, ho, ho, boy! Come, bird, come.
(1.5.115-16)

This is the beginning of Hamlet's "wild and whirling words" (133). We remember that he made his promise to the Ghost in a falcon image:

> Haste me to know't, that I, with wings as swift
> As meditation or the thoughts of love,
> May sweep to my revenge.   (1.5.29-31)

"Sweep" seems to refer to the hawk's "swooping" or "stooping" to prey from its "pitch," or apex of its flight, as Richard II admires "How high a pitch" Bolingbroke's "resolution soars" (*Richard II* 1.1.109). Since the falcon reaches its "pitch" just before it strikes, "enterprises of great pitch and moment" can suddenly "turn awry,/ And lose the name of action" (3.1.86-88).

Claudius records Hamlet's escape from certain death in England with another term from falconry: "If he be now returned,/ As checking at his voyage" (4.7.61-62). A hawk is said to "check" when it abandons its proper quarry to pursue other birds that cross its path. "Checking" is ironic in this passage, because Hamlet as hawk is not within the control of Claudius as falconer. Hamlet thinks of his uncle as the prey of kites, those base hawks that were believed to feed on carrion:

> But I am pigeon-livered and lack gall
> To make oppression bitter, or ere this
> I should ha' fatted all the region kites
> With this slave's offal.   (2.2.588-91)

From the talk of the players, we learn that the competition of the children's companies has forced them to take to the road: "an eyrie of children, little eyases, that cry out on the top of question and are most tyrannically clapped for't" (2.2.347-49). "Eyrie" is the falcon's nest, and "eyases" are the fledgling hawks trained from the nest. These domesticated birds are meant to be contrasted with "haggards," the wild hawks caught and then trained, whose fierceness was much prized by Renaissance falconers. Hamlet welcomes the players with sporting enthusiasm: "We'll e'en to't like French falconers, fly at anything we see" (439-40). Hawks were trained to fly at only one, or at most several, kinds of prey, and Hamlet is soon using his player-hawks in more orthodox fashion to "catch the conscience of the King" (617).

After the success of his play, Hamlet makes an explosively satirical reference to Claudius as a peacock:

> For thou dost know, O Damon dear,
> This realm dismantled was
> Of Jove himself; and now reigns here
> A very, very—peacock.[11]   (3.2.287-90)

This little doggerel poem is probably meant to be sung, and Hamlet's avoidance of the "was"-"ass" rhyme puts special stress on "peacock," a bird "no less undesirable morally than musically, fiend-voiced, serpent-headed, thief-paced, lecherous, and an unnatural father."[12] Hamlet's topical song offers a lesson in the "dismantling" of

[11] Hubler and many other editors read "pajock," a modernization of Quarto 2's "paiock" (Folio also has "paiocke"), but this is a nonexistent animal, and even those editors who object to "peacock" agree that it is the word intended, of which they claim "pajock" as a variant.

[12] Travers, p. 134.

the realm similar to that in the closet scene, where Hyperion, Jove, Mars, and Mercury (3.4.57-59) are replaced by the animal equivalents of the peacock: "a paddock," "a bat, a gib" (191).

Bird imagery is used to characterize Osric, whose name suggests "ostrich" (in Quarto 2 he is actually called "Ostricke"[13]). We remember that he is also a "waterfly" (5.2.83), one of the "diminutives of nature" among Thersites' worthless nothings (*Troilus and Cressida* 5.1.31-32). The contrast between waterfly and ostrich makes an excellent grotesque, especially in the light of Samuel Johnson's definition: "A *water-fly* skips up and down upon the surface of the water, without any apparent purpose or reason, and is thence the proper emblem of a busy trifler."[14] In Hamlet's contemptuous description, Osric is a "chough" (5.2.89) or jackdaw, a foolish chattering bird, and part of the "bevy ['breed' in Quarto 2] that I know the drossy age dotes on" (191). Osric's exit in this scene is marked by Horatio's satirical thrust: "This lapwing runs away with the shell on his head" (187-88). It is a triumph of subtlety on Claudius' part to use such a foolish, callow bird as messenger for his poison plot, and Hamlet and Horatio are successfully put off their guard.

As Spurgeon argues in her discussion of the dog-lick-

[13] Quarto 2's "Ostricke" may, of course, be a misprint, since the scene also has "Osrick," and both *Ostr.* and *Osr.* appear in the speech prefixes. But the birdlike name does suggest a deliberate choice, if only on the part of an inspired compositor or press-corrector. See Wilson, *The Manuscript of Shakespeare's Hamlet*, I, 149.

[14] *Johnson's Notes to Shakespeare*, ed. Arthur Sherbo, p. 178.

ing-candy sequence,[15] dogs almost always suggest something unpleasant to Shakespeare, a point she illustrates with Hamlet's refusal to flatter Horatio:

> Why should the poor be flattered?
> No, let the candied tongue lick absurd pomp,
> And crook the pregnant hinges of the knee
> Where thrift may follow fawning.   (3.2.61-64)

Although there are no dogs mentioned in the passage, the imagery suggests a spaniel or greyhound "at table, licking the hands of the guests, fawning and begging for sweetmeats. . . ."[16] Horatio, who is "e'en as just a man" (56) as Hamlet has ever met, has none of these courtier's attributes, especially not that corrupted virtue of "thrift."

The pejorative quality of the dog image usually occurs in passing or by association, and it is often expressed in proverbial form. Thus Gertrude addresses Laertes' rebels as "false Danish dogs" who run "counter" (4.5.110), or in a direction opposite to that which the game has taken, and Hamlet will allow Laertes to rant, since "The cat will mew, and dog will have his day" (5.1.294). Hamlet proposes a difficult analogy for Polonius: "For if the sun breed maggots in a dead dog, being a good kissing carrion—Have you a daughter?" (2.2.181-83). This is the lesson of *Measure for Measure*, where Angelo takes responsibility for his fall:

[15] See Spurgeon, *Shakespeare's Imagery*, pp. 195-99.
[16] Spurgeon, *Shakespeare's Imagery*, p. 197.

>   . . . but it is I
> That, lying by the violet in the sun,
> Do as the carrion does, not as the flow'r,
> Corrupt with virtuous season.
>
>   (2.2.165-68)

But Ophelia has not the resilience of Isabella in coping with Angelo, and there is no bed-trick to save her from her watery death.

The image of stinking carrion is recalled when Hamlet tells the king where he may "nose" (4.3.36) Polonius' corpse, as, at the end of the previous scene, a hound might smell out the hidden fox. "Truth's a dog must to kennel," says the Fool in *Lear* (1.4.110), but Hamlet will "unkennel" (3.2.83) his uncle's "occulted guilt" (82) with his "dozen or sixteen lines" (2.2.551) of *The Mousetrap*. There is a suggestion of malodorousness in "kennel," through its derivation from "cannel" (or "channel"), an open drain or gutter.

The references to horses are also familiar and proverbial, which has the advantage of generating a strong and deeply rooted response. Hamlet doesn't bother to complete the old saw, " 'while the grass grows,' " since "the proverb is something musty" (3.2.351-52). Whetstone's version of 1576 reads, "whilst grasse doth growe, For want of foode the steede doth sterve" (Tilley, G423). Hamlet's teasing assertion before Lucianus enters is also a proverb: " 'Tis a knavish piece of work, but what of that? Your Majesty, and we that have free souls, it touches us not. Let the galled jade winch; our

withers are unwrung" (3.2.246-49) .[17] We think of that
"poor jade" Cut in *1 Henry IV*, who "is wrung in the
withers out of all cess" (2.1.6-7) , a condition produced
by "the galling or pinching by a badly fitting saddle of
the part where the shoulder-bones join the neck."[18]

The physical soreness that galling produces (from
rubbing or chafing) becomes an image of destructive
contact. The salt of Gertrude's "most unrighteous tears"
gives her "gallèd eyes" (1.2.154-55) . Hamlet complains
that "the toe of the peasant comes so near the heel of the
courtier he galls his kibe" (5.1.142-44) , and Laertes advises his sister that "The canker galls the infants of the
spring/ Too oft before their buttons be disclosed"
(1.3.39-40) . In a more menacing sense, Laertes will
anoint his foil with a poison so powerful that "if I gall
him slightly,/ It may be death" (4.7.147-48) . These
additional examples should help us understand why a
"galled jade" will "winch."

The most brilliant equestrian passage in the play is
Claudius' description of Lamord,[19] "a gentleman of Nor-
mandy" (4.7.82) :

I have seen myself, and served against, the French,
And they can well on horseback, but this gallant
Had witchcraft in't. He grew unto his seat,
And to such wondrous doing brought his horse
As had he been incorpsed and deminatured

[17] See Tilley, H700: "Touch (Rub) a galled Horse on the back
and he will wince (kick)."
[18] A. Forbes Sieveking, "Horsemanship, with Farriery," *Shakespeare's England*, II, 426.
[19] Lamord is the name in Quarto 2; in Folio it is Lamound.

With the brave beast. So far he topped my thought
That I, in forgery of shapes and tricks,
Come short of what he did.   (4.7.83-90)

This is Claudius' only lyric and exuberant passage, and
it has a leisure and copiousness that are intended to distract Laertes and puff him up with self-love. The king
puns on "topped" as overtopped, surpassed, as well as
mounted on a horse. "Incorpsed and deminatured/ With
the brave beast" indicates that Lamord is like the Centaurs, who were known for their skill in natural magic,
especially in poisons. There is some occult link between
Lamord's "witchcraft" and Claudius' (cf. 1.5.43).

In Hamlet's inflamed imagination, Claudius himself
is represented as a "paddock" or toad, a "bat," and a
"gib" or tomcat (3.4.191), all animals that were considered the familiars of witches. It is worth insisting
that this is a moral description of Claudius; it sets forth
the fauna of the region of his soul. To take these frenzied imaginings as an accurate account of the king's
physical appearance, as some critics have done,[20] seems
to me to distort the dramatic context. The important
point about Claudius is the contrast between his regal
bearing—"Ay, every inch a king" (*King Lear* 4.6.107)
—and his inner rottenness. Although the Ghost calls
him "a wretch whose natural gifts were poor/ To those
of mine" (1.5.51-52), we should not translate this into
objective, physical terms. To make Claudius up as ugly
and repulsive, like Richard III, would destroy the unctu-

[20] See Bradley, *Shakespearean Tragedy*, p. 169, and Weston
Babcock, *Hamlet: A Tragedy of Errors* (Lafayette, Ind.: Purdue
University, 1961), p. 55.

ous hypocrisy of the "smiling, damnèd villain" (1.5.
106). It does seem, however, as if Claudius is a large
and powerfully built man, capable of overawing Laertes
and others by the sheer bulk of his royal person.

In his own role, Hamlet is troubled by the question of
"Bestial oblivion" (4.4.40), or a beast's lack of concern
for anything besides the satisfaction of its appetites:

> What is a man,
> If his chief good and market of his time
> Be but to sleep and feed? A beast, no more.
>
> (4.4.33-35)

Thus a man is in danger of becoming a beast when "reason panders will" (3.4.89). Hamlet seems acutely conscious throughout the play of this amphibious nature of
man, placed in a middle state, a little lower than the an-
gels and a little higher than the beasts. It is the great
paradox of the age that man, who should be "the beauty
of the world, the paragon of animals," is nevertheless
the "quintessence of dust" (2.2.315-17). Around him
Hamlet sees a human reality divorced from ethical values, where "a beast that wants discourse of reason/
Would have mourned longer" (1.2.150-51) than his
own mother. Therefore he can wonder, in an animal
image, "What should such fellows as I do crawling between earth and heaven?" (3.1.128-29), or he can speculate why man, like a willing ass, "would fardels bear,/
To grunt and sweat under a weary life" (3.1.76-77).
These doubts are by no means answered in the play,
but the young Hamlet is like the old Lear in insisting
so strenuously on the question "What is a man?" (4.4.
33).

Disease

Imagery of disease offers one of the most traditional ways of creating a sense of evil in tragedy. In the typical structural pattern, the dramatic action moves toward the discovery and expulsion of the disease and the return of the body politic to health. The antagonist who is the source of the disease is uncovered and destroyed, but the protagonist who sets the action in motion also becomes implicated in it and must inevitably die. I am, of course, tracing a general development, but the form of tragedy lends itself to medical and therapeutic metaphors, in which the movement is always from disease to health. The need for tragic persons to be of high station has a practical as well as snobbish basis, since there is an immediate analogy between the king's two bodies, the natural and the politic. In a king or prince, private and public may be played off against each other with interesting tragic possibilities.

What is often surprising in disease imagery is how literally disorders of a symbolic nature may be described. "The time is out of joint" (1.5.188), says Hamlet. There is a dislocation in the body of the world, in the nature of reality as well as in the body politic of Denmark, and Hamlet curses the spite "That ever I was born to set it right" (189). This is the very same image (with a double reference to carpentry) that Claudius uses for the audacity of "young Fortinbras," "thinking by our late dear brother's death/ Our state to be disjoint and out of frame" (1.2.19-20). Is the kingdom in need of medical attention? Claudius obviously does not think so, but we soon see that there may indeed be something "rotten in the state of Denmark" (1.4.90). The word "rotten" is also associated with disease in the sense, now lost, of putridity carried by the air.

The general condition of rottenness in *Hamlet* finds its most powerful expression in the imagery of skin disease, which derives from the Ghost's description of its poisoning:

> And a most instant tetter barked about
> Most lazarlike with vile and loathsome crust
> All my smooth body. (1.5.71-73)

"Tetter" is a strong word for any pustular, herpetiform eruption of the skin, such as eczema, herpes, impetigo, or ringworm. The "lazarlike" and "loathsome crust" of the "tetter" gives the elder Hamlet's "smooth body" a hideous, barklike rugosity, and it provides a model for all the other skin diseases in the play.

I have already discussed the connection between poison and disease in the second chapter. Hamlet's father is killed by a "leperous distillment" (1.5.64), as if the poison were a perverse medicine that could produce the disease. The poisonous "unction of a mountebank" (4.7.141) with which Laertes will anoint his foil is another perverse medicine, more powerful than any existing antidote:

> So mortal that, but dip a knife in it,
> Where it draws blood, no cataplasm so rare,
> Collected from all simples that have virtue
> Under the moon, can save the thing from death
> That is but scratched withal. (4.7.142-46)

Romeo first noted his fatal apothecary "Culling of simples" (*Romeo and Juliet* 5.1.40), but in *Hamlet* these old-fashioned, uncompounded herb-medicines can have no effect against a "potent poison" (5.2.354). It is an "anti-medicine," administered to kill rather than to cure, and it is significant that Laertes also refers to his poison as "this contagion" (4.7.147). He will "touch" (146) his point with it in both senses of the word: "anoint" (140) and infect, as Claudius had earlier offered Laertes "our kingdom . . ./ Our crown, our life" if he and his judges could "find us touched" (4.5.205-6). The king is boastfully disclaiming any infection or guilt from Polonius' death. In this context, Laertes' admission in the fencing match, "A touch, a touch; I do confess't" (5.2.287), is full of irony. "No med'cine in the world" (315) can do Hamlet any good after he is touched with Laertes' stronger medicine, which, like the mountebank's nostrum that it is, serves for its owner too.

With a nice moral symmetry, the images of disease can be reversed between protagonist and antagonist. Just as Hamlet will "tent" or probe Claudius "to the quick" (2.2.609) with his play, so Claudius brings Laertes "to the quick of th' ulcer—/ Hamlet comes back" (4.7.123-24), and Laertes must make his lethal demonstration of filial love. Both Claudius and Hamlet acknowledge the existence of disease, but they have contradictory claims about who is afflicted. Hamlet is "the hectic" (4.3.66), or consumptive fever, that "rages" in Claudius' blood and that he calls on England to "cure" (67). We know the nature of this attempted cure, which we can judge by Claudius' proverbial formula:

> Diseases desperate grown
> By desperate appliance are relieved,
> Or not at all.   (4.3.9-11)

In both these images, Hamlet is the disease and Claudius the body, which he wants us to understand as the body politic. In the final audit of Claudius' evil, Hamlet is confident that his revenge is just:

> And is't not to be damned
> To let this canker of our nature come
> In further evil?   (5.2.68-70)

Claudius is now the "canker" or cancer—the two words were used interchangeably until the eighteenth century—that is infecting the body of Denmark. The doubleness of the ulcer or canker image, which Hamlet and Claudius apply to each other, makes it a part of other ambiguities in the play.

The persistence of the imagery of skin disease may be seen in a number of unexpected examples. At the very beginning, the advent of the Ghost bodes "some strange eruption" (1.1.69) to the state, which Wilson glosses as "an outbreak of calamity or evil."[21] But "eruption" also has a strong secondary meaning of skin disease, as in Hotspur's impudent mocking of Glendower: "Diseased nature oftentimes breaks forth/ In strange eruptions" (*1 Henry IV* 3.1.27-28). The Clown-gravedigger, who is after all no social historian, is disturbed by the fact that "we have many pocky corses nowadays that will scarce hold the laying in" (5.1.166-68). As

[21] Wilson, p. 270. For the disease sense see Mahood, *Shakespeare's Wordplay*, p. 113.

another aspect of "the late innovation" (2.2.341) in the Danish kingship, Hamlet notes that in the last three years "the age is grown so picked that the toe of the peasant comes so near the heel of the courtier he galls his kibe" (5.1.142-44). A "kibe" is a chapped or ulcerated chilblain on the heel—the effort to keep one's kibes ungalled is not just a matter of social distinction. In Hamlet's "dram of evil" speech, the "mole of nature" (1.4.24) is not a benign or even an eccentric growth, but a "vicious mole" that, like a cancer, eats away all vigorous and healthy qualities. The point of the speech is to deny a symmetrical and balanced morality of "taints and honours" waging equally in a man (*Antony and Cleopatra* 5.1.30), since the smallest quantity of evil is able to spoil the largest quantity of "noble substance" (1.4.37).

Gertrude's moral weakness is also represented in physiological terms. Thus, her "act"

> . . . takes off the rose
> From the fair forehead of an innocent love,
> And sets a blister there. . . .   (3.4.43-45)

Schmidt defines "blister" as a pustule or ulcer, a sense that is demanded by the strong contrast between blister and rose, even as Laertes' mother may be branded a harlot "between the chaste unsmirchèd brow" (4.5.119). Hamlet also means us to understand that Gertrude, at menopause, is too old for keen sexual excitement:

> You cannot call it love, for at your age
> The heyday in the blood is tame, it's humble,
> And waits upon the judgment. . . .   (3.4.69-71)

"Blood" was a common Elizabethan word for sexuality. Although Schmidt pleasantly glosses "heyday" as "frolicsome wildness," the context insists that Gertrude can no longer be one of those dangerous lovers (as Polonius thinks Hamlet) whose "blood burns" (1.3.116).

By putting particular stress on the dullness of his mother's senses, Hamlet presents a physical analogue for her moral blindness. His comparison of the two portraits in the closet scene is punctuated by a series of alarming questions about Gertrude's capacity to perceive: "Have you eyes?" (3.4.66), "Ha! Have you eyes?" (68), which ends in a bleak, Beckett-like conclusion:

> Eyes without feeling, feeling without sight,
> Ears without hands or eyes, smelling sans all,
> Or but a sickly part of one true sense. . . .

$$(3.4.79-81)$$

This enumeration of the senses contributes to the grossness of the scene, in which Hamlet holds forth as a medical as well as a spiritual counselor.

Gertrude's inability to understand any but literal meanings seems to assure us of her tragic end. When Hamlet warns her, metaphorically, "You go not till I set you up a glass" (3.4.20), she apparently thinks that she will be forced to drink a glass of poison, and her frightened cry, "What wilt thou do? Thou wilt not murder me?" (22), leads directly to the stabbing of Polonius. "That monster custom" (162), or habit, may have something to do with Gertrude's obtuseness, since it eats "all sense" (162), all awareness or perception of what we are actually doing. Gertrude's faculties are certainly in good working order, "Else could you not have motion" (73), but, figuratively, her "sense/ Is apoplexed" (73-74). This is a strong word, meaning a sudden arrest of the powers of motion, a temporary paralysis. Hamlet is presenting his argument in neurological terms in order to mitigate his mother's moral offense.

The most persistent verbal theme within the motif of disease is that of "blasting," a word that occurs more often in *Hamlet* than in any other play of Shakespeare. The basis for the image is the infection carried by the air, especially night air and air in unhealthful places such as swamps and cemeteries. There is some literal notion of infected air in Hamlet's first words to the Ghost: "Be thou a spirit of health or goblin damned,/ Bring with thee airs from heaven or blasts from hell" (1.4.40-41). In Laertes' warning to his sister, there is also a strong sense of baleful contagion carried by the wind: "And in the morn and liquid dew of youth/ Contagious blastments are most imminent" (1.3.41-42). Laertes sweetens his purpose with mellifluous platitudes, but what he fears is Hamlet's "hot love on the wing" (2.2.132) and its power to blast Ophelia's virginity.

A blastment is a sudden pernicious influence that blights, withers, shrivels, and destroys—the "blasted heath" in *Macbeth* (1.3.77) is an expression of this cursed and desolating force. "Blast" is also the familiar word for an explosion, as in Claudius' plot, whose "back or second" will be ready if the first part "did blast in proof" (4.7.153-54). Ophelia laments Hamlet as a "blown youth/ Blasted with ecstasy" (3.1.162-63). Madness is a disease, and "Blasted" carries with it the sense of a sudden infectious gust, as of a wind, capable of extinguishing the reason. The image is supported by "blown," meaning both blooming and windswept. In the closet scene, Claudius is "like a mildewed ear/ Blasting his wholesome brother" (3.4.65-66) . There is a quibble on that symbolic ear through whose porches old Hamlet was destroyed. His brother is now the diseased ear itself, spreading his blighting fungus to the healthy ears in the corncrib. The sense of blasting as a curse is most explicit in the description of Lucianus' poison, which is "With Hecate's ban thrice blasted, thrice infected" (3.2. 264) , as if these processes were inseparable. Some of this meaning carries over to Horatio's determination to cross the Ghost, "though it blast me" (1.1.127) . One has the impression of a demon Ghost with the power to destroy the good Horatio in body and soul. By combining the notions of disease, explosion, annihilating wind, and diabolic curse, "blasting" becomes a complex word which no single meaning can adequately explain.

We have yet to answer the most pressing question of all: What ails Hamlet? Among his many difficulties, the most grievous are melancholy, heartache, and shortness of breath. Hamlet's worst complaint is, of course, melancholy,[22] the predominance of black bile, possibly even adust, which Robert Burton thought the source of all madness and all genius in this world. As generations of Romantic critics have nostalgically pointed out, Hamlet's "native hue of resolution/ Is sicklied o'er with the

[22] See Bridget J. Gellert, "Three Literary Treatments of Melancholy: Marston, Shakespeare and Burton," doctoral dissertation, Columbia University, 1966, esp. Chap. 4, on *Hamlet*.

pale cast of thought" (3.1.84-85). In its root sense, however, this image is physiological. The natural redness
and sanguinity of resolution pales to a much lighter
color ("cast") as the blood is drawn from the cheeks by
the workings of thought, a process always associated
with melancholy in the Renaissance. We remember
Enobarbus' advice to Cleopatra after her perfidy at
Actium: "Think, and die," and in his own death, if
"swift thought" cannot break his heart, "a swifter mean/
Shall outstrike thought; but thought will do't, I feel"
(*Antony and Cleopatra* 3.13.1, 4.6.35-36). Ophelia gives
pansies "for thoughts" (4.5.176), and to Gertrude,
heaven itself, in imitation of the Day of Doom, is
"thoughtsick" at her "act" (3.4.52). Hamlet fears that
his "weakness" and his "melancholy" may have made
him an easy prey to the devil, who, "As he is very potent
with such spirits,/ Abuses me to damn me" (2.2.613-15).

Heartsick matches thoughtsick as a description of what
ails Hamlet. Death is "a consummation/ Devoutly to
be wished" (3.1.63-64) because it ends the dominion
of "outrageous fortune" (58):

> To die, to sleep—
> No more—and by a sleep to say we end
> The heartache, and the thousand natural shocks
> That flesh is heir to!   (3.1.60-63)

This is the only example of "heartache" in Shakespeare,
and the *OED* marks it as the first use of the word in
English in its modern sense; it seems to have special relevance to Hamlet and his problems.

Just before the fencing match, Hamlet has an intuition of disaster that gives, in Kitto's term,[23] a "religious" dimension to the tragedy: "I shall win at the odds. But thou wouldst not think how ill all's here about my heart. But it is no matter" (5.2.212-14). There is conscious poetic artifice in those matched monosyllables, "ill-all's" and "here-heart," but the assonantal modulation is sustained by the intensity of the context. Hamlet vows to "defy augury" (220), even those oracular reports from the region of his heart, because to a true Christian "There is special providence in the fall of a sparrow" (220-21). Echoing Matthew 10:29, he also assents to its description of a "divinity that shapes our ends" (5.2.10) and an "ordinant" (48) heaven. Hamlet's ill-boding heart recalls the opening scene, where Francisco thanks Barnardo for relieving him (in a therapeutic as well as military sense): " 'Tis bitter cold,/ And I am sick at heart" (1.1.8-9). This serves as the keynote of the first scene and possibly of the entire play, in which more persons than Francisco will suffer from atmospheric *Angst*.

The vulnerability of Hamlet's heart is particularly insisted on. At the end of his first soliloquy, he says: "But break my heart, for I must hold my tongue" (1.2.159), and after the exit of the Ghost he exclaims, perhaps with a gesture: "Hold, hold, my heart" (1.5.93). Horatio marks Hamlet's death with a lyrically physiological observation: "Now cracks a noble heart" (5.2.360), which draws on the Elizabethan notion of death as a snapping of the heartstrings or sinews. In contrast to Hamlet, Claudius has a "heart with strings of steel," which he

[23] See Kitto, *Form and Meaning in Drama*, esp. Chap. 8: "Religious Drama and its Interpretation."

vainly hopes may become "soft as sinews of the newborn babe" (3.3.70-71).

There is a significant imagery of breathing in *Hamlet*, especially difficult breathing, as if to emphasize how much of a burden it is "To grunt and sweat under a weary life" (3.1.77). One of the signs of Hamlet's painful mourning for his father is his "windy suspiration of forced breath" (1.2.79). Difficult breathing is a symptom of pursiness, a malady that lends itself to moral metaphor, as in Alcibiades' reform program for Athens:

> Now breathless wrong
> Shall sit and pant in your great chairs of ease,
> And pursy insolence shall break his wind
> With fear and horrid flight.
> *(Timon of Athens 5.4.10-13)*

In the closet scene, Hamlet describes the corruption of the present age in terms of pursiness:

> Forgive me this my virtue,
> For in the fatness of these pursy times
> Virtue itself of vice must pardon beg,
> Yea, curb and woo for leave to do him good.
> (3.4.153-56)

Corpulence makes one "pursy," or short- and broken-winded.

Pleurisy (or "plurisy") is related to pursiness through the painful and difficult breathing common to both. There was some confusion over the word in Elizabethan English, since it could mean either specifically an inflammation of the pleura (the coverings of the lungs), or, through a popular derivation from the Latin *plus*, an illness caused by general superabundance and excess of humors.[24] The latter sense of superfluity is found in Claudius' discourse on the fickle nature of time and fortune:

> And nothing is at a like goodness still,
> For goodness, growing to a plurisy,
> Dies in his own too-much.   (4.7.116-18)

This idea leads to the next image in Claudius' speech. Delay in putting into effect that which we should do creates a morbid condition, "And then this 'should' is like a spendthrift sigh,/ That hurts by easing" (122-23). One of the reasons that the sigh may hurt is because in a pleuritic state any breathing at all is painful. The sigh is "spendthrift," since sighing was thought to draw drops of blood from the heart and thereby squander the body's vitality. By an effect of antithesis of which Claudius is fond, it at once hurts and eases the body. The physiological dangers of sighing may also be seen in Ophelia's description of the lovelorn Hamlet:

> He raised a sigh so piteous and profound
> As it did seem to shatter all his bulk
> And end his being.   (2.1.94-96)

The strongest examples of this theme are found in the last scene of the play, where the difficulty of breathing has more than a figurative importance. We remember that Hamlet wrenches the poisoned chalice from Horatio in order to force him to be his "abstract and brief" chronicle (2.2.535):

[24] See Wilson, p. xxxvii, and *Variorum*, I, 365.

Absent thee from felicity awhile,
And in this harsh world draw thy breath in pain,
To tell my story.   (5.2.348-50)

However pleuritically and pursily, Horatio must continue to "draw" his "breath in pain" in order to clear
his friend's "wounded name" (345). Difficult breathing seems to provide a metaphor for the human condition. By a fitting irony, Claudius will pledge the poisoned cup "to Hamlet's better breath" (272).

During the fencing match, the queen answers Claudius' hollow assertion: "Our son shall win," with a
statement that has puzzled commentators: "He's fat,
and scant of breath" (288), which seems to state two
reasons why Hamlet cannot possibly win. The context
supports the idea that "fat" means "sweaty," since Gertrude's next words are: "Here, Hamlet, take my napkin
[=handkerchief], rub thy brows" (289), and she persists
even after she has drunk the poisoned cup: "Come, let
me wipe thy face" (295). Gertrude's affectionate gesture
echoes the very words of Doll Tearsheet to Falstaff: "Ah,
you sweet little rogue, you! Alas, poor ape, how thou
sweat'st! Come, let me wipe thy face" (2 Henry IV
2.4.206-7). Despite this random association with Falstaff,
Hamlet is not necessarily overweight (as Richard Burbage, the actor who played Hamlet, seems to have been),
but he is panting and perspiring because he is "fat" in
the sense of not quite being in shape. I know that this
interpretation denies Hamlet's earlier assertion that he
has been "in continual practice" (5.2.212) since Laertes
went into France, but an audience is not supposed to

notice such contradictions. Hamlet's "fatness" may also have something to do with the physical-spiritual condition of both his father and the Player King, who are murdered after their midday dinner, when they are "full of bread" (3.3.80) .[25]

Although critics are repelled by the notion of a corpulent Hamlet, it seems to me that there is an association, perhaps only figurative, between fatness and pursiness, as in Hamlet's indignation at the "fatness of these pursy times" (3.4.154) . No one has questioned Gertrude's assertion that her son is "scant of breath," which makes Hamlet as a fencer rather different from the dashing, romantic figure one sees in most productions. We have been carefully prepared for his tragic death in this scene, and we are presumably willing to agree that, like all revengers (except a few impossibly Christian ones) , he has become tainted by the workings of his revenge. If the negative imagery of disease and physical impairment has any cumulative force, we should be able to postulate certain physical correlates of Hamlet's taint. By being a revenger, he may literally have become "fat, and scant of breath," so that now more than ever before he is ready "To die, to sleep," and by a sleep to "end/ The heartache, and the thousand natural shocks/ That flesh is heir to!" (3.1.60-63) .

[25] See R. J. Dorius, "A Little More than a Little," *SQ,* XI (1960), 13-26. See also Kittredge's judicious note, p. 295; M. P. Tilley, "Two Shakespearean Notes," *Journal of English and Germanic Philology,* XXIV (1925), 315-24; J. C. Maxwell, " 'Fat and Scant of Breath' Again," *English Studies,* XXXII (1951), 29-30; and Waldo H. Dunn's letter to the *Times Literary Supplement,* May 26, 1927, p. 375.

Food

The imagery of food and eating, like that of animals and disease, also undercuts man's claim to be a rational being. By relating hunger to the instinctive needs of animals, this imagery emphasizes man's grossness and sensuality, and there is a familiar association between gluttony and lechery. "Appetite" is always a pejorative term in Shakespeare, as in Lear's defense of the proposition, "Let copulation thrive":

> Behold yond simp'ring dame
> Whose face between her forks presages snow,
> That minces virtue and does shake the head
> To hear of pleasure's name—
> The fitchew nor the soiled horse goes to't
> With a more riotous appetite.
>
>   (*King Lear* 4.6.118-23)

"Yond simp'ring dame" might well be Gertrude, who certainly "minces virtue," and who, like Cleopatra, is "wrinkled deep in time" (*Antony and Cleopatra* 1.5. 29). Enobarbus, in fact, describes Cleopatra's paradoxical attraction in an image that seems to be picked up from *Hamlet*. Gertrude shows an exorbitant affection for her first husband:

> Why, she would hang on him
> As if increase of appetite had grown
> By what it fed on. . . . (1.2.143-45)

And Cleopatra manifests her "infinite variety" in physical terms:

> Other women cloy
> The appetites they feed, but she makes hungry
> Where most she satisfies. . . .
>
>   (*Antony and Cleopatra* 2.2.240-42)

There is a feeling of disgust in the *Hamlet* passage quite different from anything in *Antony and Cleopatra*, where sexual attraction is fatal and incomprehensible to reason, but also imperative.[26]

Gertrude's lust is the leading motif in the food imagery. The Ghost admonishes Hamlet not to let "the royal bed of Denmark be/ A couch for luxury and damnèd incest" (1.5.82-83), and throughout its revelation is preoccupied with the sensuality of the queen:

> But virtue, as it never will be moved,
> Though lewdness court it in a shape of heaven,
> So lust, though to a radiant angel linked,
> Will sate itself in a celestial bed
> And prey on garbage.   (1.5.53-57)

The imagery is drawn from the gross terms of animal feeding. "Sate" means to surfeit, as a beast might do, and to "prey on garbage" is the act of a scavenging animal. We think of Hamlet's frustrated wish to "ha' fatted all the region kites" with Claudius' "offal" (2.2.590-91), or those parts of a slaughtered animal unfit for human consumption.

In the closet scene, Hamlet takes up the Ghost's gross terms of animal feeding when he asks his mother: "Could you on this fair mountain leave to feed,/ And

---

[26] See Maurice Charney, *Shakespeare's Roman Plays* (Cambridge, Mass.: Harvard University Press, 1961), pp. 102-7.

batten on this moor? Ha! Have you eyes?" (3.4.67-68) .
In the first, pastoral image, we think of sheep or cattle
grazing "on a heaven-kissing hill" (60) , whereas in the
second the scene is a "moor," a fen or wasteland on
which one "battens," or gluts oneself—this is a specifically animal word. There is an obvious quibble on Claudius as a Moor, a darkskinned and therefore ugly and
sinister person (according to popular belief) as contrasted with his "fair" brother.

Hamlet continues his moral disquisition with revolting, physical details of his mother's "compulsive ardor"
(87):

> Nay, but to live
> In the rank sweat of an enseamèd bed,
> Stewed in corruption, honeying and making love
> Over the nasty sty. . . .   (3.4.92-95)

This imagery reveals as much about Hamlet's "imagina-
tions . . . foul/ As Vulcan's stithy" (3.2.85-86) as about
the lovemaking of Claudius and Gertrude. Its sexual
content is drawn from cooking: the middle-aged lovers
in the royal marriage bed are being "stewed" in their
own sweat and hog's lard ("enseamèd," "nasty sty") , or
possibly their "honeying" with each other and "making
love" causes them to perspire as a stewing-pot steams.
The image is specifically sexual in a way that reminds
us of the sex nausea of *Troilus and Cressida*, whose food
imagery is more extensive than that of any other play
of Shakespeare.[27]

[27] See Spurgeon, *Shakespeare's Imagery*, pp. 320-24 and Chart
VII.

Many other images of animal eating support the combined notions of grossness and prey. Fortinbras, for example, has

> Sharked up a list of lawless resolutes,
> For food and diet, to some enterprise
> That hath a stomach in't. . . .   (1.1.98-100)

As Wilson points out, "voracious and promiscuous feeding was for Shakespeare the distinctive feature of the shark tribe."[28] By an associative link, the shark image suggests "food and diet," which in turn leads to "stomach," a word that means stubborn courage. In Guildenstern's "candy deal of courtesy" (*1 Henry IV* 1.3.251) to the king, there is an unintended hint of prey:

> Most holy and religious fear it is
> To keep those many many bodies safe
> That live and feed upon your Majesty.
>
>   (3.3.8-10)

If the king's body is indeed the body politic, then all of his subjects feed upon his sustaining favor, as Rosencrantz and Guildenstern are doing in parasitic fashion —in Elizabethan English "feeder" can also mean servant. No matter how threatening they may appear as the king's agents, they will themselves be eaten in the end. Hamlet delights in deflating their aggressive postures: "But such officers do the King best service in the end. He keeps them, like an ape an apple,[29] in the corner of

---

[28] Wilson, p. xxxvi. The only other reference to shark in Shakespeare is in the witches' brew of *Macbeth* (4.1.23-24).

[29] I follow the reading of Parrott and Craig, after Farmer, which is used by Alexander and which seems to me the only one

his jaw, first mouthed, to be last swallowed" (4.2.16-19).
"Mouthed" is another gross word from animal eating,
and it recalls the mouthing of game by hunting dogs.

In his praise of Horatio, Hamlet uses the fastidious
feeding of a dog at table as a sign of court corruption:

> No, let the candied tongue lick absurd pomp,
> And crook the pregnant hinges of the knee
> Where thrift may follow fawning. (3.2.62-64)

"Candied" suggests the cloying sweetness of Polonius'
image for Ophelia, set out with her prayer book to en-
trap Hamlet:

> 'Tis too much proved, that with devotion's visage
> And pious action we do sugar o'er
> The devil himself.   (3.1.47-49)

Candying is literally a process of "sugaring o'er," so that
it makes an apt image for a deceptive appearance. We
think also of the excessive sweetness of Ophelia, sucking
"the honey" of Hamlet's "musicked vows" (3.1.159) —
the sound is too musical in this phrase and in the whole
overwrought speech.

Food imagery lends itself well to wordplay. When
asked by the king how he "fares" (3.2.94), Hamlet
chooses to understand the word as "feeds," and answers
darkly: "Excellent, i' faith, of the chameleon's dish: I
eat the air, promise-crammed; you cannot feed capons
so" (95-97). Since the chameleon was fabled to live on

---

that makes good sense out of the passage. Hubler reads "like an
ape," from Folio.

air, the rightful heir (the "air-heir" pun) [30] may thrive by cramming himself with promises, which are only of "so sweet breath composed" (3.1.98). But the fat and sexless capon, destined for the slaughter, must be fed on more substantial food; he too is "crammed," or force-fed, but not with promises.

There is unsparing wordplay on the dead body of Polonius, beginning to putrefy. Hamlet reports that he is "At supper" (4.3.17), but active and passive have changed places in the dining arrangements of man's mortality: "Not where he eats, but where 'a is eaten. A certain convocation of politic worms are e'en at him. Your worm is your only emperor for diet. We fat all creatures else to fat us, and we fat ourselves for maggots. Your fat king and your lean beggar is but variable service—two dishes, but to one table. That's the end" (19-25). The present diet of worms quibbles on the one that Emperor Charles convoked in 1521, which pronounced its ban on Luther, Hamlet's fellow student from the University of Wittenberg—a name that itself suggests a pinnacle of wits. "Politic" worms attend on Polonius, who has always himself hunted "the trail of policy" (2.2.47), and they celebrate, by feasting, the same triumph over him as over the "politician" who "would circumvent God" (5.1.79-81). As Delius points out, Hamlet may also sardonically mean that the worms become politic from feeding on so distinguished a diet.[31]

Hamlet expounds these transformations in a mock

---

[30] See Helge Kökeritz, *Shakespeare's Pronunciation* (New Haven: Yale University Press, 1953), pp. 90-91.
[31] *Variorum*, I, 318.

funeral sermon for Polonius: "A man may fish with the worm that hath eat of a king, and eat of the fish that hath fed of that worm" (4.3.27-28) —words especially appropriate for a "fishmonger" (2.2.174). The upshot of this Pythagorean metempsychosis is that by eating fish, "a king may go a progress through the guts of a beggar" (4.3.30-31). In the stage action, Polonius is literally going a "progress" from behind the arras to behind the "stairs into the lobby" (37), where he may indeed be "nosed" like any "good kissing carrion" (2.2. 182).

The "politic worms" of Polonius' feast reappear in the graveyard as subjects of Lady Worm (5.1.89), who rules all in that kingdom. There is a strong emphasis on eating and drinking to mark the end to which all flesh must come. The Clown-gravedigger recalls that this grinning skull of Yorick was "the King's jester," who "poured a flagon of Rhenish on my head once" (180-82). He might well be thinking wistfully of that wasted flagon, since his fellow Clown, sent to the imperishable Yaughan's[32] to fetch "a stoup of liquor" (61), has not yet returned—and does not return within the time of the play. These somber thoughts about the king's jester work together with the real and imagined smells around him to turn Hamlet's stomach: "My gorge rises at it" (189). The "gorge" is the crop, especially of a hawk, but it could also mean what has been swallowed, especially the chewed and partially digested food in the stomach. The rising gorge indicates vomiting, and we

[32] The name *"Yaughan"* appears only in Folio. It is not in Hubler's text.

remember that the Ghost has been "cast up" by the "ponderous and marble jaws" of its sepulcher (1.4.50-51).

If we return now to the Ghost's unforgettable description of the murder, we discover that it contains a powerful and unexpected food image. The poison "courses" through the body "swift as quicksilver" (1.5.66) :

> And with a sudden vigor it doth posset
> And curd, like eager droppings into milk,
> The thin and wholesome blood.   (1.5.68-70)

Like the ale, wine, or other liquor put into hot milk (with sugar and spices) to make a posset, the poison is also an "eager dropping," or acid, that can curdle the blood. By a deliberate irony, Shakespeare takes a familiar and comforting drink, often used as a nightcap or as a remedy for colds, to represent the effects of a hideous poison. So Lady Macbeth has drugged the "possets" of Duncan's grooms (*Macbeth* 2.2.6) . We remember that word "eager" from the scene in which Hamlet and Horatio await the Ghost: a "nipping and an eager air" "bites" (1.4.1-2) as an acid corrodes.

The milk image is especially associated with mother's milk, and hence with the "milk of human kindness" that Lady Macbeth fears will mollify her husband's ambition. She will exchange her "milk for gall" and be ready to dash out the brains of "the babe that milks me" (*Macbeth* 1.5.14, 45; 1.7.55) . This is the most significant milk imagery in Shakespeare, and it should help us understand the three examples in *Hamlet*. As a parallel figure to the Ghost, old Priam is also cruelly murdered; but just before his death there is a curious pause in the action, as Pyrrhus' sword, "Which was declining on the milky head/ Of reverend Priam, seemed i' th' air to stick" (2.2.489-90). In this context, "milky" means not only mild, but also white-haired, "reverend." The effect of Priam's murder, as heard through the clamor of Hecuba, "Would have made milch the burning eyes of heaven/ And passion in the gods" (528-29). The old form, "milch," and the conceit of tears as milk (as in Crashaw's "The Weeper"), are all part of the heightened rhetoric in this speech. Even if Hecuba's plaintive wail has no effect on the gods, it does make "milch the burning eyes" of the First Player, who is forced to break off his declamation.

Set against the "milky head" of Priam and the "milch" tears expected from the gods, there is in this narrative a brutal food imagery like that of Seneca's *Thyestes*. Hamlet begins it with a description of Pyrrhus that mixes heraldry and cooking:

> Head to foot
> Now is he total gules, horridly tricked
> With blood of fathers, mothers, daughters, sons,
> Baked and impasted with the parching streets. . . .
>
> (2.2.467-70)

Burning Troy bakes and "impastes," or makes a crust of, the blood of slaughter on the demonic Pyrrhus, who wears his "total gules" as the livery of the murderer. We remember that the poison had covered the elder Hamlet's "smooth body" "with vile and loathsome crust" (1.5.72-73), and in Richard II's grotesque description of the grave as a meat pie, the earth "serves as paste and cover to our bones" (*Richard II* 3.2.154). So Pyrrhus presses on toward his victim as if walking in a baking oven. He is "Roasted in wrath and fire" (2.2. 472), which suggests that both internal and external heat make him "thus o'ersizèd with coagulate gore" (473). There is a further allusion to food in Hecuba's sight of Pyrrhus "mincing with his sword her husband's limbs" (525). This domestic imagery of cooking and food preparation adds a special touch of cruelty to horrors of mythological proportions.

Before we leave the Ghost and its problems both in this world and the next, we should notice an odd cooking image in its account of purgatory:

> My hour is almost come,
> When I to sulf'rous and tormenting flames
> Must render up myself. (1.5.2-4)

In addition to the obvious meaning of "render" as return or yield, there is also a suggestion that the fat and dross of his "foul crimes done in my days of nature" (12) must be purged away or clarified by "sulf'rous and tormenting flames." This would make a link between old Hamlet and old Priam, between the fires of purgatory and those of burning Troy.

Although there is much talk of food in *Hamlet*, there are no scenes of feasting either on stage or off. We hear from Hamlet about two feasts that seem to have been planned as one: "Thrift, thrift, Horatio. The funeral baked meats/ Did coldly furnish forth the marriage tables" (1.2.180-81). This is the "thrift" of domestic management, the astute handling of leftovers, the sort of "base respects of thrift" that the Player Queen tells us are "instances that second marriage move" (3.2.188-89) —a virtue from *Poor Richard's Almanack*. The juxtaposition of funerals and marriages is aptly expressed by the king's mindless oxymorons:

> With an auspicious and a dropping eye,
> With mirth in funeral, and with dirge in marriage,
> In equal scale weighing delight and dole. . . .
>
> (1.2.11-13)

Like the imagery of eating, drinking is also an appetitive theme. Hamlet makes a particular point of his uncle's carousing, which represents for him everything that is "rank and gross" (1.2.136) in the new regime. Almost his very first words to Horatio are: "We'll teach you to drink deep ere you depart" (175). Claudius "drains his draughts of Rhenish down" (1.4.10) with public ceremony, as if insisting on his private vice as a national virtue. Hamlet is concerned with the slur to the Danish national character, the "dram of evil" (36) that corrupts all other aspects of reputation:

> This heavy-headed revel east and west
> Makes us traduced and taxed of other nations.
> They clepe us drunkards and with swinish phrase
> Soil our addition, and indeed it takes
> From our achievements, though performed at height,
> The pith and marrow of our attribute. (1.4.17-22)

"Pith" is the vegetable equivalent of "marrow," and both words together mean the essential or vital part, the quintessence, as when the undivulged "foul disease" feeds "Even on the pith of life" (4.1.23).

Throughout the play, Hamlet is preoccupied with the drunkenness of his uncle, the "bloat King" (3.4. 183), who is like Ophelia's "puffed and reckless libertine" (1.3.49). After *The Mousetrap*, Guildenstern reports that the king "Is in his retirement marvelous distemp'red" (3.2.307-8), to which Hamlet quips: "With drink, sir?" (309). In the prayer scene, Hamlet passes up his chance to kill Claudius in order to wait for a time "When he is drunk asleep, or in his rage" (3.3.89). In Hamlet's imagination, his uncle is a "satyr" (1.2. 140), who "Keeps wassail, and the swagg'ring upspring reels" (1.4.9). As Samuel Johnson thought, "upspring" seems to mean "blustering upstart," reeling with drunkenness, rather than that mysterious Germanic dance the "Hüpfauf," or the "upsy freeze," of which it would seem doubtful that Claudius could know the steps.[33] Again, we need to insist that this is Claudius as Hamlet pictures him in his "mind's eye" (1.2.185). There is no trace of drunkenness or any other satyric, Corybantic, or centaur-like quality in the character the audience sees—not even a hangover.

For his own drinking, Hamlet prefers potions other than the king's "Rhenish":

> Now could I drink hot blood
> And do such business as the bitter day
> Would quake to look on.   (3.2.398-400)

[33] See *Johnson's Notes to Shakespeare*, ed. Arthur Sherbo, p. 159, and *Variorum*, I, 78-79.

Hamlet is invoking strains of Teutonic warrior traditions, in which the hot blood of one's enemy is the only
really satisfying beverage.[34] In this context, we should
also remember the odd image Gertrude uses for Ophelia's death:

> . . . her garments, heavy with their drink,
> Pulled the poor wretch from her melodious lay
> To muddy death.   (4.7.181-83)

Like the drunken grooms of Duncan in *Macbeth*, Ophelia's clothes are imagined as sodden rogues, who complete the "bloody deed" (3.4.28) begun by the "envi-
ous," or spiteful, "sliver" (4.7.173) of the willow
branch. It is a strained conceit, but it is rescued from
its own artifice by the matching of "melodious" and
"muddy" and the consistent harmony of liquid and
nasal sounds.

In the final scene, the imagery of drinking enters directly into the stage action. Claudius depends upon the
social situation, since Hamlet is honor-bound to answer
the king's "health." But Hamlet sets by the cup and
excuses himself from the "custom/ More honored in
the breach than the observance" (1.4.15-16). Gertrude
drinks and is poisoned, and her last exclamations put
a strident emphasis on "the drink, the drink! O my dear
Hamlet!/ The drink, the drink!" (5.2.310-11). There
is a fitting reversal in Hamlet's forcing Claudius to
"Drink off this potion" (327), the same euphemistic
"chalice for the nonce" (4.7.160) that the king had prepared for his nephew. The catastrophe of *Hamlet* fulfills

[34] See Prosser, *Hamlet and Revenge*, pp. 181-82.

with an uncanny literalness the tragic criteria of Macbeth:

> This even-handed justice
> Commends th' ingredient of our poison'd chalice
> To our own lips.　　　　　　　(*Macbeth* 1.7.10-12)

Macbeth is trying to convince himself that he should not
murder Duncan, and, in this early scene, he already has
a moral insight far beyond that of Claudius, on whom
he is modeled. The religious overtones of "chalice"
suggest the identification of blood and wine, so that
drinking may become an appropriately symbolic means
of death.

Gardens

The well-tended garden, free from weeds and flourish-
ing in symmetrical order, reflects the perfection of that
first happy place where Adam and Eve dwelt before the
fall. Thus the garden of paradise is the model by which
to understand the corruption introduced into gardens
by man's sin. Through analogy, the body politic can be
represented in these same terms, as in the celebrated
garden scene of *Richard II*:[35]

> Why should we, in the compass of a pale,
> Keep law and form and due proportion,
> Showing, as in a model, our firm estate,
> When our sea-walled garden, the whole land,

[35] See the appendix on Shakespeare's garden symbolism in
Wolfgang Clemen, *Shakespeares Bilder* (Bonn, 1936). This chap-
ter does not appear in the English translation (1951). See also
Terry Allen Comito, "Renaissance Gardens and Elizabethan
Romance," doctoral dissertation, Harvard University, 1968.

Is full of weeds; her fairest flowers chok'd up,
Her fruit trees all unprun'd, her hedges ruin'd,
Her knots disordered, and her wholesome herbs
Swarming with caterpillars?   (3.4.40-47)

Only by strong measures can the garden be restored to its former condition, its overgrowth pruned and the "caterpillars of the commonwealth" (*Richard II* 2.3. 166) destroyed. This is a normative symbolism, which, like that of disease and health, lends itself to simple antitheses. Thus flowers may be set against weeds, nurture against neglect, and the gardener can be either diligent or slothful in his God-given work.

As the setting for the murder of Hamlet's father— "Sleeping within my orchard" (1.5.59) —gardens have pejorative connotations almost from the beginning of the play. In Hamlet's first soliloquy, his "prophetic soul" (40) anticipates the dire garden imagery of the Ghost's revelation:

How weary, stale, flat, and unprofitable
Seem to me all the uses of this world!
Fie on't, ah, fie, 'tis an unweeded garden
That grows to seed. Things rank and gross in nature
Possess it merely.   (1.2.133-37)

We should not be misled by the luxuriance of growth in this garden, which indicates nature exerting its force apart from human agency or reason; it is this "naturalism" that breeds atheism, as in Edmund and Iago. Vile weeds are especially rank and vigorous, always threatening to choke the more noble and delicate plants, which need human care and divine benediction in order to flourish.

If, as Iago says, "Our bodies are our gardens to the which our wills are gardeners" (*Othello* 1.3.321-22), then weeds represent sins, as they did in popular iconography. Thus Hamlet exhorts his mother not to "spread the compost on the weeds/ To make them ranker" (3.4. 152-53). Such weeds must either be plucked out by the roots or starved to death. The Ghost uses the weed image in a memorable way to spur Hamlet to his revenge:

> I find thee apt,
> And duller shouldst thou be than the fat weed
> That roots[36] itself in ease on Lethe wharf,
> Wouldst thou not stir in this.   (1.5.31-34)

As the river of forgetfulness, Lethe symbolizes spiritual torpor, so that the "fat weed" thriving on its banks or docks presents a revolting image of sloth.

Aside from the weed, any lush growth may represent the effects of sin. The Ghost complains that it was "Cut off even in the blossoms" of its sin (1.5.76), and when Hamlet is about to murder Claudius, he echoes the Ghost's words: "'A took my father grossly, full of

---

[36] "Roots" is the reading of Quarto 2, but many editors follow the Folio "rots" on the analogy of a passage in *Antony and Cleopatra* (1.4.44-47). This seems to me, however, to make the wrong image. See C. J. Sisson, *New Readings in Shakespeare* (London, 1956), II, 212, and Parrott and Craig, pp. 98-99. There is some orthographical confusion of "root" and "rot" and possible wordplay on "root," "rot," and "rut," as in Jaques' lines: "And so, from hour to hour, we ripe and ripe, / And then, from hour to hour, we rot and rot" (*As You Like It* 2.7.26-27). See Kökeritz, *Shakespeare's Pronunciation*, p. 238 and note 4.

bread,/ With all his crimes broad blown, as flush as May" (3.3.80-81). "Blown" means flowering, in bloom, as Ophelia calls Hamlet a "blown youth" (3.1.162). The vigor of "flush" May is used pejoratively, for the rankness of the Ghost's "crimes" or sins. This image is another expression of the powerful energy of matter without the tempering control of spirit, which should curb and inhibit such a "flush." The "puffed and reckless libertine," who is committed in principle to naturalism, treads "the primrose path of dalliance," while the true Christian follows "the steep and thorny way to heaven" (1.3.48-50). These are the same spiritual thorns that the Ghost provides for Gertrude's conscience:

> Leave her to heaven
> And to those thorns that in her bosom lodge
> To prick and sting her.   (1.5.86-88)

The symbolic garden in *Hamlet* seems to be a dangerous and threatening place. As Hamlet tells Ophelia in the nunnery scene, "virtue cannot so inoculate our old stock but we shall relish of it" (3.1.117-19). No amount of grafting can obliterate the taste of the "old stock" of old Adam's sinful nature.

The rose imagery in *Hamlet* indicates the beauty and love which have been destroyed in this new world created by Claudius' murder. To Hamlet, his mother's "act"

> . . . takes off the rose
> From the fair forehead of an innocent love,
> And sets a blister there. . . .   (3.4.43-45)

Therefore Ophelia must "To a nunnery, go, and quickly too," since even the chaste and the pure shall "not
escape calumny" (3.1.141-42, 138). Laertes warns his
sister of the perils lurking in her garden: "The canker
galls the infants of the spring/ Too oft before their buttons be disclosed" (1.3.39-40). The cankerworm or the
rose caterpillar was thought to be especially fond of
buds, so that these spring roses of Ophelia, the "rose of
May" (4.5.157), seem doomed to perish without ever
being "disclosed"—the word is used in its etymological
sense (cf. 5.1.289). Like most of the other garden images, the rose seems to mark a lost fulfillment and an
unrealized possibility. It recalls the sweeter world that
existed before the murder of Hamlet's father, in which
young Hamlet was "Th' expectancy and rose of the fair
state,/ The glass of fashion, and the mold of form" (3.1.
155-56).

Since the garden imagery is so generally pejorative
in *Hamlet*, we shall find it difficult to sentimentalize
Ophelia's flowers, although actresses playing this part
rarely allow themselves to be photographed without at
least a nosegay or disordered wreath about their persons.
We may begin with the violet image, which seems to
show a pattern of development. Laertes launches his
exhortation against Hamlet's love by calling it

> A violet in the youth of primy nature,
> Forward, not permanent, sweet, not lasting,
> The perfume and suppliance of a minute,
> No more.   (1.3.7-10)

The momentary quality of the violet's perfume is emphasized in the repetition of that fateful "No more":

> *Laertes.* No more.
> *Ophelia.*   No more but so?
> *Laertes.*   Think it no more.
>   (1.3.10)

These words echo in Gertrude's pleas in the closet scene, just before the Ghost enters to protect her: "O Hamlet, speak no more," "O, speak to me no more," "No more, sweet Hamlet," "No more" (3.4.89, 95, 97, 102). Again, at Ophelia's funeral, we have the same formula of finality:

> *Laertes.* Must there no more be done?
> *Doctor.*   No more be done.
>   (5.1.237)

We remember Lear's overwhelming, "Thou'lt come no more,/ Never, never, never, never, never" (*King Lear* 5.3.307-8).

In her mad scene, Ophelia is still thinking of violets, although she has none to offer: "I would give you some violets, but they withered all when my father died" (4.5.182-84). Her erratic fancy presents images of mourning not only for her father, but also for herself and for her unfulfilled love, "A violet in the youth of primy nature." According to Clement Robinson, "Violet is for faithfulnesse."[37] For his sister's funeral, Laertes reverses his earlier violet image:

[37] Quoted in Kittredge, p. 265.

Lay her i' th' earth,
And from her fair and unpolluted flesh
May violets spring!　　　(5.1.240-42)

Ophelia has managed to keep "her fair and unpolluted flesh" from the taint of a corrupt world by surrendering herself "mermaidlike" to "the weeping brook," "like a creature native and indued/ Unto that element" (4.7. 175, 176, 179-80). She has solved the problem of her "too too solid flesh" (1.2.129) in a way that is not possible for Hamlet. Almost by lyric style alone, she is able to obliterate all traces of involvement in her father's plots, and to convince us of her ruined perfection.

Ophelia mentions many flowers in her mad scene, but although she distributes them with symbolic appropriateness, it seems doubtful whether we can ever identify the persons for whom they are intended. In an age when flower symbolism had become extremely complex, Ophelia helps us by naming some of the attributes: "There's rosemary, that's for remembrance. Pray you, love, remember. And there is pansies, that's for thoughts" (4. 5.174-76). Rue is "herb of grace o' Sundays" (181), the "sour herb of grace" of the Gardener's lament for King Richard's queen: "Rue, even for ruth, here shortly shall be seen,/ In the remembrance of a weeping queen" (*Richard II* 3.4.106-7). Ophelia dwells on "Rue, even for ruth" for herself and for all others who feel sorrow mixed with repentance and the need for grace. This general significance goes beyond a narrow identification of rue as the flower intended for Gertrude. It also seems unlikely that Ophelia actually has specimens of rosemary, pansies, fennel, columbines, rue, daisies, and violets in her hands to distribute to persons on stage.[38] She is, after all, not a botanist like Friar Laurence, but a young maiden distracted in her wits; and most of the audience would not, at any rate, be able to distinguish exactly what flowers she is holding.

Like Polonius, Ophelia dies "Larded all with sweet flowers" (4.5.38). In Gertrude's description, the fatal scene makes the most sustained lyric passage in the play:

There is a willow grows askant the brook,
That shows his hoar leaves in the glassy stream:
Therewith fantastic garlands did she make
Of crowflowers, nettles, daisies, and long purples,
That liberal shepherds give a grosser name,
But our cold maids do dead men's fingers call them.

(4.7.166-71)

The willow is the tree of forsaken lovers. In Lorenzo's evocation, Dido stood

. . . with a willow in her hand
Upon the wild sea-banks, and waft her love
To come again to Carthage.
(*The Merchant of Venice* 5.1.10-12)

Most memorably, Desdemona sings her "song of 'willow,'" learned from the maid Barbary, whose lover "prov'd mad,/ And did forsake her" (*Othello* 4.3.26-27). Ophelia makes her "fantastic garlands" of willow twigs decorated with meadow flowers, all of which have con-

---

[38] See *Variorum*, I, 346, and William Poel, *Shakespeare in the Theatre* (London, 1913), p. 172.

notations either of grossness or deception. The "dissembling" daisy is one of the flowers of the mad scene, and we know that the nettle is a "stinging" (*Richard II* 3.2.18) and an "idle" weed (*King Lear* 4.4.5). Apparently the long purple is the *Phallus impudicus* of Shakespeare's Warwickshire countryside;[39] its associations fit well with Ophelia's bawdy ballads.

Gertrude describes the flowers that Ophelia has been preparing for her father's tomb as if they were garlands for Ophelia's own watery grave beneath the willow:

> There on the pendent boughs her crownet weeds
> Clamb'ring to hang, an envious sliver broke,
> When down her weedy trophies and herself
> Fell in the weeping brook.   (4.7.172-75)

By a fanciful pathetic fallacy, the brook is already "weeping" as a mourner at her funeral. Real flowers are used in Ophelia's "maimèd rites" (5.1.221); the literal and "churlish priest"[40] will allow her only "virgin crants" and "Her maiden strewments" (234-35). "Crants" (*Kranz*) is the German word for garland or wreath, and in Folio this unusual word is replaced by the colorless "Rites." There is an odd phonetic link between "virgin crants"

[39] See p. 57, note 5.

[40] He is a *"Doctor,"* presumably of Divinity, in the speech prefixes of Quarto 2. The Folio speech prefixes have *"Priest,"* as in 5.1.242. It seems unlikely that this difference is so crucial as Wilson represents it. "Priest" would not be at all unreasonable in a play with a vaguely pre-Reformation setting, whose Ghost speaks of purgatory. In any case, there seems to be no consistent pattern of theological references in *Hamlet*. See Parrott and Craig, pp. 220-21, and Roland Mushat Frye, *Shakespeare and Christian Doctrine* (Princeton: Princeton University Press, 1963).

and the much maligned Rosencrantz. "Strewments" are the flowers laid on the grave by the mourners, who would presumably know how to express Ophelia's virginity in the flower symbolism of the time. Gertrude scatters flowers to accompany her line: "Sweets to the sweet! Farewell" (245). Her ceremonial act reminds us of that mingling of funerals and marriages so characteristic of this play:

> I hoped thou shouldst have been my Hamlet's wife.
> I thought thy bride bed to have decked, sweet maid,
> And not have strewed thy grave.   (5.1.246-48)

We should not forget one other garden image, that old-fashioned stage property of the dumb show, "*a bank of flowers,*" on which the Player King "*lies him down*" (3.2.140 s.d.) for his after-dinner nap. We know from Henslowe's inventory of 1598 that he had "ij mose banckes" (two moss banks), which he lists together with one caduceus and a snake.[41] This is probably the sort of resting place Hermia has in mind when she says: "For I upon this bank will rest my head" (*A Midsummer Night's Dream* 2.2.40), and is undoubtedly the same property that Titania offers to Bottom: "Come, sit thee down upon this flow'ry bed" (4.1.1). In *The Merchant of Venice*, Lorenzo woos Jessica with a similar invitation:

---

[41] *Henslowe's Diary*, ed. R. A. Foakes and R. T. Rickert (Cambridge, Eng.: Cambridge University Press, 1961), p. 320. See also George Fullmer Reynolds, *The Staging of Elizabethan Plays At the Red Bull Theater 1605-1625*, Modern Language Association (New York, 1940), pp. 73-75, and Percy Simpson, "Actors and Acting," *Shakespeare's England*, II, 269-70.

> How sweet the moonlight sleeps upon this bank!
> Here will we sit and let the sounds of music
> Creep in our ears. . . .   (5.1.54-56)

These Elizabethan flower or moss banks probably resembled the vernal canvas and wood arrangements still used by florists, caterers, and ancient photographers to set off their wares. In the Quarto 1 staging of the dumb show, the Player King *"sits down in an arbor,"* which is another old-fashioned pastoral property, best remembered as the scene of Horatio's death in *The Spanish Tragedy* (1587). It seems not at all unlikely that the bank of flowers (in Quarto 2 and Folio) was used together with the arbor of Quarto 1.

The fact that garden imagery is of much less importance in *Hamlet* than the imagery of animals, disease, and food seems to point to the very limited role of nature in the play. In *King Lear*[42] and *Macbeth*, for example, we feel that evil permeates the nature of things, or at least threatens to reestablish the dominion of Chaos and Old Night:

> Light thickens, and the crow
> Makes wing to th' rooky wood;
> Good things of day begin to droop and drowse,
> Whiles night's black agents to their preys do rouse.
>   (*Macbeth* 3.2.50-53)

King Lear on the heath is "unaccommodated man," engaging himself directly with the forces of nature, trying to "Crack nature's moulds, all germens spill at

---

[42] See John F. Danby, *Shakespeare's Doctrine of Nature: A Study of King Lear* (London, 1961).

once,/ That makes ingrateful man" (*King Lear* 3.4. 106, 3.2.8-9). This universalizing dimension of nature is missing in *Hamlet*, which, like *Othello*, is a much more personal tragedy than either *King Lear* or *Macbeth*.

There are hints in *Hamlet* of a wider perspective, especially at the end of the first scene, when dawn reasserts the primacy of God and nature over "Th' extravagant and erring spirit" (1.1.154) as well as over the "bitter cold" (8) and fearful night. Shakespeare makes a determined lyric effort to modulate the anxious mood that opened the play. With leisurely and adoring fullness, Marcellus discourses about "that season .../ Wherein our Saviour's birth is celebrated," when the cock "singeth all night long" (158-60). Horatio continues with his beautiful announcement of the dawn:

> But look, the morn in russet mantle clad
> Walks o'er the dew of yon high eastward hill.
>
> (1.1.166-67)

The god of morning, dressed as a peasant in "russet mantle," can once again make his accustomed rounds despite the portentous Ghost whose appearance bodes "some strange eruption to our state" (69). But this example of nature exerting its influence over the fears and limited concerns of man is very rare in *Hamlet*, and there is little in the play that is "hallowed" and "gracious" (164).

4. Limits

IN IDEAL terms, "how infinite" man is "in faculties . . . , in action how like an angel, in apprehension how like a god" (2.2.313-15), whereas in actuality man is only the alchemist's "quintessence of dust" (317). "O God," says Hamlet, "I could be bounded in a nutshell and count myself a king of infinite space, were it not that I have bad dreams" (258-60). Man's infinity is questioned by these restrictive "bad dreams," very like those troubled "dreams" that "may come/ When we have shuffled off this mortal coil" (3.1.66-67). "A dream itself is but a shadow" (2.2.264), says Hamlet, echoing Pindar, but in these quibbling exchanges with Rosencrantz and Guildenstern, shadow may triumph over substance, and "monarchs and outstretched heroes" like Claudius and Laertes may be merely "beggars' shadows" (268-69). Man's infinite faculty of reason and imagination, that "large discourse,/ Looking before and after" (4.4.36-37), is "bounded in a nutshell," and the image suggests an association between the convoluted nut and the human brain.

These references indicate a persistent sense of limits in *Hamlet*, where the hero is not alone in feeling himself "cabin'd, cribb'd, confin'd, bound in/ To saucy doubts and fears" (*Macbeth* 3.4.24-25). We may trace the idea of limits in two themes: confinement, and money and numbers, both of which show a range of possibilities between, on one end, man's finiteness and mortality and, on the other, his attempts to break out of all confining boundaries with "thoughts beyond the reaches of our souls" (1.4.56).

Confinement

The most literal images of confinement are prisons, locked doors, or, in the stage action, physical restraint. To Hamlet, "Denmark's a prison" (2.2.247), and he asks Rosencrantz and Guildenstern what they have "deserved at the hands of Fortune that she sends you to prison hither" (244-45). These "privates" (237) of Fortune turn out to be her prisoners, who are eventually executed by order of a "changeling" (5.2.53) commission. As Claudius' spies, they are also Hamlet's jailers, who react with predictable objections to his feelings of constraint. Hamlet will agree that the whole world is a prison, "A goodly one, in which there are many confines, wards, and dungeons, Denmark being one o' th' worst" (2.2.249-51), but Rosencrantz and Guildenstern will not go beyond the political metaphor of ambition: " 'Tis too narrow for your mind" (257).

"Denmark's a prison" (247) for Hamlet in much more than a figurative sense. When the king refuses to allow him to go "back to school in Wittenberg" (1.2.113), it is because he wishes to have "Our chiefest courtier, cousin, and our son" "Here in the cheer and comfort of our eye" (116-17) —Claudius' "kingly eyes" (4.7.45), one "auspicious" and one "dropping" (1.2.11), make a surrealistic link with the poisoned ear of his brother. The "cheer and comfort" is, of course, all on Claudius' side, and the phrase is a euphemism for surveillance.

Hamlet must not be allowed to live abroad like Laertes, who eventually returns with "a list of lawless resolutes" (1.1.98) to stage a putsch.

Claudius and his agents are constantly urging a stricter control for Hamlet. "To England send him," says Polonius, "or confine him where/ Your wisdom best shall think" (3.1.189-90). The voyage to England is Claudius' "final solution" to the Hamlet problem: "For we will fetters put about this fear,/ Which now goes too free-footed" (3.3.25-26). "Fetters" are the leg-irons or gyves that will not allow Hamlet's madness to "range" (2). In a later scene, Claudius explains to Laertes why he could not go to a "public count" with Hamlet: the "general gender" "Would, like the spring that turneth wood to stone,/ Convert his gyves to graces" (4.7.17-21). We also remember the Hamlet of Ophelia's description, with his stockings "fouled,/ Ungartered, and down-gyvèd to his ankle" (2.1.79-80). In Hamlet's own report of the sea voyage, "Methought I lay/ Worse than the mutines in the bilboes" (5.2.5-6); these were a kind of shackle (used for mutinous sailors) that slid on an iron bar locked to the floor. Characteristically, Hamlet's imprisonment is represented as a fettering, and he himself is made to seem a dangerous person.

After the death of Polonius, the action against Hamlet becomes more openly menacing, since the king now has the pretext to deal firmly with his nephew's "liberty," which "is full of threats to all" (4.1.14). Claudius fears that public opinion will blame him for Polonius' murder,

> . . . whose providence
> Should have kept short, restrained, and out of haunt
> This mad young man.   (4.1.17-19)

As he tells his *"two or three"* trusted counselors at the beginning of Act IV, Scene iii, "How dangerous is it that this man goes loose!" (2), and we think immediately of the contrast between fast and loose throughout the play. A few lines further on Rosencrantz informs us that Lord Hamlet is "Without, my lord; guarded, to know your pleasure" (14). The surveillance of Act I, Scene ii has now become physical restraint; as Claudius' prisoner, Hamlet enters with guards at Rosencrantz's brusque command: "Ho! Bring in the lord" (4.3.15).

In an analogous imagery of confinement, the Ghost speaks of purgatory as "my prison house" (1.5.14), and it describes its purifying torments in terms of secular punishment:

> Doomed for a certain term to walk the night,
> And for the day confined to fast in fires,
> Till the foul crimes done in my days of nature
> Are burnt and purged away.   (1.5.10-13)

The Ghost may be ubiquitous under the stage—*"Hic et ubique"* (156)—but in the otherworldly domain it is ruled by a power greater than itself. The attempt by Marcellus and Barnardo to stop it with their partisans proves to be only "malicious mockery," "For it is as the air, invulnerable" (1.1.145-46). When the cock crows, however, "Th' extravagant and erring spirit hies/ To his confine" (154-55). "Confine" is here at once a syno-

nym for "prison house" and the literal means of re-
stricting "extravagant and erring" spirits—both adjec-
tives are used in their etymological senses.

In his first address to the Ghost, Hamlet wants to
know why it has not remained within the limits of the
grave:

> Why thy canonized bones, hearsèd in death,
> Have burst their cerements, why the sepulcher
> Wherein we saw thee quietly interred
> Hath oped his ponderous and marble jaws
> To cast thee up again.   (1.4.47-51)

The Ghost is like Jonah, cast up from the belly of the
whale, and the imagery reflects the popular iconography
of resurrection. Hamlet also prescribes limits to the
Ghost at the opening of Act I, Scene v: "Whither wilt
thou lead me? Speak; I'll go no further."

When the Ghost asks Hamlet to "lend thy serious
hearing/ To what I shall unfold," he answers with
alacrity, "Speak. I am bound to hear" (1.5.5-6). In true
Elizabethan style, the Ghost then puns on Hamlet's
word: "So art thou to revenge, when thou shalt hear"
(7). Hamlet's "bound" means ready or prepared, as
Claudius, attempting to pray, is "like a man to double
business bound" (3.3.41). But the Ghost takes "bound"
to mean obligated, which is also a sense in which Claudius uses the word:

> . . . and the survivor bound
> In filial obligation for some term
> To do obsequious sorrow.
>   (1.2.90-92)

One is "bound" by specific limits, as "The single and peculiar life is bound/ With all the strength and armor of the mind" (3.3.11-12). We also think of the king's diabolical advice to Laertes: "Revenge should have no bounds" (4.7.128), not even those imposed by Christianity or natural law. In the same kind of double image, when Horatio and Marcellus find the "escaped" Hamlet, Horatio says, "Heavens secure him!" (1.5.113), as if no mortal hand could either guarantee his safety or tie him up. Throughout the play, Horatio delights in these bantering quibbles based on man's unacknowledged limitations. He is constantly reminding Hamlet of that ordinary, commonsensical humanity he seems to have violated or forgotten.

As one might expect, the repressed and overruled Ophelia has a significant imagery of limits, especially locks. Her brother's advice is in her memory "locked,/ And you yourself shall keep the key of it" (1.3.85-86), which is a characteristic way of surrendering responsibility. Her father's "prescripts" about Hamlet include: "That she should lock herself from his resort" (2.2.143), and we already know that she repelled his letters and "denied/ His access" (2.1.109-10). One of Ophelia's mad songs sums up this imagery of constraint:

> Then up he rose and donned his clothes
>   And dupped the chamber door,
> Let in the maid, that out a maid
>   Never departed more.   (4.5.52-55)

It is a wish-fulfillment image of doors being "dupped" or opened for her. Claudius shows a more than personal interest in keeping an eye on the mad Ophelia: "Follow her close; give her good watch, I pray you" (4.5.74). We recall the king's anxieties about his nephew-son: "How dangerous is it that this man goes loose!" (4.3.2). Like Hamlet, Ophelia represents a political danger to the new regime, especially when she threatens: "My brother shall know of it" (4.5.70-71).

We may also consider the idea of limits as it is expressed in the symbolism of contraction or expansion: tightness and restriction versus freedom, boldness, and a refusal to be bound in. Claudius is the great constrictor in the play, who, like the players, attempts to be Hamlet's "abridgment" (2.2.429). In his official mourning speech for his brother, he represents the whole kingdom of Denmark as "contracted in one brow of woe" (1.2.4), a figure which is only one of the king's many grotesque images involving parts of the body. The secondary meaning of "contracted" is made explicit in the closet scene. Gertrude's "deed"

> . . . from the body of contraction plucks
> The very soul, and sweet religion makes
> A rhapsody of words!   (3.4.47-49)

"Contraction" is the marriage contract, and Hamlet means that the sacrament has become, through Gertrude's mockery of it, a mere verbal formula, a "minglemangle" (as Florio defines "rhapsody").[1]

---

[1] See *Variorum*, I, 289. This is the only use of "rhapsody" in Shakespeare. Donald M. Frame informs me in a letter that Montaigne also uses "rapsodie" only once (Book I, Chap. 13 of his *Essais*), and that Cotgrave's dictionary (1611) defines it as "an improper collection, a confused heaping up, of many sentences."

The imagery of confinement and limits is represented literally by the stage doors. In the De Witt sketch of the Swan playhouse,[2] which shows that theater in about 1596, there are two massive, hinged double doors at the rear of the stage, both with prominent locks. Presumably Shakespeare's Globe was similarly constructed. The doors are used most significantly in the scene of Laertes' rebellion, where they provide a barrier more immediate than "divinity" to "hedge a king" (4.5.123). Suddenly, the king's "Switzers" can no longer "guard the door" (97), and Laertes and his "false Danish dogs" (110) burst through: "The doors are broke" (111). In the final scene, after Hamlet discovers that Gertrude has been poisoned, he exclaims: "Let the door be locked" (5.2.312), and this stage action creates the Sartrian illusion of "No Exit."

Throughout *Hamlet* there is an acute awareness of man's limitations as a finite being, perhaps nowhere so brilliantly expressed as in Claudius' discussion of time and love:

[2] The drawing is actually a copy of Johannes de Witt's sketch (made during a visit to London) by his friend, Arend Van Buchell, who also recorded de Witt's comments on it. These names are sometimes modernized to de Wit and Van Buchel. The manuscript is in the collection of the library of the University of Utrecht, Holland (MS 842, fol. 132 recto—for the drawing). See "A Note on the Swan Theatre Drawing," *SS*, I (1948), 23-24, and Plates II, III, and IVA. See also Richard Hosley's exacting essay, "Reconstitution du Théâtre du Swan," *Le Lieu Théâtral à la Renaissance*, ed. Jean Jacquot et al. (Paris: Éditions du Centre National de la Recherche Scientifique, 1964), pp. 295-316.

> . . . I know love is begun by time,
> And that I see, in passages of proof,
> Time qualifies the spark and fire of it.
> There lives within the very flame of love
> A kind of wick or snuff that will abate it. . . .
> (4.7.111-15)

In an age when people used candles and lamps for all their lighting, this flame was one of the most familiar images of mortality, and it appears repeatedly in emblem books. We remember Macbeth's desolate image at his wife's death: "Out, out, brief candle!" (*Macbeth* 5.5.23), and in Sonnet LXXIII the fire of youth is "Consum'd with that which it was nourish'd by." The wick is essential to the flame, but the same process that makes the flame bright also chars the wick and creates the snuff that dims the flame. This is the principle of self-destruction that resides in all things and that leads Claudius to his *carpe diem* conclusion: "That we would do/ We should do when we would" (4.7.118-19), which is almost exactly the opposite of Hamlet's faith in the providence of time: "If it be now, 'tis not to come; if it be not to come, it will be now; if it be not now, yet it will come. The readiness is all" (5.2.221-24). Hamlet's "readiness" and Claudius' are radically different. Hamlet is poised to respond to a purpose that man cannot shape for himself, whereas Claudius is brutally voluntaristic. The king's consciousness of limits seems to give him a momentary advantage over Hamlet's "large discourse,/ Looking before and after" (4.4.36-37), but in the framework of the tragedy, Claudius' antiheroic practicality must yield to those "thoughts beyond the reaches of our souls" (1.4.56).

Money and Numbers

Man may be "infinite in faculties" (2.2.313), but the exigencies of daily life limit his scope. Numbers, quantities, and all measures (including money) remind us of some of the ways in which man's "Immortal longings" (*Antony and Cleopatra* 5.2.279) are circumscribed. The frequent reference to these topics in *Hamlet* is a significant aspect of the imagery of limits. Money, in particular, is a familiar sign of man's fallen state, which makes him subject to "cormorant devouring Time" (*Love's Labour's Lost* 1.1.4). The whole theme emphasizes man's fallible, measurable, material being, that condition of mortality which makes him vulnerable to tragedy.

Money and numbers may be considered together in the mention of specific sums or in the use of coins of known value. Hamlet runs Polonius through with "Dead for a ducat, dead!" (3.4.25), and using this same price scale, Fortinbras' captain speaks to Hamlet of the Polish expedition with businesslike disdain:

> We go to gain a little patch of ground
> That hath in it no profit but the name.
> To pay five ducats, five, I would not farm it,
> Nor will it yield to Norway or the Pole
> A ranker rate, should it be sold in fee.
>
> (4.4.18-22)

The worth of that land is contemptuously pegged at

five ducats—an absolute maximum, as the colloquial repetition seems to say—whether it be leased or rented ("farmed" in its old sense), or bought outright ("in fee," short for "in fee-simple").

This talk of money sets Hamlet a difficult problem about the nature of honor: "Two thousand souls and twenty thousand ducats/ Will not debate the question of this straw" (4.4.25-26), which is actually the more specific question of the value of five ducats' worth of Polish land. The numbers exactly fix the disproportion between infinite thoughts of honor and material objectives. Incidentally, in Hamlet's soliloquy we suddenly hear about "The imminent death of twenty thousand men" (60), who were only a tenth of that number in line 25. The number of ducats seems to have attracted an equal number of troops.[3]

Hamlet also complains bitterly to Rosencrantz and Guildenstern about the inflation of values that Claudius has created in Denmark: "those that would make mouths at him while my father lived give twenty, forty, fifty, a hundred ducats apiece for his picture in little" (2.2.372-74). Gertrude seems to be wearing one of these sought-after miniatures in the closet scene, for the benefit of Hamlet's lecture on "The counterfeit presentment of two brothers" (3.4.55). It is ironic that Polonius should end with the shortest measure—"Dead for a ducat"—since he makes the most notable use of money imagery in the play.

---

[3] For a comparable difficulty with money see Terence Spencer's fascinating note, "Shakespeare Learns the Value of Money: The Dramatist at Work on *Timon of Athens*," *SS*, VI (1953), 75-78.

The largest sum mentioned in *Hamlet* is the "three-score thousand crowns in annual fee" (2.2.73) that old Norway gives to his penitent nephew, Fortinbras, which Folio economizes to "three thousand crowns," perhaps to help the meter. Scholars have calculated that if Fortinbras needs at least "twenty thousand ducats" (4.4.25) for his Polish expedition, he has to have the larger number of crowns as an "annual fee."[4] The smallest sum in the play may be found in Hamlet's acknowledgment of Rosencrantz and Guildenstern's visit: "Beggar that I am, I am even poor in thanks, but I thank you; and sure, dear friends, my thanks are too dear a halfpenny" (2.2.278-80). These two are obviously not interested in halfpennies, and their visitation turns out not to be "free" (281) in the sense either of voluntary or gratis. They act, after all, not from disinterested love of the king, but to soak up his "rewards" (4.2.16).

There is an apt recognition of this double role in Gertrude's greeting:

> If it will please you
> To show us so much gentry and good will
> As to expend your time with us awhile
> For the supply and profit of our hope,
> Your visitation shall receive such thanks
> As fits a king's remembrance.   (2.2.21-26)

"Expend," "supply," "profit" are all commercial words, and we still use "remembrance" in this insinuating way, especially at Christmastime, to indicate gratuities. A "king's remembrance" bodes well for two aspiring cour-

[4] See Wilson, p. 168.

tiers, who are, according to their own admission, the "privates" (2.2.237) of Fortune—both soldiers and private parts. The word "remembrance" has a special irony in the context of the Ghost's cry: "Remember me" (1.5.91). Ophelia has "remembrances" of Hamlet that she has euphoniously "longèd long to redeliver" (3.1.93-94). These are tangible, stage-property "remembrances," which she returns to her lover at this point with a sententious jingle: "Take these again, for to the noble mind/ Rich gifts wax poor when givers prove unkind" (100-1).

In Shakespeare's numerology, one thousand appears about four times more often than does one hundred, probably because one thousand of anything still seemed an impressive amount in Elizabethan England. I suspect that our million is the inflated equivalent of Shakespeare's thousand. A thousand pounds was a proverbial sum,[5] the very amount that Falstaff owes Shallow (2 *Henry IV* 5.5.74). After the success of *The Mousetrap*, Hamlet jubilantly exclaims: "O good Horatio, I'll take the ghost's word for a thousand pound. Didst perceive?" (3.2.292-93). There is a quibble on "word," which in this context means a verbal assurance for a debt, but the play has also verified the Ghost's narration in Act I, Scene v, as well as Hamlet's own "word" or motto: " 'Adieu, adieu, remember me' " (1.5.111). Further, the thousand pounds may represent Hamlet's wager on the truth of the Ghost's word.

In his "To be, or not to be" soliloquy, Hamlet speaks of "the thousand natural shocks/ That flesh is heir to" (3.1.62-63), then proceeds to enumerate only about half

[5] See Tilley, M217, and also C601, C687, and P520.

a dozen of them. When the Clown-gravedigger asks his conundrum—"What is he that builds stronger than either the mason, the shipwright, or the carpenter?" (5.1.42-43) —he is disconcerted by the Second Clown's obviously correct answer: "The gallowsmaker, for that frame outlives a thousand tenants" (44-45). We would not be inclined today to think one thousand a very imposing number, and we would certainly not regard it as a synonym for an incalculable sum. Hamlet recalls that Yorick the jester "hath borne me on his back a thousand times" (187-88), which, if one can reckon that Hamlet was only seven years old when Yorick died, represents an average of one hundred and forty-three piggyback rides a year. Perpend!

If we accept the normative use of a thousand, then ten thousand is an intensifier. Among other "pregnant" replies (2.2.211), Hamlet tells Polonius: "To be honest, as this world goes, is to be one man picked out of ten thousand" (178-79), and we can supply a stress on "this," referring to the new regime. In its usual form, the proverb reads: "A Man among a thousand" (Tilley, M217). Rosencrantz speaks of "ten thousand lesser things/ . . . mortised and adjoined" to the "huge spokes" of the king's "massy wheel" (3.3.19-20,17), as if to indicate the population of an entire kingdom. Numbers share in the inflation of rhetoric in Hamlet's wit-combat with Laertes at Ophelia's grave. As Hamlet says in his arithmetical imagery:

> I loved Ophelia. Forty thousand brothers
> Could not with all their quantity of love
> Make up my sum.   (5.1.271-73)

Laertes is the one who has been insisting on his "quantity of love," according to Cleopatra's formula: "If it be love indeed, tell me how much" (*Antony and Cleopatra* 1.1.14). Hamlet attempts to top Laertes' measures by making "Ossa like a wart" (5.1.285): "And if thou prate of mountains, let them throw/ Millions of acres on us" (282-83).

We have now reached the hyperbolic number of a million, which Hamlet had used earlier to describe the reception of the Dido and Aeneas play, that "pleased not the million; 'twas caviary to the general" (2.2.446-47). Against the "million" of popular taste, Hamlet sets that small coterie of himself "and others, whose judgments in such matters cried in the top of mine" (448-49). We think of Hamlet's claim just before the catastrophe: "the interim's mine,/ And a man's life's no more than to say 'one'" (5.2.73-74). This is the single number one that can exert its individual and heroic force against any odds. We also remember Hamlet's ominous threat at the end of the nunnery scene: "I say we will have no moe marriage. Those that are married already—all but one—shall live" (3.1.149-51)—a special solution to the problem of the one and the many.

Monetary and enumerative themes have an important character function in *Hamlet*. Polonius, for example, thinks of worldly experience as knowing how to manage one's financial affairs. His famous "precepts" (1.3.58) to his son have a distinctly commercial flavor, suggesting that human relations are to be governed with the same discretion one uses in handling money:

Neither a borrower nor a lender be,
For loan oft loses both itself and friend,
And borrowing dulleth edge of husbandry.

(1.3.75-77)

Laertes seems to fulfill his father's advice when he tells Claudius threateningly: "And for my means, I'll husband them so well/ They shall go far with little" (4.5. 138-39) . This is "husbandry" in the sense of thrift, as in Banquo's description of the darkness: "There's husbandry in heaven;/ Their candles are all out" (*Macbeth* 2.1.4-5) . Thrift, however, is a pejorative virtue in *Hamlet*, a sign of domestic pettiness.

There is a memorable imagery of money in Claudius' soliloquy in Act III, Scene iii, where it becomes the symbol for "the corrupted currents of this world" (57) as contrasted with the incorruptibility of heaven. Claudius begins "like a man to double business bound" (41) . He wants to persuade God to accept his prayer without his having to sacrifice any ill-won gains, and the word "double" immediately suggests duplicity. But Claudius' "stronger guilt" defeats his "strong intent" (40) :

. . . I am still possessed
Of those effects for which I did the murder,
My crown, mine own ambition, and my queen.

(3.3.53-55)

It is curious that the king should list together all of his assets, both material and personal.

In his confession, Claudius testifies unmercifully to his own double-dealing, especially his bribery:

— *129* —

In the corrupted currents of this world
Offense's gilded hand may shove by justice,
And oft 'tis seen the wicked prize itself
Buys out the law.   (3.3.57-60)

The personified Offense does not have a golden hand,
but only a "gilded" one, as alchemists counterfeited gold
coins with the thinnest layer of gilding. So Ulysses establishes for Achilles the distortions of human judgment:
men "give to dust that is a little gilt/ More laud than
gilt o'er-dusted" (*Troilus and Cressida* 3.3.178-79).
"Gilt" also makes a familiar pun with "guilt," and it
has a distant phonetic association with Guildenstern.
"Offense's gilded hand" is, of course, a pleasant circumlocution for bribery, which is able violently to "shove"
justice out of its path. In Claudius' brilliant machinations, "the wicked prize itself" provides the capital that
"Buys out the law."

Hamlet addresses the Ghost "in the cellarage" (1.5.
151) as "truepenny" (150), a coin honest though small
and a trusty good fellow, the rough equivalent of Jay
Gatsby's "old sport." The Ghost speaks of its murder
in the imagery of bookkeeping:

No reck'ning made, but sent to my account
With all my imperfections on my head.
                              (1.5.78-79)

Hamlet echoes this earlier speech just as he is about to
kill Claudius:

'A took my father grossly, full of bread,
With all his crimes broad blown, as flush as May;

And how his audit stands, who knows save heaven?

(3.3.80-82)

"Audit" matches "reck'ning" and "account"; in the context of this imagery, to kill Claudius while he is praying would be like the "hire and salary" (79) of a paid assassin. When Hamlet reflects that instead of bearing "the whips and scorns of time" (3.1.70) he "might his quietus make/ With a bare bodkin" (75-76), he is using a term from accounting similar to those favored by the Ghost. *Quietus est* is the standard Latin formula for being quit of a debt, as if the "bare bodkin" were wielded by a clerk who canceled one's mortal obligations. The word also suggests the quiet of death, after all the earthly turmoils mentioned in the preceding lines.

In general, Hamlet's aristocratic virtue recoils in disdain from all talk of money or circumscribing measurement. As he tells Ophelia in his love letter: "I am ill at these numbers. I have not art to reckon my groans" (2.2.120-21). "Numbers" is a specific word for metrics, but one may see here a rejection of numbering and reckoning and all other petty limits.

Of all the characters in *Hamlet*, Laertes has the most consistently developed imagery of measure and enumeration. As the subtle Claudius so well understands, Laertes can be made an easy dupe of that symmetrical sort of justice codified as "An eye for an eye." The image invoked by Laertes when he sees the mad Ophelia is meant as a practical guide to his future conduct: "By heaven, thy madness shall be paid with weight/ Till our scale

turn the beam" (4.5.156-57). Justice is usually represented with balance scales in one hand and a sword in
the other, and Laertes intends to put the dead Hamlet
in the empty pan to overbalance the weight of his mad
sister and his murdered father. This quantitative approach to reality seems to be Laertes' tragic flaw, or,
rather, the limitation that prevents him from ever seeming tragic at all. In his prohibitions to his sister, he
stresses the need for circumspect weighing. Ophelia
"must fear" that when Hamlet's "greatness" is "weighed,
his will is not his own" (1.3.16-17), and she should
"weigh what loss your honor may sustain/ If with too
credent ear you list his songs" (29-30).

Laertes is not only a weigher, but also, as we might
expect, a hyperbolical enumerator—two aspects of the
same point of view. His immediate reaction to the sight
of his mad sister is an extremely formal apostrophe: "O
heat, dry up my brains; tears seven times salt/ Burn out
the sense and virtue of mine eye!" (4.5.154-55). Why
"seven times salt"? There is no obvious connection with
the "seven ages" of man (*As You Like It* 2.7.139ff.) or
the "sevenfold shield of Ajax" (*Antony and Cleopatra*
4.14.38), so that we are forced to conclude that Laertes'
use of the Biblical seven is only a magical intensifier for
the salty virtue of tears. Hamlet had earlier spoken of
"the salt of most unrighteous tears" "flushing" in Gertrude's "gallèd eyes" (1.2.154-55) and of her mourning
"Like Niobe, all tears" (149). When Laertes says of the
dead Ophelia, "Too much of water hast thou, poor
Ophelia,/ And therefore I forbid my tears" (4.7.185-
86), we are meant to understand that his tears, with

their sevenfold potency, insist on appearing at his eyes despite his own efforts at self-control.

Enumeration is only one of many devices of hyperbole in Laertes' ranting style at the burial of Ophelia:

> O, treble woe
> Fall ten times treble on that cursèd head
> Whose wicked deed thy most ingenious sense
> Deprived thee of!   (5.1.248-51)

These enumerations are purely expressive, and they are meant to offer an emotionally arithmetical persuasion. We see Laertes as the hyperbolic hero of his own fancy in his Jack Cade rebellion against Claudius. The messenger speaks in the appropriate high style of reported terror:

> The ocean, overpeering of his list,
> Eats not the flats with more impiteous haste
> Than young Laertes, in a riotous head,
> O'erbears your officers.   (4.5.99-102)

The first image seems to be that of an irresistible tidal wave that cannot be contained by its "list," or bounding shore; the word was most often used in the plural, for the enclosing barriers of a tournament. Further on, Laertes agrees to be "ruled" by Claudius only on condition that "you will not o'errule me to a peace" (4.7.59-60). This is a touch characteristic of his very submissive bravado, and the many words prefixed by "o'er" help to determine the degree of Laertes' rhetorical excess.[6]

---

[6] According to Bartlett's Concordance, *Hamlet* has more "o'er" (and "over") prefix words than any other play of Shakespeare. The "o'er" prefix group indicates excess, it is used most fre-

Laertes' quantifications are paralleled by those in *The Murder of Gonzago*, which begins with what is perhaps the most devastating enumerative circumlocution in Elizabethan drama.[7] The Player King announces:

> Full thirty times hath Phoebus' cart gone round
> Neptune's salt wash and Tellus' orbèd ground,
> And thirty dozen moons with borrowed sheen
> About the world have times twelve thirties been,
> Since love our hearts, and Hymen did our hands,
> Unite commutual in most sacred bands.   (3.2.160-65)

The old-fashioned wit of this passage expects the audience to do the sums quickly in their heads and to admire the invention of the arithmetical synonyms. The couplet form also helps to convey the gravity of public statement, although we know that, by writing so wholeheartedly in an archaic style, Shakespeare is amusing both himself and us. The Player Queen continues the counting:

> So many journeys may the sun and moon
> Make us again count o'er ere love be done!
>   (3.2.166-67)

There seems to be a talismanic insistence on these thirty years of marriage between the Player King and his queen.

The play within the play is full of quantitative measures, especially in the part of the Player Queen, who

---

quently in hyperboles, and it has some connection with Marlowe's device of invidious comparison. There is a concentration of "o'er" prefix words in Hamlet's advice to the players, where they mark departures from the ideal of temperance or moderation.

[7] See the analogues in Kittredge, p. 224.

wants to order her reality with symmetrical thorough-
ness:

> And women's fear and love hold quantity,
> In neither aught, or in extremity.
> Now what my love is, proof hath made you know,
> And as my love is sized, my fear is so.
> Where love is great, the littlest doubts are fear;
> Where little fears grow great, great love grows there.
>
> (3.2.173-78)

These elaborate antitheses, driven home by alliteration,
would normally be the matter of comedy in Shakespeare,
but here they are meant as a simplified psychology of
alternatives. The point of the imagery is that love can
be "sized"—an unconscious pun on Walt Whitman's
"adhesiveness." We remember the figure of Pyrrhus,
"o'ersizèd with coagulate gore" (2.2.473), as if his skin
were a cloth or canvas overstiffened with the "total
gules" (468) of clotting blood.

The most specific enumerations in the play are the
Gravedigger's calculations of Hamlet's age.[8] The Clown
became a "gravemaker" (5.1.144-45) on "that day that
our last king Hamlet overcame Fortinbras" (146-47).
This is established for us as "that very day that young
Hamlet was born" (150). The Clown then tells us: "I
have been sexton here, man and boy, thirty years" (163-
64). That is an unmistakable number, which tallies with
the thirty years proclaimed by the Player King and the

[8] See *Variorum*, I, 391-94. See also V. Østerberg, *Prince Hamlet's Age*, Pamphlet VIII, Number 4, Det Kgl. Danske Videnska-
bernes Selskab. Historisk-filologiske Meddelelser (Copenhagen,
1924), and Carl Anders Dymling, *Hamlet's Age* (Stockholm,
1956).

Player Queen. We have further confirmation in the fact that the skull of Yorick, the king's jester, "hath lien you i' th' earth three and twenty years" (174-75). Shakespeare has obviously taken pains to tell us that Hamlet is now thirty years old. That much is undeniable, but it seems to me to have no bearing at all on Hamlet's age as it may be worked out from chronological references in earlier parts of the play. He is a young man there, about the same age as all the other young men in the play: Horatio, Laertes, Fortinbras, Rosencrantz, and Guildenstern.

We should bear in mind that we are dealing with a play, and that it is not possible for an audience to make fine discriminations about the ages of the characters. In a dramatic performance, age is comparative, and it takes on meaning only in relationships of characters, or when the dramatist insists on a certain number of years. I would agree that Shakespeare insists that Hamlet is thirty years old upon his return from his sea voyage, but how old was he when he left, and how long has the voyage taken? These are the kinds of questions that are impossible to answer and unfruitful to pursue by detective methods. Hamlet is now thirty because he has matured. He is no longer the melancholy youth of the beginning of the play, thinking seriously about "self-slaughter" (1.2.132). No matter how long a time has elapsed since Act I, it is clear that Hamlet has now forever lost his impetuous innocence. After a long and bitter apprenticeship of doubts, hesitations, self-accusations, and fascination with violence, he is finally "ready; now or whensoever" (5.2.203-4).

5. Art, Acting, and the Theater

HAMLET is Shakespeare's most self-conscious play, as we may see in the quantity of professional allusions to art, acting, and the theater.[1] Instead of trying consistently to create and maintain an illusion, Shakespeare often breaks the illusion by letting us know that this is only a play and that the actors are not actually the persons they represent. Brecht would call this the *Verfremdungseffekt*, but luckily Shakespeare did not make any theoretical pronouncements about what he was doing. In terms of appearance and reality, we may say that *Hamlet* attempts to remind us of the practical realities behind its histrionic appearances. The play demands an ironic and skeptical awareness on the part of the audience, who must be able to distinguish between the persuasive truth of the dramatic fable and the artifice of the dramatic vehicle.

Shakespeare's terms of art are all consistently negative or at best ambivalent in connotation, and he follows the popular conception of the actor as a dissembler and the artist as a creator of deceptive appearances. Art is an imitation of reality; it does not perfect and idealize it, but merely puts a good face on it, paints or colors it, as "The harlot's cheek" is "beautied with plast'ring art" (3.1.51).

There is a strong analogy in Shakespeare between painting[2] and acting, since both present appearances

---

[1] See Anne Righter, *Shakespeare and the Idea of the Play* (New York, 1962), esp. Chap. 5: "The Player King."

[2] For an extensive discussion of the art of painting in Shake-

that "show fairly outwards" (2.2.382), and, as arts, they lend themselves to the Bastard's distinction between "Exterior form, outward accoutrement" and "inward motion" (*King John* 1.1.211-12). The painter's imitation or feigning of reality is like the actor's pretending to be the person whom he merely represents, and the set of terms for these two arts is steeped in moral condemnation. In the closet scene, for example, Hamlet refers to the portraits of his father and his uncle as "The counterfeit presentment of two brothers" (3.4.55). "Counterfeit" is a standard Elizabethan term for portrait, and Fairchild believes that it reflects the Platonic notion that a painting is always "an inferior representation of an original—an imitation of a perfect 'substance.' "[3] The painting itself is at least three removes from the Platonic reality, and all of Shakespeare's terms of art share in this unfavorable epistemology, even when there is no pejorative intention in the immediate context. In *The Merchant of Venice*, for example, when Bassanio opens the casket, he finds, to his triumphant joy, "Fair Portia's counterfeit!" (3.2.115). Portia herself is seductively genuine, but portraits in general are "counterfeits," as in Sonnet XVI, where "living flowers" are infinitely preferable to a "painted counterfeit."

Shakespeare was well aware of the doubleness of "counterfeit." In *Timon of Athens*, where painting is

---

speare see Arthur H. R. Fairchild, *Shakespeare and the Arts of Design* (Columbia: University of Missouri, 1937), Part Three. See also Margaret Farrand Thorp, "Shakespeare and the Fine Arts," *PMLA*, XLVI (1931), 672-93.

[3] Fairchild, *Shakespeare and the Arts of Design*, p. 117.

used more significantly than in any other of his plays, Timon offers ironic praise to the rapacious Painter and Poet:

> Good honest men! Thou draw'st a counterfeit
> Best in all Athens. Th'art indeed the best;
> Thou counterfeit'st most lively. (5.1.78-80)

There is wordplay on "lively" as signifying both animated and lifelike, or exactly represented in the painting. Shakespeare also has a series of references to counterfeit coins, which bear falsely imposed images and are therefore doubly imitations of the real thing.

As a term for acting, to "counterfeit" means to present a false appearance, to dissemble. Buckingham, in his costume of *"rotten armour, marvellous ill-favoured,"* boasts of his villainous ability to "counterfeit the deep tragedian" (*Richard III* 3.5 s.d. and 5), and Coriolanus in his "gown of humility" has contempt for his prepared role as humble suitor to the citizens: "I will practise the insinuating nod and be off to them most counterfeitly. That is, sir, I will counterfeit the bewitchment of some popular man and give it bountiful to the desirers" (*Coriolanus* 2.3.96-99). We may conclude that the negative connotations of "counterfeit" are difficult to suppress even in its neutral senses, because art and acting in Shakespeare are feigning, deception, and illusion.

"Shadow" is another deprecating Elizabethan word for a portrait, applied either to one's likeness in a mirror or a painted picture. In *The Merchant of Venice,*

Bassanio plays wittily on shadow and substance when he finds Portia's picture in the leaden casket:

> Yet look how far
> The substance of my praise doth wrong this shadow
> In underprizing it, so far this shadow
> Doth limp behind the substance.   (3.2.126-29)

The possibilities of this theme are more highly developed in Hamlet's talk with Rosencrantz and Guildenstern. Hamlet's commonplace, "A dream itself is but a shadow" (2.2.264), is topped by Rosencrantz's comment that "ambition [is] of so airy and light a quality that it is but a shadow's shadow" (265-66), to which Hamlet replies with impatient metaphysical subtlety: "Then are our beggars bodies, and our monarchs and outstretched heroes the beggars' shadows" (267-69). Since "shadow" is such a complex word, this talk has a specious air of profundity, although it is only the most elementary exercise in paradox. Its terms are not specifically those of art, but it draws on the familiar idea that a painting or a play is only a representation, an imitation, feigning, image, counterfeit, or shadow of some ulterior and objective reality.

The actor, too, is a shadow, as Duke Theseus tells us: "The best in this kind are but shadows" (*A Midsummer Night's Dream* 5.1.210), and Puck, in this most critically self-conscious scene, makes his apologies directly to the audience, "If we shadows have offended" (412). We also have Macbeth's more somber image for the deceptive illusion of life:

Out, out, brief candle!
Life's but a walking shadow, a poor player,
That struts and frets his hour upon the stage,
And then is heard no more. . . .

(Macbeth 5.5.23-26)

Macbeth may be thinking of the candles used to light
the stage in the private theaters, and more spectacularly
in court masques, so that the "strutting player whose
conceit/ Lies in his hamstring" *(Troilus and Cressida*
1.3.153-54) would be unforgettably associated with his
"walking shadow."

The references to acting and the theater in *Hamlet*
depend upon the same assumptions about appearance
and reality as in Shakespeare's terms of art. Of all
his works, *Hamlet* develops the most self-conscious
contrasts between the world of the play and the real
world. Its scenes from interpolated plays (the Player's
speech and *The Murder of Gonzago*) are written in
styles entirely different from that of the main action,
and they serve to displace our awareness of what is fictive
and what is true. If there are plays within plays, there
must also be scenes within scenes and acting within acting, so that we are immediately prevented from giving
any simple answers about the nature of the dramatic illusion in *Hamlet*.

There is a semantic difficulty in Shakespeare's theatrical terms, because they are often common words that
would normally be understood in their general rather
than technical senses. "Act," "scene," "plot," "play,"
"perform," "put on," "show," and "shape" all have this

double reference, so that we need to discern whether such words are indeed theatrical terms in any particular context. This is a simple and unsatisfactory way of putting it, because certain key words tend to carry over their connotations into unfamiliar and even inappropriate contexts.

In Hamlet's warning to Ophelia about her father: "Let the doors be shut upon him, that he may play the fool nowhere but in's own house" (3.1.133-34), "play the fool" is a general indication of folly as well as a specific dramatic role. Within the next hundred lines Hamlet has advice for "those that play your clowns" (3.2.40-41) that would apply admirably well to Polonius: let them "speak no more than is set down for them" (41-42). And in his farewell to the murdered counselor, Hamlet refers to him as a "wretched, rash, intruding fool" (3.4.32). Although there is no way of proving that Shakespeare meant to use "fool" in its theatrical sense, it seems to me that this is an inescapable secondary meaning. We see the process working in the opposite direction, from the more specific meaning to the general one, in Hamlet's comment on the Clown, whose extemporized jesting "shows a most pitiful ambition in the fool that uses it" (3.2.46-47). If this needs any explanation, we may say that the actor is both Fool and fool. In a more pointed allusion, Hamlet represents himself to the Ghost as one of the "fools of nature" (1.4.54), a bit of wordplay on naturals, or fools by birth, as distinguished from professionals like Yorick.

The most overtly theatrical passage in the play is Hamlet's soliloquy at the end of Act II, after the First Player has broken off his passionate declamation. Ham-

let wonders what the Player would do "Had he the
motive and the cue for passion/ That I have?" (2.2.571-
72). "Cue" is an actor's word, which seems to assume
that both Hamlet and the Player have only a stage existence. Hamlet's answer to his own question also equates
the stage with the world: "He would drown the stage
with tears/ And cleave the general ear with horrid
speech" (572-73), and he goes on to speak about the
emotional effects of the Player on his audience. But
Hamlet breaks off his own histrionics at the climactic
"O, vengeance!" (593, Folio). He then begins to differentiate, ironically of course, between the play world and
the real world, between "brave" (594) words and brave
action. He is being "Prompted" to his "revenge by
heaven and hell" (596), who are presumably dissatis-
fied with his "bad performance" (4.7.151). The whole
soliloquy is Hamlet's most extended excursion into the
psychology and sociology of the drama.

The actor's deceptive appearance is represented by
costume: "clothes do but cheat and cozen us." The double symbolism of clothing may be seen in the expression
"put on," which means not only to dress oneself, but
also to pretend. Thus Hamlet tells us that he will "put
an antic disposition on" (1.5.172) as if it were a costume, and the king wonders why his nephew-son "puts
on this confusion" (3.1.2). We learn later that the
"monster custom" is like the wardrobe manager, who
supplies costumes for different roles:

> ... to the use of actions fair and good
> He likewise gives a frock or livery
> That aptly is put on.   (3.4.164-66)

"Actions" is another of those ambiguous common words that may or may not have a theatrical reference, but in this context it resembles Hamlet's own "actions that a man might play" (1.2.84), or the advice to the players: "Suit the action to the word, the word to the action" (3.2.18-19).

The most significant of these common words with theatrical overtones is "shape," which could be used in Shakespeare's time to mean the makeup and costume suited to a particular part, as well as the part itself or the character impersonated. "Shape" and "form" are close in meaning and often paired, so that we may think of shape as an external, visible form—a sense in which it appears in *Love's Labour's Lost*, when we learn that the suitors, "Disguis'd like Muscovites, in shapeless gear," "will again be here/ In their own shapes" (5.2. 303, 287-88). Costume is usually the most important aspect of a "shape," but the word denotes the entire appearance or effect.

The strongest example of "shape" is in the king's disclosure of his plot to Laertes:

> Let's further think of this,
> Weigh what convenience both of time and means
> May fit us to our shape. If this should fail,
> And that our drift look through our bad performance,
> 'Twere better not assayed. (4.7.148-52)

The imagery is theatrical, and Claudius uses the familiar trope of the villain as an actor, who plays his role according to his ingenious and aesthetically satisfying plot. Like Iago and Marlowe's Barabas, Claudius takes pleasure in contrived effects; he and Laertes can only be fitted to their proper "shape" by the "convenience both of time and means." In this context, "shape" means not only the proper costume, but the whole deceptive role the two must play. It is a "performance," and one which will turn out badly if the real "drift" of the action is revealed to the spectators.

To proceed from obvious to less obvious uses of "shape" in its theatrical sense, Hamlet's first speech in the play (after the one-line thrusts) calls attention to his "inky cloak" and "customary suits of solemn black" (1.2.77-78) as only "forms, moods, shapes of grief": "For they are actions that a man might play." But Hamlet has "that within which passes show;/ These but the trappings and the suits of woe" (82, 84-86). The passage is steeped in the language of the theater: "shapes," "actions," "play," "show," "trappings." Hamlet is using acting in the traditional way to represent appearances in contrast to true inner feelings. His costume, gesture, and facial expression are all "shapes of grief," the kinds of details with which an actor would concern himself in preparing his part (the "actions that a man might play"), but they are ultimately only outward "trappings," a "show." In Hamlet's nunnery scene with Ophelia, we find the word "shape" again in a theatrical context: "I am very proud, revengeful, ambitious, with more offenses at my beck than I have thoughts to put them in, imagination to give them shape, or time to act them in" (3.1.124-28). The concurrence of "act" and "shape" suggests that Hamlet is thinking of his revenge as a part to be played, for which his "imagination" will provide the scenario.

Among Hamlet's first passionate exchanges with the Ghost is this puzzling declaration: "Thou com'st in such a questionable shape/ That I will speak to thee" (1.4.43-44). "Questionable" may mean inviting question (or conversation), or arousing it by an odd or doubtful appearance. It seems likely that the Elizabethan ghost had traditional characteristics,[4] so that the "shape" itself is not "questionable," only its otherworldly associations. Hamlet may also be thinking that the devil, as a master of theatrical disguises, "hath power/ T' assume a pleasing shape" (2.2.611-12), especially for a temptation scene. There is an extensive use of "shape" to mean a false appearance or disguise, as in the Ghost's account of Gertrude, who lacks the virtue that "never will be moved,/ Though lewdness court it in a shape of heaven" (1.5.53-54). The "shape of heaven" is only an actor's costume that cannot deceive steadfast virtue.

"Act" is the most ambiguous of all dramatic words, but when the Clown says that "an act hath three branches" (5.1.11), it is difficult to ignore the intrusive theatrical meaning. It is not essential to verify whether the Clown's "act" occurs in the real world or in the world

[4] See, for example, the interesting passage on the staging of ghosts by Angelo Ingegnieri (1598), quoted in Allardyce Nicoll, *Stuart Masques and the Renaissance Stage* (New York, 1938), pp. 204-5. See also R. A. Foakes's edition of *Macbeth*, which suggests (p. xviii) a "white-faced and perhaps white-robed ghost" in that play (The Bobbs-Merrill Shakespeare, Indianapolis, Ind., 1968).

of the play. In other parts of *Hamlet*, "act" is defined by a context of theatrical words and images. Thus, before Hamlet dies, he addresses the spectators as an on-stage audience: "You that look pale and tremble at this chance,/ That are but mutes or audience to this act" (5.2.335-36). The "mutes" are nonspeaking supernumeraries, and we recall that the Poisoner in the dumb show enters *"with some two or three Mutes"* (3.2.140 s.d., Folio). In the closet scene, Gertrude demands to know "what act" it is that Hamlet speaks of, "That roars so loud and thunders in the index" (3.4.52-53), as if her son were a ham actor like Bottom the Weaver, who "will roar that I will do any man's heart good to hear me" (*A Midsummer Night's Dream* 1.2.62-63). "Index" is a specific term for the prologue to a play, as in Iago's sexual metaphor: "Lechery, by this hand; an index and obscure prologue to the history of lust and foul thoughts" (*Othello* 2.1.252-54).

Other common words with theatrical overtones are "plot," "show," and "part." "Plot" raises interesting analogies between the stage action and what it represents, so that Shakespeare's villains are usually good actors as well as skillful plotters—one could, in fact, take a completely histrionic approach to evil in the plays. Hamlet learns quite late in the action that "Our indiscretion sometime serves us well/ When our deep plots do pall" (5.2.8-9). These are "deep plots" such as Hamlet's decision to spare the praying Claudius in order to wait for a "more horrid hent" (3.3.88). At the very end of the play, Horatio insists that all the actions he has specified

> . . . be presently performed,
> Even while men's minds are wild, lest more mischance
> On plots and errors happen.   (5.2.394-96)

"Plots and errors" suggest the complications of Plau-
tine comedy, as they are happily developed in *The Comedy of Errors*, but Horatio has already indicated what he
means:

> So shall you hear
> Of carnal, bloody, and unnatural acts,
> Of accidental judgments, casual slaughters,
> Of deaths put on by cunning and forced cause,
> And, in this upshot, purposes mistook
> Fall'n on th' inventors' heads. All this can I
> Truly deliver.   (5.2.381-87)

This is not only a summary of the action in *Hamlet*;
it is also a compendium of tragic plots.

The word "show" could be used for a play, especially
one that stresses spectacle rather than language, as in
the traditional image of the world as a theater in Sonnet
XV: "this huge stage presenteth naught but shows/
Whereon the stars in secret influence comment." There
is, of course, the dumb show or pantomime in *Hamlet*,
on which the witty prince quibbles aggressively in his
talk with Ophelia. When she asks if the Prologue will
"tell us what this show meant" (3.2.148), as prologues
were supposed to do, Hamlet taunts her: "Ay, or any
show that you will show him. Be not you ashamed to
show, he'll not shame to tell you what it means" (149-
51). Hamlet later turns Ophelia's putative lovemaking
into a puppet show, to which he will act as presenter or

chorus: "I could interpret between you and your love, if I could see the puppets dallying" (252-53). There is no doubt that this is a cruel attack on Ophelia, but Hamlet means to explode all false shows with his *Mousetrap*.

"Part" is a theatrical word for role, but it has so many other meanings that it is often difficult to tell whether it is being used histrionically—for example, when Hamlet says: "for my own poor part, / Look you, I'll go pray" (1.5.131-32). This is the sort of case that may be attracted into a theatrical meaning by its context. There is no ambiguity, however, when Hamlet says: "the humorous man shall end his part in peace" (2.2.331-32), with a glance at Corporal Nym and the humors comedies with which Ben Jonson had so recently astounded English audiences. Another clear reference is found in Hamlet's outrageous puns on Polonius' acting career. He "played once i' th' university" and "was accounted a good actor" (3.2.101-3):

> *Polonius.* I did enact Julius Caesar. I was killed
> i' th' Capitol; Brutus killed me.
> *Hamlet.* It was a brute part of him to kill so
> capital a calf there. (3.2.105-8)

To continue the prophetic puns into the speech of the Player King, Polonius is one of those ill-fated actors whose "own enactures with themselves destroy" (203). Hamlet will enact the "brute part" for the old counselor in the closet scene, where, like the good curate Sir Nathaniel in the show of the Nine Worthies, he proves to be "a little o'erparted" (*Love's Labour's Lost* 5.2.578).

Shakespeare's self-consciousness of his own theater is sometimes expressed in unexpected ways. When Hamlet vows to remember the Ghost, he speaks a line with an extraordinary allusion in it:

> Remember thee?
> Ay, thou poor ghost, whiles memory holds a seat
> In this distracted globe.   (1.5.95-97)

Hamlet makes a gesture to his head, which could familiarly be called a "globe," but this is also the name of the theater in which the play is being presented, and the word "seat" clinches the comparison. Memory, then, is personified as a member of the audience—one of those "wonder-wounded hearers" (5.1.259)—that closely attends the Ghost's recital, both in Hamlet's "globe" and in Shakespeare's Globe.[5] The phrase "holds a seat" suggests a place in the highest price category, that may have been held on subscription for influential patrons.

For a more subtle example of Shakespeare's awareness of the illusion he is creating, we may turn to Hamlet's explanation of his melancholy to Rosencrantz and Guildenstern: "I have of late, but wherefore I know not, lost all my mirth, forgone all custom of exercises; and indeed, it goes so heavily with my disposition that this goodly frame, the earth, seems to me a sterile promontory; this most excellent canopy, the air, look you, this brave o'erhanging firmament, this majestical roof fret-

[5] See Charles R. Forker, "Shakespeare's Theatrical Symbolism and Its Function in *Hamlet*," *SQ*, XIV (1963), 221.

ted with golden fire: why, it appeareth nothing to me but a foul and pestilent congregation of vapors" (2.2. 303-11). During an afternoon performance in an un-roofed theater, "this brave o'erhanging firmament" is plainly visible to all, and Hamlet's "look you" seems to invite the audience to verify the words of the play. Hamlet is making his demonstration in terms of visual realities just outside the theater, but "this most excellent canopy" and "this majestical roof fretted with golden fire" may also refer to the projecting canopy or "shadow" over the stage, with its zodiacal decorations.[6]

In Hamlet's cloud speech to Polonius, there is a similar reciprocation between the play world and the real world, and even the illusion that certain objects identifiable to the audience may be appropriated to theatrical use. Hamlet begins: "Do you see yonder cloud that's almost in shape of a camel?" (3.2.384-85). Polonius looks up, as the audience is encouraged to do, and politely agrees with this description of "yonder cloud." According to the meteorological conditions on the Bankside in Southwark on any particular day in the very early seventeenth century, "yonder cloud" might look like a camel, a weasel, or a whale—"Very like a whale" (390), as Polonius says obligingly—or like Antony's

> . . . cloud that's dragonish;
> A vapour sometime like a bear or lion,
> A tower'd citadel, a pendent rock,

[6] See Nevill Coghill, *Shakespeare's Professional Skills* (Cambridge, Eng.: Cambridge University Press, 1964), Chap. 1: "Visual Meaning," esp. pp. 8-9. See also C. Walter Hodges, *The Globe Restored* (New York, 1954), p. 31.

A forked mountain, or blue promontory
With trees upon't that nod unto the world
And mock our eyes with air.
                    (*Antony and Cleopatra* 4.14.2-7)

These are excellent, if not fortuitous, examples of
what Bethell calls the "popular dramatic tradition," that
"multi-conscious" counterpoint between the desire to
create a convincing illusion on stage and the contrary
impulse to keep the audience aware that this is only a
play, "a fiction" and "a dream of passion" (2.2.562) .[7]
This counterpoint may seem to violate modern assumptions about psychological verisimilitude, but it does allow the audience to share in the playwright's own self-
consciousness and to participate wholeheartedly in
strong histrionic emotions.

On one side of this "multi-consciousness," we may
see how Hamlet, from the Player's "passionate speech"
(2.2.441-42) , arrives at the central question of all mi-
metic art: "What's Hecuba to him, or he to Hecuba,/
That he should weep for her?" (569-70) . Through a
series of self-accusations, this question leads to an understanding of how pity and fear—or, more practically, a
guilty conscience—can be "caught" by a play:

                I have heard
That guilty creatures sitting at a play
Have by the very cunning of the scene
Been struck so to the soul that presently
They have proclaimed their malefactions.
                    (2.2.600-4)

---

[7] See S. L. Bethell, *Shakespeare and the Popular Dramatic Tradition* (London, 1944).

There were many "real life" anecdotes to support this confessional effect, including one in *Der Bestrafte Brudermord* (the German *Hamlet*), and three others in Heywood's *Apology for Actors* (1612), which defended the moral utility of the theater against Puritan attacks.[8]

"Cunning" means professional skill or art purposively applied, as in Hamlet's earlier remark that the Dido and Aeneas play was "set down with as much modesty as cunning" (2.2.450-51). "The very cunning of the scene" is the ability of the stage representation to work its emotional effects against the conscious will of the guilty spectator, who is caught unaware in the play's cathartic coils. But for every king who cries, "Give me some light. Away!" (3.2.275), and for every conscience-stricken wife who suddenly exclaims, "O my husband!", revealing a well-hidden murder, there are all the other persons in the audience who refuse to be ensnared by "the very cunning of the scene." They agree with Hamlet's mocking deflation of illusion: "No, no, they do but jest, poison in jest; no offense i' th' world" (240-41).

[8] See Kittredge, pp. 204-5, and *Variorum*, I, 198.

PART TWO
STAGING AND STRUCTURE

I T WOULD be a pleasant exercise to speculate on that question Martin Holmes has proposed: "What sort of a play was *Hamlet* in the eyes of its original spectators?"[1] Or, if we accept Shakespeare as our contemporary, we may return with Jan Kott to that hypothetical moment when the members of Shakespeare's company first meet to discuss *Hamlet*, which is to be the next presentation at the Globe.[2] They will have the "book" of the play in their hands, but decisions must still be made about the appearance of the characters, their costumes, the gestures they will use, and the sound effects and music needed in the stage action. A list of properties must be drawn up, and they must be cued into the text. The pattern of entrances and exits, stage groupings, doubling of minor roles, and use of traps must be made practicable for a performance. All permissive, authorial stage directions—for example, Quarto 2's entrance in the dumb show for *"The poisoner, with some three or four"* (3.2.140 s.d.) , which Folio reduces to *"some two or three Mutes"*—must be revised into a precise form.

Many of these indications are already in the text of the written play, and some effects are so much a matter of accepted practice that they can be noted in abbreviated form: for example, the trumpet fanfare or "flourish" to announce the entrance of royalty, or the clearing

[1] Martin Holmes, *The Guns of Elsinore* (London, 1964), p. 13.
[2] Jan Kott, *Shakespeare Our Contemporary*, tr. Boleslaw Taborski (London, 1964), Chap. 2: *"Hamlet* of the Mid-Century."

of corpses from the stage before a new scene begins. In the dumb show, where all the directions are unusually explicit, we are told: *"The dead body is carried away"* (3.2.140 s.d.). Since there is no possibility of either a "blackout" or a lowered curtain in the Elizabethan theater, the dead must be disposed of in full view of the audience.

There is a *Hamlet* of words that we all know almost by heart, and there is a *Hamlet* without words that may be unfamiliar, but these two *Hamlets* cannot be separated in the play we see in the theater. The poetic play is a puzzling genre, since so much in it is a matter of presentation rather than of words. What are we to make of the dumb show in *Hamlet?* The description in our text does not exist in performance. It is, literally, only a set of directions to actors, written instructions on how to execute the pantomime. We regret losing that wonderful line that tells the Player Queen to make *"passionate action"* (3.2.140 s.d.) when she finds the Player King poisoned. The actor must be able to translate the stage directions into their proper nonverbal form. Whoever acted the part of Ophelia would be able to profit from Quarto 1's vivid description of her entrance in the mad scene: *"Enter Ophelia playing on a lute, and her hair down, singing"* (at 4.5.20). This recalls the Folio directions in *Troilus and Cressida: "Enter Cassandra with her hair about her ears"* (2.2.100 s.d.), and in *Richard III: "Enter* QUEEN ELIZABETH, *with her hair about her ears"* (2.2.33 s.d.) —a conventional sign of grief-stricken, distracted ladies.

One of the most graphic Shakespearean directions is

for the entrance of Apemantus into the banqueting hall of Timon: *"Then comes, dropping after all,* APEMAN-TUS, *discontentedly, like himself"* (*Timon of Athens* 1.2 s.d.). This splendid line, which does not exist in the presented play, is meant to aid Apemantus in preparing his part and to help the poor reader "Piece out" his own "imperfections" (*Henry V* Prol. 23). We are grateful, of course, for this verbal scaffolding, but we may still wonder what sort of Janus-faced genre is this that has one form when read and another when performed? Which is indeed the play that Shakespeare wrote?

I do not propose to answer these teasing questions. Merely to formulate them suggests how difficult it is to speak about the style of a Shakespearean play. We are forced to think simultaneously about the written text and its realization in performance. Sometimes a line in the written text is not complete without the gesture that accompanies it. I am thinking of Polonius' triumphant revelation of Hamlet's love melancholy to the king and queen: "Take this from this, if this be otherwise" (2.2.156). It is not a very impressive line, yet it is unintelligible without the stage direction supplied by Theobald: *"Pointing to his head and shoulder."* The gesture is implicit in Shakespeare's text, yet in what sense can a gesture be said to exist in a literary work? We have also a problem in grammar, since the first two demonstrative pronouns refer not to other nouns, but to parts of the body of the actor playing Polonius.

There is another example in the Quarto 2 stage direction for the second appearance of the Ghost: *"It spreads his arms*"³ (1.1.127 s.d.) . The Ghost does not speak at all in this scene, but this gesture is intended as a reply to Horatio's bold line: "I'll cross it, though it blast me" (127) . The Ghost answers by "crossing" Horatio—a dangerous procedure, according to all pneumatologists —and thus warning him that it will not be trifled with. How are we, in our accepted literary categories, to deal with a nonverbal reply?

Since most studies of Shakespeare's style choose to ignore these uncategorizable details, I should like to go to the opposite extreme to see what can be said about the *Hamlet* without words. So much has already been written about the words of the play that it might be interesting, as an experiment, to confine our attention to the play as Shakespeare intended it to be produced at the Globe. I don't for a moment believe that we can literally recover Shakespeare's intentions, but the attempt might stimulate some fresh insight. In the first two chapters on staging, I shall be concerned with gesture and stage action, sound effects and music, costumes, and stage properties. I shall then briefly discuss structure in relation to dramatic scenes.

³ This stage direction, omitted in Folio, is emended in the Quarto of 1676 to *"He spreads his arms."* Most editors assume that the gesture is made by Horatio rather than by the Ghost.

6. Gesture and Stage Action

MODERN editions of *Hamlet* are filled with editorial indications of the movements to be made by the actors, such as Theobald's *"Pointing to his head and shoulder,"* discussed above. In these stage directions, the editor records what he takes to be the implication of the lines, but often he is adapting Shakespeare to the theatrical practice of a later age. This is especially true of those eighteenth-century versions of Shakespeare on which so many modern editions are based. I believe that a careful reader of plays should be able to supply for himself the gestures and stage action demanded by the text, and, by so doing, avoid the distortions of editorial staging. In the present discussion, I shall ignore the inventions of imaginative actors, chronicled by theatrical history, in order to concentrate on those examples of gesture and stage action that are either mentioned or clearly implied in the text.

There are certain demonstrative words that need a gesture to complete their meaning. The word "thus," for example, generates at least five gestures in *Hamlet*. Laertes, who is much given to broad gesturing to support his ranting style, tells the king how he will honor his father's memory:

> To his good friends thus wide I'll ope my arms
> And like the kind life-rend'ring pelican[1]
> Repast them with my blood.   (4.5.145-47)

[1] Folio has "politician" for Quarto 2's "pelican," an error so wild and so difficult to account for textually that it seems as if

Laertes opens his arms in a gesture of friendship to illustrate his sanguinary words, a conventional movement that could serve as pantomime or dumb show without any accompanying words.[2] There is another example of gesture illustrating text in Hamlet's warning to the players against obvious and excessive hand gestures: "Nor do not saw the air too much with your hand, thus" (3.2.4-5). The added "thus" is for the demonstration, which follows the example of proper speaking, "as I pronounced it to you, trippingly on the tongue" (1-2). Right after the Ghost departs, Hamlet insists that his friends swear not to give away the secret of his "antic disposition" by such knowing movements as, "With arms encumb'red thus, or this headshake" (1.5.174). Hamlet is miming possible action, which he accompanies by brief phrases of "ambiguous giving out" (178). In Ophelia's report of Hamlet's frantic visit to her in her closet, she uses two gestures introduced by "thus":

> And with his other hand thus o'er his brow
> He falls to such perusal of my face
> As 'a would draw it. Long stayed he so.
> At last, a little shaking of mine arm,
> And thrice his head thus waving up and down. . . .
>
> (2.1.89-93)

---

the compositor is playing tricks with us (see Parrott and Craig, p. 197). The "kind life-rend'ring politician" makes a splendid image of Laertes overreaching his politic father.

  [2] See B. L. Joseph, *Elizabethan Acting* (2 edn.; London: Oxford University Press, 1964). First published, 1951. Joseph discusses, with illustrations, many of these conventional gestures.

Both examples of "thus" are unnecessary for Ophelia's narration; their only function is to call attention to the actor's gestures.

"This" and "that," and "these" and "those" are also words that frequently require an accompanying gesture. When Polonius produces Hamlet's letter to Ophelia, he does it with a triumphant lawyer's emphasis:

I have a daughter: have, while she is mine,
Who in her duty and obedience, mark,
Hath given me this. Now gather, and surmise.
                                        (2.2.106-8)

There is a pause at "this," during which Polonius might wave the letter significantly in the direction of the king and queen. In this example and in a great many others like it, the gesture calls attention to the stage property. The dialogue about Yorick's skull has a number of these demonstrative pronouns:

Clown. This same skull, sir, was, sir, Yorick's
          skull, the King's jester.
Hamlet. This?
Clown. E'en that.   (5.1.181-84)

"This?" and "E'en that" need a referent to complete their meaning.

"Here" and "there" are an analogous pair of direction words. They may indicate a property, as in Claudius' "we have here writ" (1.2.27), motioning to his letter to old Norway, but most often they serve to locate action on the stage. Like Launce in his patient representation of parting (The Two Gentlemen of Verona 2.3), the

Clown-gravedigger reenacts Ophelia's drowning: "Here lies the water—good. Here stands the man—good" (5.1.15-16).

The imperative "look" or "look you," when it is not merely an interjection, implies the double action of pointing and observing. The word is of greatest importance in the closet scene, where Hamlet is urgently trying to make his mother see the Ghost: "Look you, how pale he glares!" (3.4.126). "Do you see nothing there?" (132), he asks unbelievingly, but Gertrude's blindness to the spiritual world is not to be broken by exhortation: "Nothing at all; yet all that is I see" (133). Hamlet makes one final attempt to show Gertrude the Ghost as it exits through the stage door:

> Why, look you there! Look how it steals away!
> My father, in his habit as he lived!
> Look where he goes even now out at the portal!
>
> (3.4.135-37)

Hamlet is describing what he observes, but Gertrude, although anxiously looking in the direction of her son's pointing finger, sees nothing, and confidently attributes the presence of the Ghost to madness.

"Covering" lines also indicate stage actions, usually ones that are completed during the time the lines are being spoken. They often "cover" quick costume changes or the donning of a disguise, or make it possible for a character to ascend or descend the upper stage by an inner staircase. The lines themselves may be extremely lyrical, but this does not alter their practical function. Similarly, there are many passages in Shakespeare that serve mainly to locate the scene and to set the time, and which could be replaced on the modern stage by effects of lighting and scenic illusion.

The Ghost's entrance and exit lines in Act I, for example, are conditioned by the slowly ascending and descending trap by which it presumably arrives and departs. Although there are no directions regarding the trap—and it is clear that the stage doors are also used (as in the exit at 1.4.86 and the entrance at the beginning of 1.5) —this was the conventional means of producing and withdrawing an Elizabethan dramatic spook. The Ghost's exit line in Act I, Scene v makes for an excellent slow "fade-out": "Adieu, adieu, adieu. Remember me" (91). Once the Ghost has reached the "cellarage" (151), we next hear it crying *"under the stage"* (148 s.d.), which confirms our impression of an exit by a trap.

The first appearance of the Ghost is charted by means of a star, in Barnardo's narration:

Last night of all,
When yond same star that's westward from the pole
Had made his course t' illume that part of heaven
Where now it burns, Marcellus and myself,
The bell then beating one—
                            Enter Ghost. (1.1.35-39 s.d.)

The precise astrological details locating the event in time help to develop its portentousness, and they also serve to distract us, so that the Ghost's entrance can be sudden and unobtrusive. Shakespeare will work changes on this dramatic technique for every appearance of the Ghost in the play. Each has its own variety of distraction, or what I have been calling its "covering" device.

One other important source for understanding the stage action is the description in the text of what the characters look like and what they do. These clues should be followed strictly by any director in order to avoid embarrassing or absurd contradictions. When Polonius tells us of the First Player, for example: "Look, whe'r he has not turned his color, and has tears in's eyes" (2.2.530-31), we accept this as an account of what we have just seen. Hamlet's soliloquy continues the description of the First Player's reaction to his "passionate speech" (441-42):

> . . . all his visage wanned,
> Tears in his eyes, distraction in his aspect,
> A broken voice, and his whole function suiting
> With forms to his conceit?   (2.2.564-67)

We have no reason to doubt Hamlet's word, so that the actor preparing the role of the First Player should derive useful suggestions from these two speeches.

There are many comparable examples, some very brief, scattered throughout the play. The queen tells us how Hamlet killed Polonius: "Behind the arras hearing something stir,/ Whips out his rapier, cries, 'A rat, a rat!' " (4.1.9-10). We already know most of this from the closet scene, but "Whips out his rapier" is a graphic detail that exactly describes Hamlet's unthinking alacrity. After Horatio has seen the Ghost, Barnardo comments: "How now, Horatio? You tremble and look pale" (1.1.53). The breaking of Horatio's stoic calm and skeptical banter must therefore be an immediate, physical reaction. We have a few hints for Ophelia's part in the report of the anonymous gentleman, who says that she

> . . . hems, and beats her heart,
> Spurns enviously at straws, speaks things in doubt
> That carry but half sense.   (4.5.5-7)

He also tells us of "her winks and nods and gestures" (11). All these details could profitably be put to use by an actor or serve to stimulate the histrionic imagination of a reader.

In the closet scene, Gertrude gives us a full account of how her son looks as he speaks to the Ghost:

> Alas, how is't with you,
> That you do bend your eye on vacancy,
> And with th' incorporal air do hold discourse?
> Forth at your eyes your spirits wildly peep,
> And as the sleeping soldiers in th' alarm
> Your bedded hair like life in excrements
> Start up and stand an end.   (3.4.117-23)

We know that Gertrude believes her son to be suffering from "ecstasy" (139), so that all of her details fit the idea of uncontrollable emotion: the fixed stare, the wild eyes, the hair standing on end. If we follow through our assumptions about the relation of such passages to the stage action, we will want to know something more about Hamlet's "bedded hair" and how it can "Start up and stand an end." The passage draws on Elizabethan notions of hair as "excrements" or outgrowths, which, although lifeless themselves, were nevertheless capable of extension. In an earlier scene, the Ghost anticipates the effect that a disclosure of its experiences in purgatory would have on Hamlet. Such a recital, it says, would make

> Thy knotted and combinèd locks to part
> And each particular hair to stand an end
> Like quills upon the fearful porpentine.
>
> (1.5.18-20)

There is no equivocation about the proper stage expression for Hamlet's fright; it is simply a question of how it could have been realized in performance. From what we know of the Elizabethan theater, there is no indication that Burbage or any other actor of that time was able to carry out these specific instructions in the text. But the great Garrick, so Arthur Colby Sprague informs us, was able to accomplish the effect with a mechanical wig,[3] the so-called "fright wig" operated by strings.

Hamlet's gestures may best be studied in the scene immediately after the departure of the Ghost. The young prince suddenly totters on his feet—"And you, my sinews, grow not instant old,/ But bear me stiffly up" (1.5.94-95)—and clasps his hands to his heart— "Hold, hold, my heart" (93)—to keep it from cracking its "frail case" (*Antony and Cleopatra* 4.14.41). This is a conventional gesture for an overmastering passion, just as Gertrude's "wringing" of her "hands" (3.4.35)

---

[3] Arthur Colby Sprague, *Shakespeare and the Actors* (Cambridge, Mass.: Harvard University Press, 1945), p. 382, note 43.

after the death of Polonius is a conventional expression of grief.

Hand gestures are frequent in *Hamlet*, especially the swearing of an oath, which is probably the most repeated gesture in Shakespeare. Hamlet's most memorable oath is his satirical protestation of love to Rosencrantz, "by these pickers and stealers" (3.2.343). This parody of the Anglican catechism, "Keep my hands from picking and stealing,"[4] is probably emphasized by the contemptuous gesture of opening the hand and spreading the fingers.

The most extensive use of hand gestures belongs to the Ghost, who stands at one of the stage doors and "waves" (1.4.61) Hamlet to follow: *"Ghost beckons Hamlet"* (57 s.d., Folio). Like the crossing of Horatio (1.1.127 s.d.), the beckoning is a reply to a series of urgent questions put to the Ghost by Hamlet: "Say, why is this? Wherefore? What should we do?" (1.4.57). The comments of the other characters remind us that the Ghost continues to gesture until Hamlet finally exits with it. Horatio says:

> It beckons you to go away with it,
> As if it some impartment did desire
> To you alone.   (1.4.58-60)

Marcellus tells us that the Ghost "waves" Hamlet "to a more removèd ground" with "courteous action" (60-61), a helpful and unexpected detail for a Ghost that has been unflinchingly martial up to now. In Hamlet's speech, "It waves me forth again" (68) and "It waves

---

[4] See Kittredge, p. 231.

me still" (78) and "Still am I called" (84), in a manner
not to be denied. "My fate cries out" (81), says Hamlet,
and in his last line he must fight off Horatio and Marcellus—"I say, away!"—before he can promise the
Ghost: "Go on. I'll follow thee" (86).

The Ghost's ubiquity raises an interesting problem
about how to create the illusion of stage movement.[5]
The Ghost is about to speak when *"The cock crows"*
(1.1.138 s.d.), at which signal the upstage trap on which
it presumably has been standing begins to descend. We
learn later from Horatio how close the Ghost is to speaking at this point and how strangely it seems to disappear:

> It lifted up it head and did address
> Itself to motion like as it would speak:
> But even then the morning cock crew loud,
> And at the sound it shrunk in haste away
> And vanished from our sight.   (1.2.216-20)

Nothing in this speech is inconsistent with the Ghost's
exit by a trap. Horatio says immediately: "And then it
started, like a guilty thing/ Upon a fearful summons"
(1.1.148), and Marcellus adds: "It faded on the crowing
of the cock" (157). "Shrunk in haste away," "vanished,"
"started," "faded"—all those words suggest something
extraordinary about this exit, and "shrunk" and "faded"
have some literal application to a descent.

As the Ghost is disappearing, Horatio shifts to a new
set of imperatives: "Stay and speak. Stop it, Marcellus"

---

[5] See William J. Lawrence's ingenious, but very literal essay,
" 'Hamlet' as Shakespeare Staged It," *Pre-Restoration Stage Studies,* pp. 107-8.

(1.1.139). Marcellus, however, does not immediately pursue the Ghost, but asks Horatio a question: "Shall I strike at it with my partisan?" (140). We could consider this a covering line, since it allows the Ghost sufficient time to complete its exit. Horatio agrees on the use of weapons: "Do, if it will not stand" (141), but they can now no longer locate the Ghost:

> *Barnardo.*   'Tis here.
> *Horatio.*   'Tis here.
> *Marcellus.* 'Tis gone.   (1.1.141-42)

In a daylight performance the Ghost cannot lose itself in stage obscurity either natural or created by effects of lighting, nor even in the perfumed mists that were being produced at this time in masques. Everything must be plainly visible, which makes it clear that the Ghost has made its exit and that these "vain blows" are indeed "malicious mockery" (146). This passage is also a good one to illustrate the kinds of spatial effects possible on a broad, projecting stage, since Barnardo, Horatio, and Marcellus successfully give the illusion of actively—and "maliciously"—pursuing the Ghost over a wide area.

The second demonstration of the Ghost's ubiquity is much simpler to stage, since the spirit's sudden movements in the "cellarage" (1.5.151) are mostly a matter of sound effects. The *"Ghost cries under the stage"* (148 s.d.): "Swear" (149), and a few lines further on it cries again: "Swear" (155), this time from a different part of the cellarage. Hamlet and his friends attempt in vain to elude the sepulchral voice: *"Hic et ubique?* Then we'll shift our ground" (156). When they have moved,

however, the tricky, puckish Ghost, old "truepenny"
(150), is suddenly heard beneath them yet once more.
Hamlet's amusing lines record another excursion across
the stage: "Well said, old mole! Canst work i' th' earth
so fast?/ A worthy pioner! Once more remove, good
friends" (162-63). The compliment to the "old mole"
on its speed in tunneling suggests a comparable swiftness on the part of the three swearers. After all these
merry pranks, Hamlet's "Rest, rest, perturbèd spirit"
(182) implies that the Ghost needs rest after its frantic
activity under the stage.

The obvious way of staging this scene is probably the
correct one, with the Ghost taking up three different
stations in the cellarage for its first three cries (no special movement is indicated for the fourth). There are
at least five covering lines between each cry, so that no
unusual demands are made even on a supernatural
"pioner." On the modern stage the effect could be produced effortlessly by three separate loudspeakers. It
seems to be the accepted practice now to have ghosts
speak through microphones with exaggerated bass amplification, although everyone in the classical tradition
thought that shades "Did squeak and gibber" (1.1.116).

Elizabethan staging was not symbolic in our sense of
the term; in fact, in certain areas—such as the use of
costumes, the representation of trades, and the showing
of tortures and violence—it was extremely literal. The
complex staging of the fencing match in *Hamlet*, for
example, is accurate enough to satisfy even the "elder
masters of known honor" (5.2.249). John Dover Wilson
observes: "It was a fence fought by expert swordsmen

before an understanding audience, many of them expert swordsmen themselves and all of them trained from boyhood to use eye, hand, wrist and arm in self-defence. Thus, every motion of the combatants, every turn of the fight, was followed with concentrated attention and the keenest appreciation. To such watchers, the exchange of swords must have seemed the most thrilling moment of the play."[6] One detail, "They bleed on both sides" (5.2.305), could probably be verified by the spectators, as it seems to me all such details should be. Small concealed bladders filled with animal blood could easily be pricked to create a bloody stain, an effect that promotes the immediacy of the pity, terror, and wonder expected from the audience, and prevents any unnecessary fatigue to our credulity.

The large topic of social ceremony offers a way of extending the discussion of gesture and stage action. One difficulty here is that the ceremony is often of the trivial sort that Hamlet satirizes in Osric: " 'A did comply, sir, with his dug before 'a sucked it" (5.2.189-90). "Comply" is an amusing word for a courtier's compliments; Osric's uncovering to Hamlet with his plumed hat, for example, "complies" to a social superior. Occasionally, however, the use of social ceremony or the denial of it is an important expression of a character's status at a particular point in the dramatic action. The fall of Richard II, for example, is graphically represented by his failure to receive from Northumberland the homage due to a king:

[6] Wilson, *What Happens in Hamlet*, p. 287.

— *173* —

We are amaz'd; and thus long have we stood
To watch the fearful bending of thy knee,
Because we thought ourself thy lawful king;
And if we be, how dare thy joints forget
To pay their awful duty to our presence?
(*Richard II* 3.3.72-76)

The defeated Cleopatra says to Caesar's messenger:

What, no more ceremony? See, my women!
Against the blown rose may they stop their nose
That kneel'd unto the buds.
(*Antony and Cleopatra* 3.13.38-40)

This is the "idol Ceremony," "thrice gorgeous cere-mony" (*Henry V* 4.1.236, 262), whom Henry V so deferentially apostrophizes.

In *Hamlet* ceremony is used ironically, as a form of disguise. Beneath the absurdities of the Osric scene, for example, lurk the poisonous realities of the king's plot, and Claudius is never more studiously gracious to his nephew-son than when he is about to ship him to his doom in England (cf. 4.3.40-46). Rosencrantz and Guild-enstern approach Hamlet with all the effusiveness of practiced courtiers, but the prince soon has "an eye" (2.2.298) of them and their crude signaling to each other. Hamlet's first spontaneous greeting to them is very different from his later formal welcome, after he knows that they are not making a "free visitation" (281). We may set the two passages side by side to show the contrast in social ceremony and style:

My excellent good friends! How dost thou, Guildenstern? Ah, Rosencrantz! Good lads, how do you both?
(2.2.227-29)

Gentlemen, you are welcome to Elsinore. Your hands,
come then. Th' appurtenance of welcome is fashion
and ceremony. Let me comply with you in this garb,
lest my extent to the players (which I tell you must
show fairly outwards) should more appear like entertainment than yours. (2.2.378-83)

There is a formality unusual for Hamlet in the second
passage, and he even uses the affected word "comply,"
with which he will later scoff at Osric. "Your hands,
come then" suggests that Rosencrantz and Guildenstern
are holding back, perhaps out of shame at their discovery, and Hamlet needs to spur them on to shake
hands.

Ceremony is closely associated with the court and the
falsities of the court style, so that it is not through any
anachronistically democratic impulse that Hamlet for-
swears ceremony in the scene with Horatio and Marcellus. When they are about to exit, Hamlet says: "Let
us go in together" (1.5.186), meaning not according to
rank, but as equals. In the very last line of the scene his
companions are still hesitating, but Hamlet insists that
they should not be bound by decorum: "Nay, come,
let's go together" (190). This is like the ending of
The Comedy of Errors, where the Dromio twins solve
the question of precedence by abolishing it:

We came into the world like brother and brother,
And now let's go hand in hand, not one before
another.   (5.1.423-24)

Since there is so much false and treacherous ceremony
in *Hamlet*, we feel something salubrious in the prince's
colloquial denial of it: "Nay, come."

I have been trying to describe a *Hamlet* of pantomime
and gesture that works beneath the surface of the play to
shape its style. This is, of course, to interpret style in its
widest sense, but it seems to me that readers of Shakespeare should participate in the effects immediately
available to an audience. If the techniques of gesture
and stage action seem at times simple and self-evident,
it is also true that in the drama what is most obvious
is also most likely to be overlooked by readers.

7. Sound Effects and Music, Costumes, and Stage Properties

ANY performance of *Hamlet* must necessarily be different from the *Hamlet* one reads. The validity of the presented play, however, is not something independent of language, but rather a combination of verbal and nonverbal resources. Sound effects and music, costumes, and stage properties all function as directly as gesture and stage action to express the meanings of the play. Words are only one aspect of the style of *Hamlet,* and there is special need to call attention to a dimension of the play that may not be immediately apparent in the written text.

Sound effects are not properly part of the text at all, except those that we can surmise from stage directions and from verbal clues, but our surmises differ in kind from what we actually hear in the theater. I have already spoken about the way in which the military sounds of *Hamlet*, especially the firing of cannon, support the imagery of war, weapons, and explosives. In this context, it is worth noting the importance of sound effects in Laertes' uprising of Act IV, Scene v; its discordant noises clash with the martial music for Fortinbras and his army. The first sounds of Laertes' "giantlike" (121) rebellion are indicated as *"A noise within"* (96 s.d.), at which Gertrude exclaims in fear: "Alack, what noise is this?" (96). The unexpected disturbance completes Claudius' simile of the "murd'ring piece," which gives him "superfluous death" (95-96).

The menace of popular insurrection could be expressed by a confused din of shouting and clanging of weapons offstage. Some of these shouted phrases are reported by a messenger:

> They cry, "Choose we! Laertes shall be king!"
> Caps, hands, and tongues applaud it to the clouds,
> "Laertes shall be king! Laertes king!"   (4.5.106-8)

We have returned to the threatening exuberance of the mob in *Julius Caesar* just after the murder of Caesar. There is another direction for "*A noise within*" (108 s.d.)[1]—presumably a medley of cries like those reported by the messenger—and Gertrude answers this sound with queenly scorn: "How cheerfully on the false trail they cry!/ O, this is counter, you false Danish dogs!" (109-10). I imagine that Gertrude speaks this loudly enough so that it becomes a direct address to those offstage revolutionaries. Right afterward, there is a sudden crash as the massive doors are broken open and Laertes and his rabble come rushing onto the stage.

"*A noise within*" (4.5.152 s.d.) also precedes the second appearance of the mad Ophelia. Folio adds " '*Let her come in*' " as an additional stage direction,[2] probably

---

[1] This stage direction comes after line 109 in Quarto 2 and after line 110 in Folio. The queen's two lines (109-10) are clearly a response to the "*noise within*." The difficulty of placement probably arises from the fact that the noise overlaps with some or all of the queen's lines. I do not think that it is a single burst of sound, as one might surmise from the written stage direction.

[2] My interpretation of "Let her come in" differs from that of Harold Jenkins, who believes that it should be part of the king's speech ("Two Readings in 'Hamlet,'" *Modern Language Review*, LIV [1959], 391-95). Jenkins' argument depends upon the

shouted offstage by Laertes' men, who are restive at being excluded from the presence chamber and the promise of bloody action. It is an unusual stage direction, yet
not essentially different from the previous noises *"within"* (96, 108). From my own limited experience as a
supernumerary with the Metropolitan Opera Company,
I can attest that the chorus always interprets a "confused
murmur" as actual words spoken at random as the spirit
moves. Of course, the problem of how the audience is
to distinguish these shouted phrases still remains, but
with only one short command like "Let her come in"
there is no real difficulty.

The Folio text of *Hamlet* seems to show a penchant
for offstage shouting. Before Hamlet appears in the
closet scene, Folio adds his wild cry, "Mother, Mother,
Mother!" (3.4.6) to prepare us for his vehement eloquence, and in the search for Hamlet after the murder
of Polonius, we hear *"Gentlemen within"*—Rosencrantz
and Guildenstern are certainly among them—calling:
"Hamlet! Lord Hamlet!" (4.2.2). This is not what we
ordinarily think of as an indispensable line, but Hamlet's questions, "soft, what noise? Who calls on Hamlet?" (3), seem to make it necessary. In an earlier
pursuit of Hamlet, Folio also places *"within"* the exclamations of Horatio and Marcellus: "My lord, my lord!"
(1.5.113).

Hamlet begins, I believe, with the sound of the big

assumptions of his important essay, "Playhouse Interpolations in
the Folio Text of *Hamlet*," *Studies in Bibliography*, XIII (1960),
31-47.

bell in the theater tower:[3] " 'Tis now struck twelve," says Barnardo, "Get thee to bed, Francisco" (1.1.7). This is the bell on which military "alarums" were rung, and its solemn tolling here helps to mark the spiritual alarm of the soldiers. Some lines further on, the bell tolls the hour of one and the Ghost appears. Another possible occasion for use of the tower bell is the funeral of Ophelia. Her "maimèd rites" include "the bringing home/ Of bell and burial" (5.1.235-36), and the ringing of the death bell would provide a fitting accompaniment for the entrance of her funeral procession.[4]

There is another sound associated with Ophelia's death that has not often been noticed. While the king is setting forth his plot to Laertes, he is suddenly interrupted: "But stay, what noise?" (4.7.162). This line occurs only in Quarto 2; Folio has the colorless "How, sweet queen," which editors emend to "How now, sweet queen!" But I think that the sound the king hears is some sort of howl or shriek or loud wail, possibly made by Gertrude herself, to mark the death of Ophelia.[5] The staging in *Hamlet* anticipates that terrifying mo-

[3] See W. J. Lawrence, "Bells in the Elizabethan Drama," *Those Nut-Cracking Elizabethans* (London, 1935), pp. 84-96.

[4] See Shirley, *Shakespeare's Use of Off-Stage Sounds*, pp. 162-65.

[5] A few lines further on, of course, Gertrude will describe the death scene with all the lyrical detail of an eyewitness, but one is as little prompted to inquire why she made no efforts to save the drowning girl as one is to question the integrity of the chorus in Euripides' *Medea*, who listen to the murder of the children offstage with such tragic equanimity. There is a fault in logic here that the dramatist is skillful enough to gloss over.

ment in *Macbeth* when we hear "*A cry within of women*" (5.5.7 s.d.) , and we learn that Lady Macbeth is dead.

The second coming of the Ghost is framed by Horatio's insistent expletives: "But soft, behold, lo where it comes again!" (1.1.126) . This time, "It lifted up it head and did address/ Itself to motion like as it would speak" (1.2.216-17) ; but then, according to Quarto 2, "*The cock crows*" (1.1.138 s.d.) , and at the sound "it started, like a guilty thing/ Upon a fearful summons" (148-49) . The crowing of the cock was probably imitated offstage by an experienced mimic, and in the earliest extant promptbook for *Hamlet* (about 1740) , there is a direction at this point for "*One to Crow.*"[6] This is a tricky stage effect, which, if done badly, will certainly get a laugh, and that is perhaps why the direction is omitted in Folio. Horatio tells us that "the morning cock crew loud" (1.2.218) , which doesn't allow for any weakness in execution. It seems appropriate that in an open-air afternoon performance, the passage of time should be marked by sound effects; the progress from night to day in the first scene of *Hamlet* occurs swiftly, between the tolling of the midnight bell and the crowing of the cock. This representation of the passing of time by means of sound rather than light (as on our modern stage) was one of the received traditions of Elizabethan staging.

The music of *Hamlet* has been fully discussed by lit-

[6] James G. McManaway, "The Two Earliest Prompt Books of *Hamlet,*" *Papers of the Bibliographical Society of America*, XLIII (1949), 311. See also Lawrence, "Illusion of Sounds in the Elizabethan Theatre," *Pre-Restoration Stage Studies*, pp. 199-220.

erary musicologists,[7] so that we need only notice a few special examples. There is a good deal of conventional trumpet play for the flourishes or fanfares announcing royal entries, but there is also an unexpected *"Flourish for the Players"* (2.2.376 s.d., Folio[8]) . As Wilson informs us, "Trumpets were used as a means of advertisement by Elizabethan players both in the streets of London and when travelling in the country."[9] In the Induction of *The Taming of the Shrew*, the entrance of itinerant players is preceded by the direction: *"Sound trumpets"* (Scene i, line 71, Folio) .

Quarto 2 of *Hamlet* calls for trumpet play to announce the dumb show: *"The trumpets sounds. Dumb show follows"* (3.2.140 s.d.) . This is replaced in Folio by a more appropriately soft music that can both introduce and accompany the pantomime: *"Hoboyes play. The dumb show enters."* In *Gorboduc* (1562) , for example, which is the sort of old play that *The Murder of Gonzago* imitates, we have the following direction for the dumb show that precedes Act IV: "First the musick of howboies began to plaie, during which there came from vnder the stage, as though out of hell, three Furies. . . . After that the Furies and these had passed about the stage thrise, they departed; and than the musicke

---

[7] See F. W. Sternfeld, *Music in Shakespearean Tragedy* (London, 1963), esp. Chap. 10, which discusses the critical literature. See also Peter J. Seng, *The Vocal Songs in the Plays of Shakespeare* (Cambridge, Mass.: Harvard University Press, 1967), pp. 131-62 and Bibliography.

[8] Quarto 2 also has *"A Flourish"* at this point.

[9] Wilson, p. 179.

ceased."[10] There is a general Renaissance association of oboes with the supernatural and the portentous, as in *Antony and Cleopatra* (4.3) and *Macbeth* (4.1), while the trumpet is considered a piercing and startling instrument. In *Richard II* we hear of the "harsh-resounding trumpets' dreadful bray" (1.3.135), and in *King John* Blanch speaks of "braying trumpets" (3.1.303; cf. *Hamlet* 1.4.11).

Another unusual musical effect in *Hamlet* is the *"Danish March"* (3.2.91 s.d., Folio) by which the royal couple and their court enter for the play. This was possibly added after 1603 as a compliment to Queen Anne of Denmark, the wife of James I, although *Hamlet* has little enough in it that is flattering to the Danes. The kettledrums used for Claudius' rouse and for other impressive occasions were thought to be distinctively Danish instruments,[11] and the *"Danish March"* was probably played on the *"Trumpets and Kettledrums"* listed in Quarto 2 at this point.

The recorder enters importantly into the stage action in Act III, Scene ii, when Hamlet attempts to catch the consciences of Rosencrantz and Guildenstern with it.

[10] Quoted from Joseph Quincy Adams, ed., *Chief Pre-Shakespearean Dramas* (Boston, 1924), p. 521. The dumb show itself was at the height of its popularity at the time of *Hamlet*, but *The Murder of Gonzago* is intended to be in an old-fashioned, antiquated style, and its dumb show looks back to a more formal and symbolic manner. See B. R. Pearn, "Dumb-Show in Elizabethan Drama," *RES*, XI (1935), 385-405. See also Dieter Mehl, *The Elizabethan Dumb Show* (London, 1965), esp. pp. 110-20 on *Hamlet*; first published in German (Heidelberg, 1964).

[11] See *Variorum*, I, 79, and Travers, p. 42.

Hamlet had called for music soon after the play—
"Come, the recorders!" (297-98) —a consort of instruments of different range. When the players bring them
on (350 s.d., Quarto 2[12]), Hamlet takes one for his object lesson on the difference between men and things
and demonstrates how to play it: "Govern these ventages
with your fingers and thumb, give it breath with your
mouth, and it will discourse most eloquent music. Look
you, these are the stops" (365-68).

The most striking musical direction in *Hamlet* is
that for the Quarto 1 staging of Ophelia's mad scene:
*"Enter Ophelia, playing on a lute, and her hair down,
singing"* (at 4.5.20). If Quarto 1 is a reported text and
represents what was actually seen on stage, this direction
is very apt for a maiden overwhelmed by grief. I don't
think we need to insist on a reference to lute lessons for
Ophelia to believe that she could hold the instrument
properly and strum a few distracted chords, even though
"a lute could only be played clumsily, if at all, by a
standing player."[13] Her madness would excuse any de-
ficiencies in technique.

There are no formal songs in *Hamlet* that are called
for and sung as set pieces, so that, as much as we regret
it, Polonius has no aria to match the splendid performance of Pandarus in Act III, Scene i of *Troilus
and Cressida*. But there is a great deal of informal sing-

[12] Everything in the text of this scene indicates that we must
follow the Quarto 2 direction: *"Enter the Players with recorders,"*
rather than the economizing direction in Folio: *"Enter one with
a recorder."*

[13] Peter J. Seng, "Ophelia's Songs in *Hamlet*," *Durham University Journal*, XXV, N. S. (1964), 78, note 4.

ing in the play, especially of snatches from old ballads, not only by the mad Ophelia, but also by the Clown-gravedigger and by Hamlet himself. I think that all of Hamlet's little poems or fragments of poems are intended to be sung, which would add another dimension to his already wide gamut of possible styles. By Elizabethan standards, it would seem odd to hear him recite as poems what seem to be obvious ballad stanzas, while Ophelia and the Clown sing theirs. After intoning to Polonius a few scattered but pointed lines from the old Jeptha ballad, Hamlet breaks off at the arrival of the players: "The first row of the pious chanson will show you more, for look where my abridgment comes" (2.2. 428-29). Since "chanson" was a self-conscious French word not current in Elizabethan English, there is no reason for Hamlet to use it if he has just recited these lines. Quarto 1's "godly Ballet" (or ballad) confirms the musical interpretation of "pious chanson." From Laertes' warning to his sister about Hamlet, we learn of the dangers to her virginity "If with too credent ear you list his songs" (1.3.30). This implies that Hamlet's Donne-like poem, " 'Doubt thou the stars are fire. . .' " (2.2.116),[14] is one of these perilous serenades.

In Hamlet's exhilaration over the success of his *Mouse-trap*, he sings extempore the ballad, "Why, let the strucken deer go weep" (3.2.277), which presents an im-

[14] Is it possible that John Donne remembered Hamlet's little poem to Ophelia in "An Anatomy of the World," written in 1611? The best-known lines of Donne's poem read: "And new Philosophy cals all in doubt, / The Element of fire is quite put out . . ." (ll. 205-6, ed. Frank Manley [Baltimore: Johns Hopkins Press, 1963]). See Levin, *The Question of Hamlet*, p. 54.

age very like Jaques' grotesquely "sobbing deer" in *As You Like It* (2.1.66). Hamlet also presumably sings, "For thou dost know, O Damon dear" (3.2.287), and adds a couplet flourish that parodies *The Spanish Tragedy* (1587):

> For if the King like not the comedy,
> Why then, belike he likes it not, perdy.
>
> (3.2.299-300)

There is no way to prove that all of these examples were sung, except to say that songs would contribute to the triumphant excitement of the context. The distinction between speech and song is an artificial one, and singing can be used quite naturally to extend the possibilities of expression for the human voice.

WE MAY also approach the *Hamlet* without words through a study of costumes, which offer another means of characterization. "The apparel oft proclaims the man" (1.3.72) in more ways than Polonius intends. Even modern-dress productions acknowledge the importance of costume by abandoning overworked conventions of historical period in favor of a direct and easily comprehended symbolism. Gertrude's mink coat in the rehearsal-dress *Hamlet* directed by Gielgud (1964) is an almost perfect expression of her complaisant vulgarity, although Claudius' blue blazer in the same production failed to convey any notion of a king. Costumes may reflect interpretations of the play that have long since been discredited, for example the late-nineteenth-century interest, both visual and antiquarian, in *Hamlet* as a Scandinavian saga. Thus the reader of a play has a much wider range of possibilities for interpreting character than the spectator, who sees the dramatis personae fully clothed and fully conceived.

Costume is used to mark significant changes in the role of Hamlet. He first appears in Act I, Scene ii in mourning for his father. His "nighted color" (68), "inky cloak" (77), and "customary suits of solemn black" (78) contrast strongly with the brilliant apparel of Claudius' court. The staging of the scene is designed to isolate this peevish malcontent. In Quarto 2 he enters after all the others, rather than according to social precedence (as in Folio), and he does not speak until the bitter aside of line 65: "A little more than kin, and less than kind!" His first substantial speech calls attention to his appearance as only an outward "show" (85) that cannot truly "denote" (83) his inner "woe" (86). The couplet endows his sentiments with a special emphasis and finality; we know that he cannot be reconciled to this shallow court.

Hamlet's next change of costume is for his "antic disposition" (1.5.172), but I think we should not take too literally the figure Ophelia describes:

> My lord, as I was sewing in my closet,
> Lord Hamlet, with his doublet all unbraced,
> No hat upon his head, his stockings fouled,
> Ungartered, and down-gyvèd to his ankle,
> Pale as his shirt, his knees knocking each other,
> And with a look so piteous in purport,
> As if he had been loosèd out of hell
> To speak of horrors—he comes before me.
>
> (2.1.77-84)

It is well to keep in mind that Ophelia is narrating a scene that takes place offstage. We never actually see Hamlet costumed in this way, and it would seem to me risky for a director to show such a slovenly figure to the audience, although there must obviously be some disorder in Hamlet's dress to correspond with his feigned madness. The king speaks of

> . . . Hamlet's transformation: so call it,
> Sith nor th' exterior nor the inward man
> Resembles that it was.   (2.2.5-7)

More important for our purposes, Anthony Scoloker, a minor poet who saw *Hamlet* and was influenced by it, tells us in his *Daiphantus, or The Passions of Love* (1604) that his mad hero "Puts off his cloathes; his shirt he onely weares,/ Much like mad-*Hamlet*; thus as Passion teares."[15]

To say, however, as J. Q. Adams does, that "Hamlet's 'madness,' as it impressed the audience of the Globe, was conspicuously a madness 'in clothes,' "[16] seems to me to exaggerate the dramatic point. Everyone in the play thinks of Hamlet's madness as chiefly a matter of words and wit. A little loosening and untrussing of his original costume or sagging of his stockings should serve well enough to represent his "antic disposition." Or we might choose to follow Scoloker and show Hamlet in his shirt,

[15] Anthony Scoloker, *Daiphantus, or The Passions of Love*, reprinted by the Roxburghe Club (London, 1818), E4^v.

[16] Joseph Quincy Adams, ed., *Hamlet* (Boston, 1929), p. 224; the whole argument is on pp. 221-24. See also Wilson, *What Happens in Hamlet*, pp. 96-98, and Francis Berry, *The Shakespeare Inset* (London, 1965), pp. 8-9.

which, while not quite the equivalent of our undershirt, was still a notable offense against decorum.

When Hamlet returns from his voyage to England, there is an important difference in his costume, which reflects a development or regeneration[17] in his character. I agree with William Poel and Granville-Barker that Hamlet should appear in the graveyard with his "sea gown scarfed about" him (5.2.13).[18] There is a new resoluteness and informality about this costume that makes a visual link with the dress of the pirate sailors in Act IV, Scene vi. Cotgrave defines a "sea gown" as "a course, high-collered, and short-sleeued gowne, reaching downe to the mid leg, and vsed most by sea-men, and Saylors."[19] It is a rough sort of cloak appropriate for the outdoor scene that begins Act V, but inappropriate for the interior scene that follows. Since there is no time for a change of costume between these two scenes, I assume that Hamlet is wearing the standard male attire of doublet and hose beneath his sea gown. He should have long since abandoned the black mourning suit of the earlier part of the play, since a considerable interval of time has elapsed.

[17] See S. F. Johnson, "The Regeneration of Hamlet," *SQ*, III (1952), 187-207; Peter G. Phialas, "Hamlet and the Grave-Maker," *Journal of English and Germanic Philology*, LXIII (1964), 226-34; Irving Ribner, *Patterns in Shakespearian Tragedy* (London, 1960), pp. 80-82; and Prosser, *Hamlet and Revenge*, Chap. 9.

[18] See Poel, *Shakespeare in the Theatre*, pp. 173-74, and Harley Granville-Barker, *Prefaces to Shakespeare* (Princeton: Princeton University Press, 1947), I, 233. *Hamlet* is in the third series of Prefaces (London, 1937).

[19] *Variorum*, I, 415. The French word in Cotgrave is *Esclavine*.

The costume of Osric is very different not only from Hamlet's, but also from that of Laertes, as this is set forth in Polonius' advice: "Costly thy habit as thy purse can buy,/ But not expressed in fancy; rich, not gaudy" (1.3.70-71). Osric's "habit" is costly and fanciful, rich and gaudy, and his apparel "oft proclaims the man" (72) with an exclusiveness appropriate to a minor fop. Hamlet calls him "this waterfly" (5.2.83), which may have some visual relation to the short, winglike cloak then in vogue[20] or to some other item of fantastic dress. We know from John Webster's Induction to Marston's *The Malcontent* (1604), where Will Sly burlesques some of Osric's lines, that Osric has a foolish hat with a long plume. When asked to be covered, he replies: "No, in good faith, for mine ease. Look you, my hat's the handle to this fan"[21]—a veritable "forest of feathers" (3.2.281), which he stuffs into his pocket right afterwards. It must be an absurd hat, a conversation piece, to draw so much attention to itself, and he exits with it once again triumphantly on his head.

THE MOST elementary question of all still remains to be answered: What stage properties are needed to produce *Hamlet*? Since most of these properties have already been considered in Part One, we may now turn to special aspects of the topic. The properties are part of the imagery of the play in a direct, presentational sense. Ad-

---

[20] See Travers, p. 234, and Percy Macquoid, "Costume," *Shakespeare's England*, II, 105.

[21] John Marston, *The Malcontent*, ed. M. L. Wine, Regents Renaissance Drama series (Lincoln: University of Nebraska Press, 1964), p. 9 (Induction).

mittedly, properties are more literal and less complex in their reference than language, but they still interact with language and give it important support. To understand the iconography of *Hamlet*, we must consider all the means, verbal and nonverbal, for expressing symbolic theme.

As we might expect, there are many writings or literary properties in the play, beginning with Hamlet's pocket notebook or "tables" (1.5.107) , in which he can record one fixed truth in a whirling world. We have a nice symmetry between Hamlet *"reading on a book"* (2.2.167 s.d., Folio) and Ophelia ordered by her father to "Read on this book" (3.1.44) . There are quite a few letters in the play: Claudius' letter to old Norway (1.2) and the reply (2.2) to it, Hamlet's love letter to Ophelia (2.2) , Hamlet's letter to Horatio, delivered by the pirate sailors (4.6) , his menacing letters to the king and queen (4.7) , and Polonius' notes for Laertes in Paris (2.1) . Voltemand and Cornelius give the king a written report of their mission to Norway (2.2) , and Claudius sends a "grand commission" to have Hamlet killed in England, which Hamlet steals and replaces with his own forged invention (5.2) . Interestingly enough, he gives the king's document to Horatio to read "at more leisure" (5.2.26) , which seems to prove that Hamlet has a scholar's concern for the preservation of holograph manuscripts.

The portraits on which Hamlet discourses in the closet scene are the most puzzling properties in the play. That there are two visible portraits on stage seems clear from Hamlet's demonstrative words: "Look here upon this picture, and on this" (3.4.54). The most practicable staging of this scene is that favored by theatrical tradition: the use of painted miniatures, the pictures "in little" of which Hamlet has already spoken (2.2.374). Miniature portraits were, after all, the most distinctive Elizabethan contribution to the fine arts, especially in the work of Nicholas Hilliard (ca. 1547-1619). According to this staging, Hamlet would most probably take from his pocket, or from a chain about his neck, a miniature of his father, properly set in a frame of gold and precious stones, but he would seize the miniature of the detested Claudius from the locket his mother is wearing, as Fechter, Rossi, and Edwin Booth did, with their own idiosyncratic variations.[22]

The most impressive properties in *Hamlet* are those

[22] See *Variorum*, I, 290. It would be temptingly simple to stage this scene according to the illustration in Rowe's edition (1709): two large, framed, half-length portraits hang on the wall at the back of the stage—with the added Elizabethan touch of dust curtains that Hamlet can thrust open (see W. J. Lawrence, " 'Hamlet' as Shakespeare Staged It," *Pre-Restoration Stage Studies*, pp. 111-16). There have been strong objections to this staging, especially on the questions of where the portraits would be placed in the Elizabethan public theater and when they would be brought on (see Hazelton Spencer, "How Shakespeare Staged his Plays . . . ," *The Johns Hopkins Alumni Magazine*, XX [1932], 205-21, and Fairchild, *Shakespeare and the Arts of Design*, pp. 122-24). One teasing but highly speculative way out of these difficulties is to follow Davies' conjecture of 1784 (*Variorum*, I, 290), recently supported by Martin Holmes (*The Guns of Elsinore*, pp. 46-47, 131): that the two full-length portraits were woven into (or perhaps painted on) the arras itself. There is good warrant for this conjecture in the series of tapestry kings in Kronborg castle, some of which may be seen in the National Museum at Copenhagen.

used for regal scenes, which allow a kind of staging that Shakespeare fully exploited in his English history plays. In *Henry V*, for example, the king catalogues for us, negatively, all the customary aspects of royal pomp:

> . . . I know
> 'Tis not the balm, the sceptre, and the ball,
> The sword, the mace, the crown imperial,
> The intertissued robe of gold and pearl,
> The farced title running fore the king,
> The throne he sits on, nor the tide of pomp
> That beats upon the high shore of this world—
> No, not all these, thrice gorgeous ceremony,
> Not all these, laid in bed majestical,
> Can sleep so soundly as the wretched slave. . . .
>
> (4.1.255-64)

By combining so many possible elements, this passage evokes an image of kingship that satisfies Henry V's romantic imagination. In *Hamlet*, however, we are made acutely conscious that the splendors of royalty are an empty show that conceals ugly realities.

In the large court scenes, placed so symmetrically at the beginning (1.2), middle (3.2), and end (5.2) of the play, the king and queen sit on the chair of state or throne, which was set on a dais with a few steps leading up to it. A double throne was probably used to accommodate them both, as in *Macbeth*. In these formal court scenes, we must imagine that Claudius and Gertrude invoke all the ritual and pageantry at their command to display their divine sanction: crown, royal robes, scepter and golden ball, and the ceremonious attendance of courtiers and servants, who rush to execute the most minor of royal velleities. If we may follow up a hint in Act IV, Scene v, it is likely that the king and queen are guarded by "Switzers" (97), those impressive mercenaries still active in the Vatican. All this regal show has a special ironic application to

> A cutpurse of the empire and the rule,
> That from a shelf the precious diadem stole
> And put it in his pocket. . . .   (3.4.100-2)

The royal accoutrements of *The Murder of Gonzago* and its dumb show are meant to parody those of the Danish court and also to suggest an exchange of identity between actors and spectators. Who is the Player King and who is the real king? We think of Ugo Betti's *The Queen and the Rebels* (1949) and Pirandello's *Henry IV* (1922). If Claudius' claim to the throne rests on murder and adulterous marriage, then he too only "plays the king" (2.2.328). It is noteworthy that the Ghost never appears in royal robes and crown; these properties have been tainted by Claudius and Gertrude. When the poisoner woos the Player Queen *"with gifts"* (3.2.140 s.d.), we are reminded of Claudius' winning of Gertrude,

> With witchcraft of his wits, with traitorous gifts—
> O wicked wit and gifts, that have the power
> So to seduce!   (1.5.43-45)

As Gascoigne tells us so pithily, "Lyberall gyfts are the glewe of everduring love" (Tilley, W704), and in *The Two Gentlemen of Verona*, Valentine counsels the duke how to succeed as a wooer: "Dumb jewels often in their silent kind/ More than quick words do move a woman's mind" (3.1.90-91) .

In this chapter and the previous one, I have been pursuing an elusive *Hamlet* without words, a fiction designed to startle those who can see the play only as words on a printed page. I do not wish, however, to go to the other extreme and defend the promptbook as the only authentic document, or champion the rights of the audience as sole arbiters of the play. I have tried, by deliberately narrowing the scope of inquiry to *Hamlet* "when new,"[23] to reconstruct a production of the play possible in the early seventeenth century. For this purpose, I have attempted to limit myself to the indications of staging in Quarto 2 and Folio, with occasional glances at the much maligned Quarto 1. I acknowledge that I have strayed beyond the strict bounds of the subject at almost every point, since the very act of criticism violates the "without words" stipulation. My aim has been to imagine an ideal *Hamlet* performed in the Globe theater of the mind before particularly alert and exigent spectators, who may indeed already know the play from their reading. To this end, I have freely invoked that power of "histrionic sensibility"[24] by which readers and spectators can meet on common ground.

[23] This is William Empson's title phrase for two articles in the *Sewanee Review*, LXI (1953), 15-42, 185-205.

[24] See Fergusson, *The Idea of a Theater*, pp. 250-55.

8. "The Very Cunning of the Scene"

SCAENA is the Latin word for stage, but in Elizabethan usage "scene" could mean either the stage itself or the place where the dramatic action is imagined to occur. The latter is the most frequent Shakespearean sense, although there is a natural confusion between the physical stage and what is happening on it. "In Troy, there lies the scene," begins the Prologue to *Troilus and Cressida*, which I take to mean both that the stage is to be imagined as located in Troy, and that the dramatic representation one is about to see is set in Troy. These are not quite the same thing, although very close. There is a similar ambiguity in the prologues to *Henry V*: "Unto Southampton do we shift our scene" (Prol. II, l. 42), *Romeo and Juliet*: "In fair Verona, where we lay our scene" (Prol. I, l. 2), and *Pericles*:

> Now to Marina bend your mind,
> Whom our fast-growing scene must find
> At Tharsus. . . .   (Prol. IV, ll. 5-7)

In the staging of the Elizabethan public theater, Troy, Southampton, Verona, and Tharsus are the fictive places of their respective plays, rather than actual "scenes" painted on canvas. The introduction of changeable scenery after the Restoration altered radically the earlier definitions of "scene."

Since the Elizabethan public theater did not try to represent specific locality,[1] it is difficult to insist on

[1] On the representation of place in Elizabethan drama see Harley Granville-Barker, "A Note upon Chapters XX. and XXI.

a change in place for every change of scene. There are a great many unlocalized, placeless scenes in the plays of Shakespeare and the other dramatists, which editors usually tag as "another room in the castle" or "another part of the forest," as if there actually were a castle or a forest to begin with. The art of the movie has made it especially hard for us to conceive of scenes that are set nowhere more specific than on the stage itself. The dramatic sense of place is, of course, a matter of the degree of illusion the playwright wishes to create. There is always some sense of place implied in the words of the dialogue or even in the costumes. Where the sense of place is weak, however, we may need to define "scene" in terms of persons and the significant encounters of those persons rather than in terms of setting. New persons in different kinds of encounters would make a new scene without any change in locale.

The beginning of *Hamlet*, for example, is usually visualized on the battlements of the castle of Elsinore. This is a convenient and perhaps inescapable assumption about the scene's location for modern readers and spectators, but it is only a fiction. In Shakespeare's play, we begin with the changing of the guard at midnight; it is very cold and the soldiers are extremely anxious about the state of the nation. All this is performed on a

---

of *The Elizabethan Stage," RES,* I (1925), 60-71; Arthur Sewell, "Place and Time in Shakespeare's Plays," *Studies in Philology,* XLII (1945), 205-24; Richard Southern, *The Open Stage and the Modern Theatre in Research and Practice* (London, 1953), esp. pp. 94-121; and Bernard Beckerman, *Shakespeare at the Globe 1599-1609* (New York, 1962), pp. 64-69, 220.

bare stage in the afternoon, without even the remotest scenic illusion of Kronborg castle in Elsinore. Time, place, and mood must all be created by the words themselves and their expressive sounds and rhythms. We know that we are ending one scene and beginning another when Horatio, Barnardo, and Marcellus leave the stage at one door, and Claudius and his court appear, with Hamlet trailing behind, at the other. The royal *"Flourish"* to which this procession enters immediately blows away the anxieties of the previous scene. The costumes are entirely different from the military dress of the first scene, and there is a throne (probably thrust out from backstage) as well as other appurtenances of royalty. We feel that we are in a different place because of the change in persons, costumes, and style rather than because of any change in setting. On the modern realistic stage the order is reversed, and the visual picture, emphatically lighted, takes precedence.

As a test case for understanding the relation of setting to scene, let us look at the theatrical distinction between interior and exterior scenes. In a theater of scenic illusion and in the movies (which are derived from it), indoors and outdoors are polar terms, and completely different staging, lighting, and visual representation are appropriate to each. But in *Hamlet* the separation is blurred, and we can recognize exterior scenes only from the subject matter. Assuming, as is customary, that *Hamlet* contains twenty scenes, we have five that do not take place within the castle: the scenes with the Ghost (1.1, 1.4, 1.5), Hamlet's departure for England (4.4), and the graveyard scene (5.1). Aside from the knowledge that it is "bitter cold" (1.1.8) while the soldiers await the Ghost, nothing much is done to give a sense of the out-of-doors, and even in the scenes with the Ghost the atmospheric detail is meant to create a certain mood and set of expectations rather than any feeling of particular place.

Act IV, Scene iv is usually located on "*A plain in Denmark,*" following Capell, although Rowe puts it in "*A camp*" and Theobald in "*A camp, on the Frontiers of Denmark.*"[2] But there is nothing in this scene that has anything even remotely to do with either a plain or a camp or even an exterior place. The scene exists as a *raison d'être* for Hamlet's long soliloquy, "How all occasions do inform against me" (32ff.), which furnishes just about half the lines. For all practical purposes the scene is unlocated, even though we know that Hamlet is about to embark for England, and the distinction, therefore, between exterior and interior scenes breaks down.

If we agree to suspend our intrusive modern demand that a scene be a place that can be visualized, we may try out our definition of "scene" as a significant encounter (or series of related encounters). Act I, Scene iii takes place in the household of Polonius, and its domestic tone notably lowers the tension created by the first two scenes of the play. The portentous concerns of heaven and earth are scaled down here to the private matters of the Polonius family, especially Hamlet's wooing of Ophelia. She is at the center of this scene, even though she speaks so few lines, and her encounters with

2 *Variorum*, I, 322.

her brother and her father define her role. Polonius' advice to Laertes acts as a bridge between these analogous encounters; it allows us to grasp the Polonian morality in full detail.

The next scene (1.4) reinvokes the mood and even some of the language of the first scene of the play, as we once more prepare for the appearance of the Ghost. The fifth scene continues the fourth in what seems to be a single sequence, so that we do not return to the household of Polonius until Act II, Scene i, a scene from which Laertes is absent. The domestic setting, like that in Act I, Scene iii, also serves to distract our attention from more weighty and vehement concerns, but Polonius is an analogue for Claudius, and Reynaldo an anticipation of Rosencrantz and Guildenstern.

In ordinary terminology, a scene is a subdivision of an act, but in the Elizabethan public theater the acts are much less clearly defined than the scenes. Hamlet even seems to use the two words interchangeably in his plotting with Horatio:

> There is a play tonight before the King.
> One scene of it comes near the circumstance
> Which I have told thee, of my father's death.
> I prithee, when thou seest that act afoot,
> Even with the very comment of thy soul
> Observe my uncle.   (3.2.77-82)

Hamlet may, of course, be using "act" for "action," but the equation with "scene" seems to fit better with the logic of his speech. It is possible that Shakespeare's much-heralded five-act structure may be a piece of wishful thinking on the part of critics, who want to make Shakespeare a more "regular" dramatist and improve his literary standing by claiming for him the sanction of classical models. The five-act structure is a reality in the Italian court theater and in English plays such as *Gorboduc* (1562) that are influenced by classical precedent; the entr'actes in such plays are clearly marked either by dumb shows or by spectacular inter-mezzi. But in Shakespeare one must look hard for the act divisions, about which there is no general agreement. The dramatic action in his plays certainly has well-defined movements; I would only question whether these movements form pentagonal structures.

The act divisions of *Hamlet* are essentially the product of the "Players' Quarto" of 1676, followed by Rowe in his influential edition of 1709 and perpetuated by all later editors. Thus, Shakespeare's five-act structure is the result of the adaptation of an Elizabethan dramatist to the stage practice of the Restoration, with its picture-frame theater and its exploitation of scenic illusion.[3] A few act and scene divisions in *Hamlet* are marked in the Folio text (1.1, 1.2, 1.3, 2.1, 2.2), but they are casual and incomplete and have no particular authority.

Of the act divisions followed by most modern editors, the worst is the one between Acts III and IV. As Samuel Johnson says in his note to Act IV, Scene i: "This play is printed in the old editions without any separation of the acts. The division is modern and arbitrary; and is here not very happy, for the pause is made at a time

[3] See Granville-Barker, *Prefaces*, I, 32-38: "The Five Acts of the Editors."

when there is more continuity of action than in almost any other of the scenes."[4] Hamlet has just concluded the closet scene, and he exits *"tugging in Polonius"* (3.4.218 s.d.). The Folio, which has no exit for Gertrude at this point, has the king enter immediately after Hamlet leaves, to comment on her "sighs" and "profound heaves" (4.1.1). In other words, not only is Act IV, Scene i not the beginning of a new act, but it is not even a separate scene. If we follow the Folio staging, Act IV, Scene i represents the logical conclusion of Act III, Scene iv and a necessary part of it. Quarto 2 has an *"Exit,"* presumably for Hamlet, at the end of Act III, Scene iv, but the next direction is: *"Enter King, and Queen, with Rosencrantz and Guildenstern."* Perhaps this is the sign of an intermission in the Quarto 2 text, since it is pointless to have Gertrude exit and reenter so quickly and not plausible that she is able, nevertheless, to produce enough "sighs" and "profound heaves" for Claudius to take notice of in his first line of Act IV.

Separate acts imply prominent pauses, and although no other act division in *Hamlet* is so flagrant as this one, they all seem to violate the swift and continuous movement that is a feature of Elizabethan staging. We may make an exception for the break between Act II and Act III, where Hamlet's exit couplet makes a strong cadence: "The play's the thing/ Wherein I'll catch the conscience of the King" (2.2.616-17). This may indicate an intermission, a use to which it has frequently been

[4] *Johnson's Notes to Shakespeare,* ed. Arthur Sherbo, p. 172.

put since Shakespeare's time. The next scene (3.1) begins in a low-keyed, businesslike way, with Rosencrantz and Guildenstern reporting back to Claudius.

Between Acts I and II and also between Acts IV and V there are logical links that obviate any feeling of act division. The Polonius-Reynaldo scene (2.1) is almost a parody of the scene with Hamlet and the Ghost that has just preceded it (1.5). In both, fathers have messages to impart to sons, about whose conduct they are doubtful. By the familiar device of undercutting and abrupt scenic contrast, the portentous concerns of Act I, Scene v—"O all you host of heaven! O earth! What else?/ And shall I couple hell?" (92-93) —are reduced in scale to the comfortable domestic atmosphere of Act II, Scene i, in which Polonius can lose his way in a manner unthinkable for the Ghost: "What was I about to say? By the mass, I was about to say something!" (50-51). There is an even bolder contrast between Scene vii of Act IV and the first scene of Act V, in the shift from the court to a graveyard, where two clowns we have never seen before and will not see again are engaged in witty logic-chopping in the style of Shakespeare's early comedies. But the scenes are closely related in subject matter; the report of Ophelia's death in Act IV, Scene vii leads naturally to the graveyard in which she will be buried.

Although the five acts of *Hamlet* are not strongly demarcated as units, the scenes generally are, especially through the use of scene-ending couplets. In blank verse, the shift into couplets creates a special emphasis. The couplet is usually exclamatory, epigrammatic, or sententious, and it conveys a sense of finality. *Hamlet* is customarily divided into twenty scenes, of which only six do not end with a couplet. We may rule out Scene iv of Act I, which is continuous with Scene v, and we may also consider as special cases the two shortest scenes in the play: Scene ii (31 lines) and Scene vi (34 lines) of the fourth act, where speed of movement to the next scene is important. The absence of a couplet in Act IV, Scene vii is difficult to explain, although Shakespeare may have wanted a quick transition to the clowns of Act V, Scene i. Scenes i and iii of Act I, the other units without cadence couplets, both end with a sense of suspended action that will need to be completed.

Significantly, the couplet is not usually the very last line of the scene. Shakespeare seems eager to avoid a too-formal close by adding a few extra-metrical words. Hamlet concludes Act I, Scene v, for example, with an energetic exclamation:

> The time is out of joint. O cursèd spite,
> That ever I was born to set it right!
>
> (1.5.188-89)

But he adds immediately his forswearing of precedence, in order to tone down the rhetorical quality of his couplet: "Nay, come, let's go together" (190). The last line is deliberately anticlimactic and antiheroic. Claudius uses an almost identical form at the end of Act IV, Scene v: "So you shall;/ And where th' offense is, let the great ax fall" (215-16). He then tells Laertes: "I pray you go with me" (217), which is commonplace enough to neutralize the effect of the "great ax." Polonius, too, has a couplet of this sort, the most complex in the play:

> This must be known, which, being kept close, might move
> More grief to hide than hate to utter love.
>
> (2.1.118-19)

The effect of the couplet is undercut by the addition of a colorless and unnecessary imperative, "Come" (120).

In the same way, Fortinbras also makes a dignified close with a couplet:

> Take up the bodies. Such a sight as this
> Becomes the field, but here shows much amiss.
>
> (5.2.402-3)

But the play actually ends with a prosaic military order: "Go, bid the soldiers shoot" (404). Shakespeare wants to frustrate our expectations of noble diction for the very last words. In the closet scene, Hamlet seems to be making a well-turned, epigrammatic close:

> Indeed, this counselor
> Is now most still, most secret, and most grave,
> Who was in life a foolish prating knave.
>
> (3.4.214-16)

To this, however, he appends a rhetorically excrescent line and a half: "Come, sir, to draw toward an end with you./ Good night, Mother" (217-18). All of this could have been placed before, but in its position after the couplet it has a deflating quality.

Another idiosyncratic aspect of the couplets in *Hamlet* is the strong caesura in the first line. Actually, the most frequent logical and syntactical form of the couplet is only one and a half lines long (seven or eight accented feet). I count eight and a half of these "broken couplets"[5] out of fourteen (the half based on the double couplet close of Act III, Scene iii). If we put some of Hamlet's line-and-a-half couplets together, we may note a remarkable similarity in rhythm among them:

Foul deeds will rise,
Though all the earth o'erwhelm them, to men's eyes.
(1.2.257-58)
O cursèd spite,
That ever I was born to set it right! (1.5.188-89)
The play's the thing
Wherein I'll catch the conscience of the King.
(2.2.616-17)
O, from this time forth,
My thoughts be bloody, or be nothing worth!
(4.4.65-66)

These are all exclamations in a rhetorical and hortatory style; the couplet form does not lend itself to colloquial informality.[6]

---

[5] Levin, *The Question of Hamlet*, p. 86.

[6] There are other couplets in the play, most notably in *The Murder of Gonzago*, which imitates the end-stopped, singsong style of an old-fashioned, moralistic tragedy. Gertrude's sententious couplets (1.2.72-73, 4.5.17-20) and Ophelia's (3.1.100-1) have some relation to this antiquated manner, even Ophelia's haunting couplet of lamentation for Hamlet's "ecstasy": "O, woe is me / T' have seen what I have seen, see what I see!" (3.1.163-64). There is an extraordinary felicity in the patterned sound and antithesis—Ophelia in her brief role is as artful a stylist as her father—although we would not be surprised to hear her couplet spoken by the Player Queen. We may also note in *Ham-*

A stage that does not use changeable scenery to create the illusion of setting can have one scene moving swiftly into another, so that whatever is lost in visual stimulus may be more than regained by the intensity and concentration with which the play seems to progress. There are no blackouts or curtain drops during which the clattering flats and cumbersome interior decorations are moved into position, while the audience is expected willingly and cheerfully to think only that "this play is playing" (3.2.90). The "two hours' traffic of our stage" that the Prologue to *Romeo and Juliet* speaks of is not so unbelievable when the staging is uninterrupted. It is not likely that the full text of *Hamlet* could have been presented in two hours, but modern directors would be well advised to follow the Elizabethan example and abbreviate the visual representation rather than the text.

Time is an illusion, but in plays time is a calculated illusion used to produce certain effects. Even writers following a strict unity of time, such as Jonson in *The Alchemist* (1610), need to practice some deception in order to be convincing. Shakespeare's *Hamlet*, however, is not bound by the unity of time; in all senses of Polonius' phrase, it is a "poem unlimited" (2.2.408-9). One temporal trick that Shakespeare uses is to divide what seems to be a single scene into two parts, separated by a short bridge. This breaking of the scene in two gives the impression of a much longer duration than would be possible if it were a single unit, and it allows for important economies in exposition.

---

let a good many speech-ending couplets, which are analogous in function to the scene-ending ones.

I am thinking of the sequence of scenes showing Laertes' rebellion and its consequences: Scenes v, vi, and vii of Act IV. Scenes v and vii are essentially the same scene, but if one looks at the end of Scene v and the beginning of Scene vii, one is struck by how much intervening material has been omitted. At the close of the earlier scene, Claudius promises that he will give Laertes a satisfying account of his father's death. By the time the later scene opens, this account has already been rendered, and Claudius is now ready to make Laertes a tool in his plot against the unexpectedly returned Hamlet. Time has been foreshortened here by the use of a brief intervening scene (4.6) setting forth Hamlet's escape from the fateful voyage arranged by the king.

We may also study the illusion of elapsed time in the Ghost scenes of Act I. The first appearance of the Ghost in the first scene is suspended (rather than broken, as in the sequence of Scenes v, vi, and vii in Act IV), while two extremely different kinds of scenes intervene (Act I, Scenes ii and iii). The Ghost then reappears in Scenes iv and v for an extended interval. The stylistic intention in Scene iv seems to be to recapitulate the mood of Scene i, as we may see by setting two passages side by side:

> *Barnardo.* 'Tis now struck twelve. Get thee to bed, Francisco.
> *Francisco.* For this relief much thanks. 'Tis bitter cold,
> And I am sick at heart.
> *Barnardo.* Have you had quiet guard?

Francisco.   Not a mouse stirring.
Barnardo. Well, good night.
              If you do meet Horatio and Marcellus,
              The rivals of my watch, bid them make
                   haste.   (1.1.7-13)

Hamlet. The air bites shrewdly; it is very cold.
Horatio. It is a nipping and an eager air.
Hamlet. What hour now?
Horatio.   I think it lacks of twelve.
Marcellus. No, it is struck.
Horatio. Indeed? I heard it not. It then draws
              near the season
              Wherein the spirit held his wont to walk.
                                             (1.4.1-6)

These passages are so similar because Shakespeare
wants to give the impression of beginning again, but
much has happened since those tentative part-lines of
the opening scene. Scene iv has the two previous scenes
as its context, while Scene i must create its own context
as it goes along. By separating the Ghost scenes, Shakespeare generates a momentum that reaches its climax
in the Ghost's narration of its murder (1.5) . The revelation of the hidden truth is certainly crucial in Act I,
but even more important is the idea of the Ghost as it
develops in Hamlet's consciousness. This idea is built
up slowly and discretely, and one has the feeling that a
substantial period of time has elapsed between Scene i
and Scene iv. The ambiguity of the Ghost, established
by the structure of these early scenes, persists even after

Hamlet confirms the truth of the Ghost's narration and is certain that it is not a devil.

One other deceptive illusion of time is created by Hamlet's absence during his English voyage. He is away for all of Scenes v, vi, and vii of Act IV, although Scene vi is devoted to Hamlet's letter to Horatio about his adventurous escape. There is nothing in these three scenes that would factually suggest a long interval, yet when Hamlet returns, Shakespeare takes pains to tell us that he is now thirty years old and no longer the young man of the earlier part of the play. I have already discussed the pseudo-rational question of Hamlet's age, but I should like to insist that the matter can only be resolved by the logic of scenes and not by the logic of overt and covert allusions to time in the text. From the spectator's point of view, Hamlet has so overwhelmingly dominated the action until his departure in Act IV, Scene iv that the duration of his absence from the stage tends to be exaggerated.

We could say that there is a Hamlet time and a non-Hamlet time in the play, as there would be a separate time sense for each character. This is not to argue that Hamlet was ten years at sea on his voyage to England or even five. Hamlet is obviously no Odysseus, but in both characters there is an equally strong notion that time is fictive and chronology is a matter of dramatic and rhetorical emphasis. Hamlet makes an unanticipated appearance in the graveyard, entering with Horatio from *"afar off"* (5.1.56 s.d.) —and the authorial direction of Folio makes an unexpected theatrical pun on *"afar"*: as a stage term (=from far upstage) and as an indication of distance (=from a faraway place). Hamlet's return via the graveyard suggests an orphic delivery from "The undiscovered country, from whose bourn/ No traveler returns" (3.1.79-80). He is the mythic adventurer, who, by triumphing over death, has also triumphed over time.[7]

[7] See J. Gold, "Hamlet's Sea-change," *English*, XV (1964), 53-55.

PART THREE
DRAMATIC
CHARACTER

CHARACTER analysis is in disfavor in Shakespearean criticism as well as in the criticism of the novel, where it would be more naturally at home. The excesses of this approach to Shakespeare were so grievous that, like those mathematical studies of collaboration, the method itself was discredited by its own practitioners. L. C. Knights's essay, "How Many Children Had Lady Macbeth?" (1933), dealt a death-blow to the kinds of concerns posed in the title. Knights is parodying the questions so earnestly debated in Note EE of A. C. Bradley's *Shakespearean Tragedy* (1904): "Duration of the Action in *Macbeth*. Macbeth's Age. 'He Has No Children.'" We may well add Bradley's Note B: "Where Was Hamlet at the Time of His Father's Death?" and Note DD: "Did Lady Macbeth Really Faint?"

Everyone who has read Bradley closely and profited from his resilient and logical mind knows that these are the quirks of his criticism rather than its substance. But even if they are quirks, they do reflect the kinds of interests that fill the pages of the New Shakespere Society Transactions, the Variorum editions of Horace Howard Furness and his son, and the nineteenth-century issues of *Notes and Queries*. The whole approach is brilliantly typified by Hartley Coleridge in his *Blackwood's Magazine* article of 1828: "Let us, for a moment, put Shakespeare out of the question, and consider Hamlet as a real person, a recently deceased acquaintance."[1]

[1] Quoted in L. C. Knights, *Explorations* (New York, 1947), p. 30.

To consider Hamlet as "a recently deceased acquaintance," we must indeed "put Shakespeare out of the question," and this is precisely where character analysis, with
its juicy human concerns, parts company with literature.
In his essay, Knights tries to reestablish Shakespeare's
status as a dramatic poet rather than a creator of unforgettable imaginative persons. But in his zeal to replace
character by poetry, Knights completely ignores the
nature of dramatic illusion. He speaks only of the play
as read and never as acted ("We start with so many
lines of verse on a printed page which we read as we
should read any other poem"), and he is constantly
using that limiting phrase, "the words on the page."[2]

If we think of the play as presented by actors in a
theater, then the notion of character does not seem so
farfetched as Knights would have us believe. There is
no essential conflict between the idea that "our actors"
"were all spirits, and/ Are melted into air, into thin
air" (*The Tempest* 4.1.149-50) and the fact that the
"poet's pen" turns "The forms of things unknown" into
"shapes, and gives to airy nothing/ A local habitation
and a name" (*A Midsummer Night's Dream* 5.1.15-17).
Duke Theseus presents a justification for dramatic character a few lines further on in this same speech:

> Such tricks hath strong imagination
> That, if it would but apprehend some joy,
> It comprehends some bringer of that joy. . . .
>
> (5.1.18-20)

---

[2] Knights, *Explorations*, pp. 31 and 20. Compare the more
eclectic approach in Knights's essay, "The Question of Character
in Shakespeare," *Further Explorations* (London, 1965), pp. 186-
204.

In other words, emotions are embodied in persons, and we can only "apprehend some joy" through the medium of "some bringer of that joy." Or in *Hamlet*, if the Player could "in a fiction, in a dream of passion" (2.2.562) produce such a powerful reaction in himself, what would he do if he had the "motive and the cue for passion" (571) that Hamlet has? There is a world of difference between the fictive Hecuba and the real Gertrude, or at least we are made to acknowledge a distinction between characters described in the poetry and those actually present on stage.

There is a brief but illuminating example of Shakespearean characterization in the pirate sailors of Act IV, Scene vi, who come to Horatio with a letter from Hamlet. These colorful figures have been equally neglected by poetic analysis and by stage production. According to Quarto 2: *"Enter Sailors"* (6 s.d.), but Folio, in its consistent search for economies, reduces this to *"Enter Sailor,"* since there is only one speaking part. The Sailor begins inoffensively enough, with a greeting to Horatio: "God bless you, sir" (7); but Horatio, who is always keen on incongruity, gives his salutation a personal turn: "Let Him bless thee too" (8), as if the pirate's formidable appearance marked him out for one in need of worldly and otherworldly aid. The pirate is, of course, a proscribed outlaw who could be seized and put to death at once by the authorities.

The Sailor is not very flattered by Horatio's concern for his salvation, and he answers with masterful aplomb: "'A shall, sir, an't please Him" (9), with stress on "Him" to separate God's will from Horatio's. He continues his message with calculated and amused impertinence: "There's a letter for you, sir—it came from th' ambassador that was bound for England—if your name be Horatio, as I am let to know it is" (9-12). How cool and unyielding is that "let to know!" The pirate's costume would, of course, give an additional emphasis to his words, and the presence of a second or third pirate— all "thieves of mercy" (21-22) —would strengthen the illusion of a distinctive role. In these five lines of the Sailor's part, we have a delightful characterization that has nothing to do with poetic imagery, but which nevertheless shows an important aspect of Shakespeare's art.

For all the complexity of *Hamlet*, the psychological processes in the play are deliberately simplified and stylized to suit the demands of the brief, swift, and unequivocal communication demanded in the theater. Claudius' brilliant device against Hamlet, for example, suggests itself to him with the sudden inspiration of comic strips:

> Soft, let me see.
> We'll make a solemn wager on your cunnings—
> I ha't! (4.7.154-56)

Hamlet hits on the idea of a play to "catch the conscience of the King" (2.2.617) with an equally unsubtle flash:

> About, my brains. Hum——[3] I have heard
> That guilty creatures sitting at a play. . . .
> (2.2.599-601)

[3] I follow the lineation of Quarto 2 rather than the adaptation of Folio that appears in Hubler. There is no warrant for the dra-

"I ha't!" and "Hum——" indicate certain limits in the psychological range of Shakespearean tragedy. They are not the sort of expressions that would give comfort to Bradley and his followers.

We may attempt to resuscitate character analysis by approaching it through style[4] rather than through physical and psychological attributes. We may ask some of the following questions: How is the character identified and individualized as a dramatic speaker? What are some of his special modes of expression? What is his own attitude to language, as this might be seen in relation to other attitudes? For example, is language for him a form of revelation or a means of deception, or some combination of these at different times? Does the character use a single dominant style, or a series of different and inconsistent styles, including parody? I shall try to apply some of these questions to Claudius, Polonius, and Hamlet.

By putting the emphasis on style, I hope to avoid the pitfalls of a psychological approach to dramatic character. Although the actors who play the parts are real people, the persons in a play are, after all, only impersonations. This creates a knotty paradox about the nature of drama as a literary form—a paradox that ceases to be so troubling in films, where we see the actors

---

matic flourish of giving "Hum——," a word that does not occur in Folio, a line to itself.

[4] See Mikhail M. Morozov, "The Individualization of Shakespeare's Characters Through Imagery," *SS*, II (1949), 83-106, esp. pp. 93-106 on *Hamlet*. Imagery, of course, provides only one means of stylistic characterization.

through the fixed medium of the photograph. Once we assume the presence of live actors, it is difficult not to believe in the active force of characterization: the actors will naturally endow the playwright's fictions with the illusion of human purpose and consistency. In this sense, the actors themselves are exercising the same willing (or professional) suspension of disbelief that is demanded from the spectators.

9. Claudius: "Break not your sleeps for that"

CLAUDIUS is not a self-conscious stylist like Hamlet and Polonius, who are acutely aware of words in their multiple significations and who at times even seem to be amusing themselves with verbal extravagance. Although he is subtle and calculating in his speech, Claudius' stylistic intentions are never difficult to discern. He uses little wordplay, his imagery inclines to illustrative similes, and both his language and his acts are the expression of a resolute sense of purpose.

Claudius alternates between two styles: an embellished, rhetorical style—his "most painted word" (3.1. 53)—for formal occasions, and a simple, direct, even colloquial style to express his determinations. I do not think that these are public and private styles, as Miss Ellis-Fermor claims,[1] because there is not very large scope in the play for revealing the private aspect of the king. In addition, Claudius shifts abruptly from one style to another, sometimes in the same speech, to show something strong and menacing behind the pleasant embellishments of his court manner. Whenever the king uses complex syntax and polysyllabic diction, there is an immediate suspicion of hypocrisy, which is dispelled when he speaks simply. If the king seems harsh and coercive in this simple style, it is at least free of verbal deception. Since the main lines of Claudius' style are so

[1] See Una Ellis-Fermor, *The Frontiers of Drama* (2 edn.; London, 1964), pp. 88-89. First published, 1945.

apparent, I shall discuss it in terms of three scenes: Act I, Scene ii, and Act IV, Scenes v and vii, with some attention to his soliloquies and his aside.

Claudius begins his part with a formal oration very much in the manner of Polonius. It has farfetched conceits, such as "an auspicious and a dropping eye" (1.2. 11) and "our whole kingdom/ To be contracted in one brow of woe" (3-4); strained paradoxes: "With mirth in funeral, and with dirge in marriage" (12); and a division of imagery and syntax into attractive antitheses: "In equal scale weighing delight and dole" (13). It is, presumably, the first public address of the new king to his court, so that its ceremoniousness is part of the state occasion. He moves from platitudes of mourning for the late king to business of state, especially young Fortinbras' presumption

> . . . to pester us with message,
> Importing the surrender of those lands
> Lost by his father, with all bands of law,
> To our most valiant brother.   (1.2.22-25)

There is already a hint of something disdainful in that less than formal word "pester."

Fortinbras is disposed of in four strong and unexpected monosyllables: "So much for him" (25). This phrase exactly matches the conclusion of Claudius' gratitude to the court: "For all, our thanks" (16), which may pass for bluff sincerity, but the dismissal of Fortinbras is curt and threatening. It seems to say: "Enough words about such a trivial matter; now that we are aware of what Fortinbras is up to, we will soon crush him." From the thirty-nine lines of Claudius' first speech, we learn that he can not only use the imperial style, but that he can also transact the business of state with energy, firmness, and unambiguous command. Despite his ornamental rhetoric dressed up for the occasion, we know that he bears no resemblance at all to Richard II.

After the formalities of Claudius' first speech, there is something offensively familiar in his tone with Laertes. He repeats the name unctuously, caressingly,[2] as if he could not offer too much flattery: "And now, Laertes, what's the news with you?/ You told us of some suit. What is't, Laertes?" (1.2.42-43), he asks, and "What wouldst thou beg, Laertes. . . ?" (45), and yet again, "What wouldst thou have, Laertes?" (50). As Hamlet says in a different context, "Something too much of this" (3.2.76). Claudius knows how to ingratiate himself with the son of his chief counselor; indeed, the king speaks to Laertes a period so characteristically Polonian that it sounds like parody:

> The head is not more native to the heart,
> The hand more instrumental to the mouth,
> Than is the throne of Denmark to thy father.
>
> (1.2.47-49)

The nine lines of Claudius' speech to Laertes (42-50) provide a very good example of how unpredictably the king can alternate between his simple and his embellished style. As we have seen, the first five lines are emphatically colloquial, if not studiedly so. The three

[2] See Granville-Barker, *Prefaces*, I, 50; 124; 125, note 8; 185, note 13; 186.

lines that follow are the elaborate triple figure quoted above, while the last line reverts to the colloquial: "What wouldst thou have, Laertes?"

The king puts off to the end his difficult interview with Hamlet, who is not only a grieving son, but also a dispossessed prince. Claudius' oration on comfort continues the formal high style of his first speech. Since it is a collection of pious (or perhaps impious) platitudes about mourning, it must be given gravity and magnitude by rhetorical means. In other words, the style is deliberately heightened, especially by Latinate polysyllables, as in the following:

> But to persever
> In obstinate condolement is a course
> Of impious stubbornness.   (1.2.92-94)

These words are almost purely oratorical, without much relation to ordinary speech. Another device of elevation is witty syntax, in which Claudius anticipates his lord chamberlain's "foolish figure" (2.2.98) : "But you must know your father lost a father,/ That father lost, lost his" (1.2.89-90).

Claudius also gains strong emphasis by repetition and by long speech periods that produce breathless climaxes:

> Fie, 'tis a fault to heaven,
> A fault against the dead, a fault to nature,
> To reason most absurd, whose common theme
> Is death of fathers, and who still hath cried,
> From the first corse till he that died today,
> "This must be so."   (1.2.101-6)

The king rises to the height of his exhortatory persuasion, and we can imagine the admiration of the whole court for his brilliant performance. All except Hamlet, of course, who persevers in stony silence as well as "obstinate condolement" (93). When he tells his mother, "I shall in all my best obey you, madam" (120), the king seizes on this grudging fragment and magnifies it into "a loving and a fair reply" (121). The resourceful Claudius wants to mitigate Hamlet's cruel anticlimax and to maintain his own image as a "smiling public man."

Claudius' great moment in the play is his triumph over Laertes in Act IV, Scene v, at a time when the headstrong youth has the king and queen completely in his power, so that Claudius can only defend himself with words. This scene is a remarkable example of the efficacy of his rhetoric. Most commentators exaggerate Claudius' physical courage here, as if Laertes were afraid that the king might at any moment pinion him in his bearlike grip. Claudius never once in the play even vaguely hints at anything so chivalric as single combat; although he is obviously no coward, his persuasion of Laertes is more a matter of cunning and bluff than of any heroic qualities. There is much more spontaneous courage in Gertrude, who tries to restrain Laertes by force, only to be rebuked by the husband she is attempting to protect: "Let him go, Gertrude. Do not fear our person" (4.5.122), and again four lines further on: "Let him go, Gertrude" (126). The queen's direct approach threatens to spoil Claudius' very different plan of attack. As Claudius tried to imprison Hamlet, so with

Laertes he exercises an even more powerful restraint by allowing him a useless and deceptive liberty. It is the masterstroke of an expert in fast and loose.

If interrogation is one of the ruling devices of the play, as Levin tells us,[3] then Claudius' questions in this scene match those of Hamlet in significance. Laertes is prepared to fight for what he imagines to be his right, but he is not ready to answer the king's paralyzing questions: "What is the cause, Laertes,/ That thy rebellion looks so giantlike?" (4.5.120-21). Laertes has no written manifesto that he can read from, and Claudius has deflated his pretensions by that diminutive "giant*like*." When Laertes asserts with characteristic bravado: "Let come what comes, only I'll be revenged/ Most throughly for my father" (135-36), Claudius disarms him by assent: "Who shall stay you?" (136). Obviously, Laertes cannot manage this kind of psychological warfare, which weakens the very foundations of his assault. How can you fight with an enemy who agrees with you? Claudius then proceeds with his pacifying interrogatives:

> Good Laertes,
> If you desire to know the certainty
> Of your dear father, is't writ in your revenge
> That swoopstake you will draw both friend and foe,
> Winner and loser? (4.5.139-43)

There is only one possible answer to this question, which Laertes makes: "None but his enemies" (144). The king then moves to the final stage of his diversionary

---

[3] Levin, *The Question of Hamlet*, Part I: "Interrogation."

tactics: "Will you know them then?" (144). Now that he is completely exonerated, he can prepare the onslaught against Hamlet.

Claudius not only asks a series of questions himself, but he also encourages Laertes to "demand his fill" (129), so that by the end of the scene one has the impression that all of Laertes' unthinking heroic energies have been drained by questions and answers. Laertes begins by asking: "Where is my father?" (128), to which the king replies at once with masterful simplicity: "Dead" (128). This is the mark of Claudius' rhetorical skill, to know when to be evasive and when to be brutally direct. His unexpected frankness here takes Laertes by surprise and encourages the illusion of bluff honesty. Gertrude's "But not by him" (128) is, of course, superfluous—"The lady doth protest too much, methinks" (3.2.236). "Let him demand his fill" (4.5.129), says Claudius, to emphasize that there is absolutely nothing to hide. Laertes' "How came he dead?" (130) is never answered, and his next questions relate to his sister's madness. To Laertes' "Do you see this, O God?" (199), the king says only: "Laertes, I must commune with your grief,/ Or you deny me right" (200-1). In a practical sense, Claudius has such an unswerving sense of purpose that he is able to exclude everything that does not further his own ends.

One ideological technique that Claudius uses to overawe Laertes is the assertion of divine sanction. Since he knows how useless it is to reason with an angry man, he appeals to Laertes' instinctive prejudices:

> Let him go, Gertrude. Do not fear our person.
> There's such divinity doth hedge a king
> That treason can but peep to what it would,
> Acts little of his will. (4.5.122-25)

Laertes is reduced to the ignominious status of a Peeping Tom before the divine hedge of royalty, and the word "treason" must give him pause. He is soon, however, speaking the direst sort of treason and blasphemy:

> To hell allegiance, vows to the blackest devil,
> Conscience and grace to the profoundest pit!
> I dare damnation. (4.5.131-33)

But the king makes no attempt to interrupt him and may, in fact, be secretly delighted that Laertes is letting off steam with this swaggering talk. Claudius will know how to divert this bravado onto Hamlet.

Not only does Claudius encourage Laertes to speak his mind, but he also pampers him, verbally, in the same shameless manner as in Act I, Scene ii. He offers an excessive, even puerile, approval of his devotion to his father's cause: "Why, now you speak/ Like a good child and a true gentleman" (4.5.147-48). The king is able to mollify Laertes' strong passions, and he makes his justification for Polonius' death in a simplified, illustrative simile:

> That I am guiltless of your father's death,
> And am most sensibly in grief for it,
> It shall as level to your judgment 'pear
> As day does to your eye. (4.5.149-52)

The image is vague enough not to arouse any possible

dissent. At the end of the scene, Claudius appeals to Laertes' legalistic and ceremonial sense of honor, offering to abide by the arbitration of whatever specialists Laertes may wish to consult:

> Make choice of whom your wisest friends you will,
> And they shall hear and judge 'twixt you and me.
>
> $(4.5.202\text{-}3)$

If the king is found to be "touched,"

> . . . we will our kingdom give,
> Our crown, our life, and all that we call ours,
> To you in satisfaction. . . . $(4.5.205\text{-}7)$

Laertes is meant to be dazzled by strong temptation. If he is indeed "A very noble youth" $(5.1.226)$, as Hamlet says, then he should not be corrupted without suitable provocation, which is provided by the king's irresistible flattery. By the time Act IV, Scene vii opens, in the midst of a conversation, Laertes is Claudius' ally, but the king never seems sure of him, even in the fencing match. Persuading him, therefore, becomes a continuous effort, with the king constantly adding new reasons and new safeguards. The change in Laertes is more remarkable than Hamlet's "transformation" $(2.2.5)$, because Laertes passes from heroics to villainy almost without conscious intention. In Act IV, Scene vii, we feel very strongly that he is being caught in a web of rhetorical tricks; Claudius is nowhere more artful, various, and elusive.

At the beginning of the scene, we see him taking Laertes into his confidence and patiently explaining to him the two reasons that he has not proceeded publicly against Hamlet. These reasons are supported by characteristic illustrative imagery. The first concerns the triangular love between himself and Gertrude, and Gertrude and Hamlet:

> She is so conjunctive to my life and soul,
> That, as the star moves not but in his sphere,
> I could not but by her.   (4.7.14-16)

This kind of simile is Claudius' favorite trope: commonplace, vague, unexceptionable, with the vehicle exactly applied to the tenor.

In explaining his next reason, however, he seems to get lost in the turgid proliferation of his figures:[4]

>   The other motive
> Why to a public count I might not go
> Is the great love the general gender bear him,
> Who, dipping all his faults in their affection,
> Would, like the spring that turneth wood to stone,
> Convert his gyves to graces; so that my arrows,
> Too slightly timbered for so loud a wind,
> Would have reverted to my bow again,
> And not where I had aimed them.   (4.7.16-24)

We know immediately that tropes are a sign of duplicity in Claudius, an attempt to disguise the literal truth. The first simile is intended to illustrate the power of "affection" to transform "faults," to "Convert . . . gyves to graces," as various petrifying springs in England are

---

[4] See *Johnson's Notes to Shakespeare*, ed. Arthur Sherbo, p. 175, and Ellis-Fermor, *The Frontiers of Drama*, note 3 on pp. 88-89.

able to turn "wood to stone." Claudius wants to restrict the image to the powers of metamorphosis alone, but other qualities intrude, as they also do in the metaphor that follows. In Claudius' representation, the loud "wind" is the public clamor in favor of Hamlet, which would blow the lightly shafted arrows that the king aims at Hamlet back to the bow from which they were shot. The intent of the figure to depict useless effort is clear, but the visual action it suggests is inept and grotesque. In Claudius' desire to be weighty, his imagery is escaping his control; it seems only strained, factitious, and therefore dishonest. The whole speech provides a good example of how figures of speech may be used negatively as a device of characterization.

Claudius' shifts from embellished rhetoric to stark simplicity are one of the most notable features of his style. After the figures we have just considered, his next speech is the simplest in the play. Laertes has just said: "But my revenge will come" (29), which Claudius confirms with an understated, colloquial menace:

> Break not your sleeps for that. You must not think
> That we are made of stuff so flat and dull
> That we can let our beard be shook with danger,
> And think it pastime. You shortly shall hear more.
> I loved your father, and we love ourself,
> And that, I hope, will teach you to imagine—
>
> (4.7.30-35)

Claudius shows a remarkable control over those twenty-nine monosyllables leading up to "danger," and his overpowering egotism is displayed frankly and without self-indulgence: "I loved your father, and we love ourself." This is an antagonist whose stature makes him worthy to be pitted against Hamlet, and who, in fact, makes us fear for Hamlet with an intensity proper to tragedy. There is a trace of sarcasm in the king's tone, as if he needed to correct the false image Laertes might have of him as a magnanimous Christian prince. He is, of course, getting Laertes ready for the imminent news of Hamlet's execution, but then, in the midst of Claudius' dark hints, comes the *coup de théâtre* of Hamlet's letter.

With a wonderful resourcefulness, the king proceeds to a new stage of persuasion in which Laertes will become the instrument of Hamlet's death. It is notable in Shakespearean tragedy how much the villain works by fortuitous circumstances on which he must improvise, rather than by a premeditated rational plan. Claudius shares this creative quality most obviously with Iago, and there is much in the corruption of Laertes that resembles the more protracted fall of Othello. All of Shakespeare's villains are masters of rhetoric, especially the simple, insinuating style whose efficacy can be immediately measured. On a moment's notice, Claudius has a fully formed plan to trap Laertes by praising his skill with the rapier and, intertwined with this, a double plot against Hamlet that will seem to be an "accident," "Under the which he shall not choose but fall" (4.7. 68, 65). Claudius seems to be making everything up as he goes along, and this improvisational feeling endows the dialogue with a good deal of dramatic excitement.

The king now moves into a deliberately broken discourse, full of insinuating hints. After Lamord's fulsome report of Laertes' fencing—and Claudius expatiates here with a leisure found nowhere else in the play—there is a sudden break that is all the more emphatic in its chatty and smoothly articulated context:

> Sir, this report of his
> Did Hamlet so envenom with his envy
> That he could nothing do but wish and beg
> Your sudden coming o'er to play with you.
> Now, out of this—   (4.7.102-6)

The unexpected pause in the king's speech rouses Laertes to ask the appropriate question: "What out of this, my lord?" (106). As in Act IV, Scene v, the king refuses to answer, but shifts instead into teasing interrogation:

> Laertes, was your father dear to you?
> Or are you like the painting of a sorrow,
> A face without a heart?   (4.7.107-9)

The king's suspended sentence, "Now, out of this—" (106), remains suspended in an atmosphere of doubts and perturbations never to be satisfied. Instead, Claudius delivers his most contemplative speech in the play, on the theme of love, time, and purpose, whose upshot is: "That we would do/ We should do when we would" (118-19). It is an eloquent persuasion to action.

That Claudius should speak two soliloquies (3.3.36-72, 97-98, and 4.3.58-68)[5] and an aside (3.1.49-54)[6] might

---

[5] It seems unlikely that Claudius' eleven lines at the beginning of Act IV, Scene iii are a soliloquy. Quarto 2 has: *"Enter King, and two or three,"* whereas in Folio the king enters alone. This may be another of Folio's economies in the number of super-

seem out of character to us, but Shakespeare wants to enlarge the scope of his role by making him conscious of his own "shuffling" (3.3.61). The forms of soliloquy and aside allow Claudius to examine passionately his spiritual state. There have been strong objections to the king's aside, because it is too brief and too unprepared to be convincing. Granville-Barker says that it "has all the look of a subsequently applied patch,"[7] since it comes out of nowhere and leads nowhere. It is triggered by Polonius' observation that "we do sugar o'er/ The devil himself" (3.1.48-49). We suddenly discover that the king is a villain with moral sensitivity:

> O, 'tis too true.
> How smart a lash that speech doth give my conscience!
> The harlot's cheek, beautied with plast'ring art,
> Is not more ugly to the thing that helps it
> Than is my deed to my most painted word.
> O heavy burden! (3.1.49-54)

In a few moments we will hear Hamlet speaking his "To be, or not to be" soliloquy (3.1.56ff.), in which he will examine "conscience" in its multiple meanings.

---

numeraries, since it is more reasonable for the king to discuss affairs of state with a few of his trusted advisers than with himself.

  [6] I omit the king's speech to Laertes at the end of Act V, Scene i, which is technically a "conversational" rather than a "solo" aside (see Beckerman, *Shakespeare at the Globe*, p. 186). Since this kind of aside is spoken apart to another character, it is really dialogue, whereas the solo aside is close to the soliloquy in form —in both the character speaks to himself and is overheard by the audience.

  [7] Granville-Barker, *Prefaces*, I, 218.

Against this speech, Claudius' aside seems pat and moralistic. By the machinations of dramatic irony, we now know that Hamlet can "take the ghost's word for a thousand pound" (3.2.292-93) and that there is no need to use *The Mousetrap* as a test. But this information is primarily for the audience's benefit, so that we may still complain that Claudius' aside has not been properly integrated into its context. We may make the same complaint about the asides of Gertrude and Laertes, which are also revelations of conscience. The idea of repentance or contrition was so firmly established as a moral convention in Elizabethan drama that no full explanation was required for it, but the penitent asides of Claudius, Gertrude, and Laertes seem abrupt even by Elizabethan standards. Since all of these asides are so closely related functionally, it may be useful to look at them as a group.

Gertrude's remorseful aside occurs in Act IV, Scene v, in the context of her refusal to speak with the "importunate, indeed distract" (2) Ophelia. She is persuaded, perhaps by the political argument of Horatio, to "Let her come in" (16). Gertrude's didactic and epigrammatic aside, delivered in two couplets, may well be a soliloquy, although the distinction is a technical one. She has a sudden access of conscience[8] that carries over from the closet scene:

[8] Ophelia's first line in this scene seems to confirm Gertrude's fears: "Where is the beauteous majesty of Denmark?" (4.5.21). This is a splendid example not only of the dark discourse of mad folk, but also of the ambiguity of the English language. As "prologue to some great amiss" (18), Ophelia is unable to recognize the once "beauteous majesty of Denmark" because of the changes

To my sick soul (as sin's true nature is)
Each toy seems prologue to some great amiss;
So full of artless jealousy is guilt
It spills itself in fearing to be spilt.

(4.5.17-20)

The moral terms—"sick soul," "sin's true nature," "guilt"—are similar to those in Claudius' aside, although the artful patterning of sound and polished antitheses also remind us of the Player Queen.

Laertes' aside comes unexpectedly, during the fencing match. He has lost the first two bouts, and when he tells the king, "My lord, I'll hit him now" (5.2.296), Claudius discourages him: "I do not think't" (296). There is nothing unusual here. Although the king is plotting with Laertes, he has placed a heavy wager on Hamlet, and we might expect him to be publicly cheering on his favorite and disconcerting his opponent. Laertes has private misgivings about his resolve to "hit him now": "And yet it is almost against my conscience" (297). This is spoken aside and has no relation to what precedes or follows, since Laertes is shortly to prick Hamlet by what seems to be foul play. But the smart "lash" that Laertes gives his "conscience" (3.1.50) is important structurally, to prepare us for his reconciliation with Hamlet. He must once more, just before he

---

Gertrude's "sick soul" has wrought. "Where, indeed, in this haggard, fearful woman, is the 'beauteous majesty' that has been the cause of all this ill?" (Granville-Barker, *Prefaces*, I, 120). Ophelia may also be speaking distractedly of herself; under different circumstances, she might have become "the beauteous majesty of Denmark."

dies, become "A very noble youth" (5.1.226), and we must be willing to accept the simplified morality of "The King, the King's to blame" (5.2.321).

In all three asides, Shakespeare wants us to feel that Claudius, Gertrude, and Laertes are troubled by guilt and conscience, "the agenbite of inwit," but he doesn't wish to carry this point too far. The form of the aside as a private declaration offers a convenient one-line or half-dozen-line statement, although all of the examples suffer from their brevity and their strong dependence on moral conventions. Since they have no vital relation to their contexts, these three asides seem sententious and mechanical.

Claudius' aside does, however, help to prepare us for his long soliloquy in Act III, Scene iii, which develops the earlier sense of guilt and gives us, as it were, his private response to *The Murder of Gonzago*. Here, too, Claudius moves into his soliloquy abruptly, without even a perfunctory "Now I am alone" (2.2.559). There is no transition at all from "Thanks, dear my lord" (3.3.35) to "O, my offense is rank" (36). The style of the soliloquy is simple and passionate, very like the expression of pent-up emotion that we find in Hamlet's soliloquies. There is a whole series of monosyllabic declarations: "Pray can I not" (38), "Then I'll look up./ My fault is past" (50-51), "All may be well" (72), "My words fly up" (97). If there is no "shuffling" "above" (61, 60), then even "In the corrupted currents of this world" (57) a man must occasionally forswear his "most painted word" (3.1.53).

Claudius raises again the moral question of style already present in his first aside. He is searching for the proper form of prayer that "Can serve" his "turn" (3. 3.52). " 'Forgive me my foul murder' " (52) is his first tentative formulation, but he discovers that the words do not correspond to any reality, "since I am still possessed/ Of those effects for which I did the murder" (53-54). He is forced to the bitter conclusion that prayer, or any form of words, is useless when it does not represent any spiritual truth: "My words fly up, my thoughts remain below./ Words without thoughts never to heaven go" (97-98). "Words without thoughts" are the equivalent of "my most painted word," and both phrases help to define Claudius' embellished style. These are the "colors" of what Berowne disdainfully calls "painted rhetoric" (*Love's Labour's Lost* 4.3.235).

The king's soliloquy is presented in the form of a debate, in which man's "offense" is set against God's "mercy," as in Claudius' question: "Whereto serves mercy/ But to confront the visage of offense?" (3.3.46-47). Everything in the soliloquy has its corresponding opposite, so that although Claudius has forsworn the arts of rhetoric, antithesis still dominates his thinking. In his only simile here, he says that he is "like a man to double business bound" (41), and one feels the effect of this doubleness throughout the speech. "O limèd soul, that struggling to be free/ Art more engaged!" (68-69) is a paradox that illustrates how trapped Claudius is by his own dualistic logic. The soul, caught in the birdlime of its own black deeds, is trying to set itself at liberty, but it also wants to be "free" in the sense of guiltless, innocent, and blameless. "My stronger guilt defeats my strong intent" (40) , says Claudius, trying to balance one force against another. "This cursèd hand/ . . . thicker than itself with brother's blood" (43-44) cannot be made "white as snow" (46) , nor "heart with strings of steel,/ Be soft as sinews of the newborn babe" (70-71) . There is an admirable toughness in Claudius that refuses to indulge itself in pipe dreams of an impossible salvation. He knows "how his audit stands" (82) , so that he need never again trouble himself with spiritual questionings, not even just before his ignominious death in the fencing scene.

One of the most memorable gestures in *Hamlet* is Claudius' holding up the hand that "hath the primal eldest curse upon't" (37) :

> What if this cursèd hand
> Were thicker than itself with brother's blood,
> Is there not rain enough in the sweet heavens
> To wash it white as snow?   (3.3.43-46)

These lines are echoed in Macbeth's more lyric soliloquy:

> Will all great Neptune's ocean wash this blood
> Clean from my hand? No; this my hand will rather
> The multitudinous seas incarnadine,
> Making the green one red.   (*Macbeth* 2.2.60-63)

It is worth noting how close Claudius and Macbeth are in spirit as well as in words. Both are redeemed by their own unmitigated self-awareness, although Macbeth shows Shakespeare's better understanding of how to make a villain sympathetic, mysterious, and tragic by making him so eloquent.

Claudius' soliloquy is intertwined with Hamlet's, which is actually a soliloquy within a soliloquy. Although Hamlet may be standing close enough to stab Claudius in the back, the king is not able to overhear Hamlet's homicidal hesitations nor feel "the whiff and wind of his fell sword" (2.2.484). It is a mistake to deny dramatic convention and to put Claudius so far upstage as to be, for all practical purposes, out of earshot of Hamlet's speech. Elizabethan staging would probably do just the opposite, and place Claudius far downstage and a little to one side, but within easy reach of Hamlet's words and sword.

Having two such different soliloquies set back to back is a bold stylistic experiment, especially because Claudius seems to be speaking in the passionate, reflective style of Hamlet's other soliloquies, and Hamlet in the brusque and menacing style of his antagonist. We are also expected to be sympathetic with the villain and deeply disturbed by the protagonist's sentiments. Claudius' couplet conclusion after Hamlet's exit seems to comment on both soliloquies at once; Hamlet's words also "fly up" and "never to heaven go" (3.3.97-98).

The king's second soliloquy at the end of Act IV, Scene iii is a brief but characteristic expression both in subject matter and style. Claudius follows the Elizabethan convention of soliloquy as the villain's direct self-explanation to the audience, a means of providing a swift and effective exposition. The speech begins with an earnest appeal to the king of England:

And, England, if my love thou hold'st at aught—
As my great power thereof may give thee sense,
Since yet thy cicatrice looks raw and red
After the Danish sword, and thy free awe
Pays homage to us—thou mayst not coldly set
Our sovereign process, which imports at full
By letters congruing to that effect
The present death of Hamlet.   (4.3.58-65)

There is a calculated paradox on "free awe" paying "homage," and the "love" in this passage, with its "cicatrice . . . raw and red," is more of the Marquis de Sade than the Sermon on the Mount.

The weighty redundancy of the legal "process, which imports at full/ By letters congruing to that effect" disappears with the mention of "The present death of Hamlet." At this point, Claudius shifts to the intense simplicities of a man of action:

Do it, England,
For like the hectic in my blood he rages,
And thou must cure me. Till I know 'tis done,
Howe'er my haps, my joys were ne'er begun.
                              (4.3.65-68)

These emphatic monosyllables and aggressive verbs are radically different from the earlier part of the soliloquy, and they allow Claudius to express the sort of controlled frenzy, like that of Macbeth, that would be inappropriate in ordinary discourse. In its forceful, passionate, percussive, and even musical assertion, this passage represents Claudius' style at its best.

10. Polonius: " 'Beautified' is a vile phrase"— " 'Mobled queen' is good"

POLONIUS' part ends abruptly behind an arras in Act III, Scene iv, according to his own prediction: "I'll silence me even here" (4). But up until this point, he has been, stylistically, second in interest only to Hamlet. They are both self-conscious rhetoricians, who engage in wordplay, conceit, and other witty turns with skill and pleasure. The comparison does not extend to the subject matter of their discourse, since Polonius represents everything that Hamlet is most inclined to satirize and parody, yet both think of style as an art.

As a literary critic, Polonius' taste is radically different from Hamlet's. In the letter to Ophelia that he reads aloud with so much demonstrative satisfaction, he objects to Hamlet's affected diction: "That's an ill phrase, a vile phrase; 'beautified' is a vile phrase" (2.2. 111-12). Polonius is thinking of the word in its modern connotation of beauty created by the cosmetic art, but in Elizabethan usage this pejorative meaning is not very strong. All the other Shakespearean examples are laudatory. Valentine is "beautified/ With goodly shape" (*The Two Gentlemen of Verona* 4.1.55-56), and Juliet's mother represents Paris as a "fair volume": "This precious book of love, this unbound lover,/ To beautify him, only lacks a cover" (*Romeo and Juliet* 1.3.88-89). We should understand that Polonius is twisting "beautified" to a special punning sense in order to prove his

own refined sensibility in words, a quality he shares
with Osric.

We can also imagine Osric's pleasure at that odd word
"mobled," meaning muffled, in the First Player's speech:
" 'But who (ah woe!) had seen the mobled queen—' "
(2.2.513) . Hamlet is puzzled: " 'The mobled queen'?"
(514) . Either he doesn't understand it, or he thinks it
strange, but Polonius asserts his unhesitating approval:
"That's good. 'Mobled queen' is good" (515) . There is
not much else in this play that he likes, but " 'Mobled
queen' is good," presumably because it is one of Holofernes' "odoriferous flowers of fancy, the jerks of invention" (*Love's Labour's Lost* 4.2.118-19) . "Beautified"
and "mobled" make an apt pair of examples in which
Polonius and Hamlet come to opposite conclusions on
specific points of style.

So far as we can tell, Polonius inclines to neoclassical
criteria, as in his notable catalogue of genres: "The best
actors in the world, either for tragedy, comedy, history,
pastoral, pastoral-comical, historical-pastoral, tragical-
historical, tragical-comical-historical-pastoral" (2.2.405-
8) . The Folio addition of "tragical-historical, tragical-
comical-historical-pastoral" continues the fun, since the
whole speech is a parody of Renaissance rhetoric, with
every subdivision mercilessly subdivided.

Polonius' announcement of the players is a compendium of post-Aristotelian dramatic criticism, as it might
have come to Shakespeare through English adaptations
of Italian Renaissance commentators. Besides every con-
ceivable genre, the "best actors in the world" can also
play "scene individable, or poem unlimited. Seneca can-

not be too heavy, nor Plautus too light. For the law of writ and the liberty, these are the only men" (2.2.408-11) . The punctuation of the last two lines depends on a suggestion of Theobald that has been challenged,[1] but the unity of place implied in "scene individable" seems to be part of the "law of writ," whose strict rules were meant to accommodate plays to the single-perspective setting of comedy, tragedy, or pastoral. "Poem unlimited" is an example of "liberty," or freedom from the unities of place, time, and action derived from Aristotle. "Liberty" would apply to the English popular theater, whereas the English academic and court theaters would, like the Italian theaters, be closer to the "law of writ." Seneca and Plautus are, of course, the most widely imitated exemplars of tragedy and comedy. I recognize that I am pursuing a thankless task in explicating the commonplaces of Polonius, but the lecture on dramatic form that he gives Hamlet, Rosencrantz, and Guildenstern perfectly exemplifies the pedantic quality of his interest in style.

Polonius is also a critic of acting. He has spontaneously high praise for Hamlet's rendition of the Aeneas speech: "Fore God, my lord, well spoken, with good accent and good discretion" (2.2.477-78) . This judgment is echoed in Hamlet's advice to the players: "let your own discretion be your tutor" (3.2.17-18) , but Hamlet makes "your own discretion" a more personal guide than the lord chamberlain's "good discretion." Polonius has some advice of his own for the First Play-

[1] See Wilson, pp. 181-82; Parrott and Craig, p. 128; and Sisson, *New Readings in Shakespeare*, II, 217.

er, as he rises to the height of his invocation against
"strumpet Fortune" (2.2.504) : "This is too long"
(509). It is ironic to hear the chief representative of
"These tedious old fools" (221) complain about prolix-
ity, but his taste is not different from that of "the million," whom this play "pleased not" (446).

Hamlet twits the old man on his inability to appre-
ciate something fine; if it is too long, "It shall to the
barber's, with your beard.—Prithee say on. He's for a
jig or a tale of bawdry, or he sleeps" (510-12). In one
sentence, Hamlet has put his finger on the musical-
comedy, bedroom-farce formula of the commercial theater, for which Polonius would have made the ideal tired
businessman with expense account unlimited. Hamlet
had earlier warned us that in this play "there were no
sallets in the lines to make the matter savory" (451-52),
or spicy. If there is no "bawdry," or "country matters"
(3.2.119), there is also no "jig," or farcical ballad sung
and danced by the clowns after the play, which is in the
same scale of literary values as the "inexplicable dumb
shows and noise" (12-13). Taken together, these are the
only dramatic effects that appeal equally to the "groundlings" and to Polonius.

As a stage manager, Polonius rehearses his daughter
for the decoy scene with Hamlet: "Ophelia, walk you
here" (3.1.43), and he insists on the right properties
for his tableau:

> Read on this book,
> That show of such an exercise may color
> Your loneliness.   (3.1.44-46)

His theatrical specialty, however, is concealments, of
which he arranges one with the king, and another by
himself in the closet scene, where Gertrude will entreat
her son "all alone" (3.1.185), as Polonius so diplomati-
cally puts it. This piece of staging comes to grief, and
"the enginer" is "Hoist with his own petar" (3.4.207-
8). By some prophetic fatality of his university days,
Polonius "was accounted a good actor" and "did enact
Julius Caesar. I was killed i' th' Capitol; Brutus killed
me" (3.2.102-3, 105-6). If Brutus is a prototype of
Hamlet,[2] then the stabbing scene in the Capitol and
the killing of "so capital a calf" (107-8) has a final reenactment in Act III, Scene iv.

Polonius is a self-conscious rhetorician, who speaks
by art rather than by nature. His most ambitious effort
is his oration on the cause of Hamlet's madness, which
he delivers as "the fruit to that great feast" (2.2.52) —
a grandiose overstatement—of Voltemand and Cornelius' report from Norway. Polonius has prepared a formal
discourse so full of witty elaboration and epigrammatic
amplification that one wonders if the wily old statist is
not aware of what he is doing. The queen calls for
"More matter, with less art" (95), but Polonius protests:
"Madam, I swear I use no art at all" (96). "Art" has
an unfavorable connotation of policy and cunning as

---

[2] S. F. Johnson suggests a possible in-joke here for those of the
audience at the Globe who had recently seen *Julius Caesar*. It is
likely that the same actor played both Julius Caesar and Polonius, as Burbage undoubtedly played Brutus and Hamlet. In
general, Shakespeare's allusions to his contemporary theater are
probably more pointedly topical than we can now hope to recover.

well as artificiality. The ideal of the good stylist is to achieve the art that conceals art and convincingly imitates nature. Right after this protest, however, Polonius moves almost by reflex into another set of pointed inversions:

> That he's mad, 'tis true: 'tis true 'tis pity,
> And pity 'tis 'tis true—a foolish figure.
> But farewell it, for I will use no art.
>
> (2.2.97-99)

Polonius' farewell to foolish figures is short-lived. In the next lines he plays on the etymological sense of "effect" and "defect," with an exaggerated shuffling of a few words to produce unexpected and outlandish antitheses.

Polonius never falters in his linguistic display, and he manages to use an astonishing variety of devices including "brevity" as "the soul of wit" (90). "I will be brief" (92), he asserts, and he is brief, even curt and monosyllabic, but his brevity is lost in endless proliferations, identities, circular definitions, circumlocutions, inversions, exact stipulations, paradoxes, superfluous ornaments, and pointless emphases. Polonius may be self-consciously parodying the art of rhetoric, since he does call one of his little turns "a foolish figure" (98), and to his definition of madness—"to define true madness,/ What is't but to be nothing else but mad?" (93-94) — he adds: "But let that go" (95). This is parody in a different sense from Hamlet's, yet there is some *arrière-pensée* in the old counselor's stylistic foolishness, which may be what Samuel Johnson meant when he said:

"This idea of dotage encroaching upon wisdom, will solve all the phaenomena of the character of Polonius."[3]

His precepts to Laertes make another oration, but everything in the immediate context of this speech emphasizes its inappropriateness. It is apparent from Laertes' first words to his father that the ceremony of leave-taking has already been successfully concluded:

> A double blessing is a double grace;
> Occasion smiles upon a second leave.
>
> (1.3.53-54)

Polonius begins by chiding his son for tarrying:

> Yet here, Laertes? Aboard, aboard, for shame!
> The wind sits in the shoulder of your sail,
> And you are stayed for.   (1.3.55-57)

There is a pleasant colloquial air about this, which shows that Polonius is not such a stuffy orator after all. The father gives his son his blessing again, with some parting words of advice: "And these few precepts in thy memory/ Look thou character" (58-59) . But "these few precepts" grow to twenty-two solid lines of moral commonplaces, delivered seriatim and without any diversions. The speech is unexpected in its present proportions, and one has the impression that Polonius himself could not have anticipated its length.

This endless discourse seems to be the mark of senility, since the rational control over expression has begun to slip and the free expatiation is becoming ever freer and more and more independent of the will. Ped-

---

[3] *Johnson's Notes to Shakespeare*, ed. Arthur Sherbo, p. 163.

antry and garrulousness (as well as love of flattery) are all vices of old men, so that there is some psychological basis for Polonius' style in the character type of the *senex*. This is also true of Nestor in *Troilus and Cressida,* who is the classical exemplar of the old man, and of Justice Shallow in 2 *Henry IV*.

Polonius' style is at its most characteristic in Act II, Scene i, where he is giving his servant Reynaldo money and notes for Laertes in Paris, with an elaborate set of instructions on how to spy out the secrets of his son's life abroad. Polonius' insinuating method, "With windlasses and with assays of bias,/ By indirections find directions out" (65-66), may also describe the windings of his own discourse, which reach their apotheosis in total incoherence:

And then, sir, does 'a this—'a does—
    What was I about to say? By the mass, I was about
    to say something! Where did I leave?   (2.1.49-51)

Reynaldo then, with an attempt at parody, leads him back to the meandering trail of his speech: "At 'closes in the consequence,' at 'friend or so,' and 'gentleman'" (52-53). This is the most explicit touch of senility in all of Shakespeare.

It is not surprising that the *senex* should be one of the stock figures of comedy, where his foolishness, because it is buttressed with wealth, may the more easily be shown up in the desiccated wooing of a young wench. But there is no amorous pursuit for Polonius, although he does confess that "truly in my youth I suffered much extremity for love" (2.2.191-92). Although Polonius exhibits some features of the *senex*, the comic element in his character has been much exaggerated by a long tradition of imperceptive acting. His status as Claudius' chief minister would immediately exclude any direct buffoonery, and there are times when he is as menacing as the king. In general, however, we think of him as a misplaced purist, who has come to love the techniques and rhetoric of "policy" more than its avowed aims.

In Act II, Scene i particularly, Polonius uses Machiavellian methods that are grotesquely out of proportion with their objectives. The most striking quality of this scene is its overfullness and overcompleteness of detail, as if nothing were too trivial to be omitted. Just before Polonius loses the thread of his speech completely, he wanders off into the vagueness of excessive specification. The hypothetical informant whom Reynaldo is pumping

> . . . closes with you in this consequence:
> "Good sir," or so, or "friend," or "gentleman"—
> According to the phrase or the addition
> Of man and country—   (2.1.45-48)

When Polonius takes up his broken discourse, he is still foundering in meaningless formulas:

> At "closes in the consequence"—Ay, marry!
> He closes thus: "I know the gentleman;
> I saw him yesterday, or t'other day,
> Or then, or then, with such or such. . . ."
>
>   (2.1.54-57)

To the imaginary but cooperative informant, Laertes will be guilty of the "prenominate," or aforementioned, "crimes" (43), among which will be:

> "I saw him enter such a house of sale,"
> Videlicet, a brothel, or so forth.   (2.1.60-61)

We cannot believe that Reynaldo needs to have explained to him what a "house of sale" is, but in Polonius' amplified rhetoric nothing is taken for granted.

Like Hamlet, Polonius is much given to wordplay of all sorts, especially puns, although he seems to have no interest in exploring the possibilities of language for their own sake. His quibbles are generally more formal than Hamlet's, and have a certain sarcasm in them, or at least that sense of superior sophistication that he shows toward Ophelia. When she tells him directly that Hamlet "hath, my lord, of late made many tenders/ Of his affection to me" (1.3.99-100), Polonius mocks his daughter's innocence:

> Affection pooh! You speak like a green girl,
> Unsifted in such perilous circumstance.
> Do you believe his tenders, as you call them?
>   (1.3.101-3)

"Affection pooh!" is an abrupt deflation of a young girl's illusions—and we should not forget that Ophelia is about the same nubile age as Juliet, although she is without any of Juliet's resourcefulness or wit.

Polonius dwells on Ophelia's word "tenders" or offers "as you call them," just as Hamlet gives an ironic emphasis to Osric's word: "Why is this all impawned, as you call it?" (5.2.164-65) . He means to give his daughter a little lesson in the ways of the world, and "tenders" provides a splendid opportunity to improvise:

> Marry, I will teach you. Think yourself a baby
> That you have ta'en these tenders for true pay
> Which are not sterling. Tender yourself more dearly,
> Or (not to crack the wind of the poor phrase)
> Tend'ring[4] it thus you'll tender me a fool.
>
> (1.3.105-9)

As a "green girl,/ Unsifted in such perilous circumstance" (101-2) , Ophelia is likely to accept Hamlet's "tenders" of affection, which are only legal offers of money rather than the "true pay" itself in palpable "sterling." "Tender yourself more dearly" (107) , says Polonius, as if Ophelia were a valuable commodity that should not be either sold for less than it is worth or delivered without cash payment. The word "dearly" has a strong connotation of "expensively"; it is the same "higher rate" at which Ophelia is to set her "entreatments" (122) . Ophelia must therefore "tender" herself (with some auditory suggestion of "attend to" or "care for") at a higher price if she doesn't want to end by making her father a fool and presenting him with a bastard. Polonius is enough of a stylist to know that he

---

[4] Hubler follows the Quarto 1 reading advocated by Sisson (*New Readings in Shakespeare*, II, 210), which, with a slight shift in the second parenthesis, makes at least as good sense as Collier's emendation "Running," adopted by most modern editors. "Tend'ring" is a characteristically tedious extension of wit by Polonius.

is cracking "the wind of the poor phrase" as if it were a nag ridden too hard, but once embarked on his "foolish figure" (2.2.98), he cannot stop until he has completed it.

Polonius' imagery is ornamental and illustrative, with the vehicle exactly applied to the tenor. In other words, the image is limited to its single witty point without any imaginative resonance, as in the following: "See you now—/ Your bait of falsehood take this carp of truth" (2.1.62-63). The image is pictorial and it offers the sort of moral allegory one sees in emblem books. Polonius' lesson to Ophelia is constructed from a whole series of these kinds of images. Hamlet's vows of love are "springes to catch woodcocks" (1.3.115), which were simple birds, proverbially easy to snare, just as Ophelia has been easily snared by Hamlet. Every image has its exact referent, so that it is merely a question of translating the figurative term into its nonfigurative equivalent. Hamlet's "blood" or sexual desire is a flame that "burns" (116), but Polonius warns his daughter not to take "These blazes," "Giving more light than heat" (117-18), for true fire, since a bright blaze will soon be burnt out. I am completing the image for Polonius merely to indicate the commonplace from which it derives. Most of Polonius' imagery follows this symmetrical pattern, which is sometimes helped along by an "as 'twere" to make sure that we shift into the figurative mode.

Polonius also uses a direct and simple style that is usually forgotten in the gross caricaturing of his role. For one thing, he wants to confirm whether his not very difficult rhetoric has been understood. "You have me, have you not?" (2.1.68), he asks Reynaldo at the end of his endless explanations. With Ophelia, he appends the baldly stated message that his figures were intended to illustrate:

This is for all:
I would not, in plain terms, from this time forth
Have you so slander any moment leisure
As to give words or talk with the Lord Hamlet.
Look to't, I charge you. Come your ways.

(1.3.131-35)

The "plain terms" are very plain indeed, with many monosyllables, especially in that last menacing line, spoken in the imperative manner of Claudius. "This is for all" for daughter matches "This above all" (78) for son, both phrases being concluding summaries as well as final admonitions.

If Polonius is a master of "indirections" (2.1.66), he also knows how to ask direct questions at the proper time: "What is't, Ophelia, he hath said to you?" (1.3.88) and the more peremptory: "What is between you? Give me up the truth" (98). This is vigorous and threatening, without the slightest touch of senility. Polonius also knows how to give commands in a manner that will not brook opposition: "From this time/ Be something scanter of your maiden presence" (120-21), and "In few, Ophelia,/ Do not believe his vows" (126-27). How effective that "In few" is for a garrulous man!

Polonius can speak lucidly when the occasion demands, so that there is no doubt at all of his capacity

— 254 —

for high public office. His talk with Claudius after their eavesdropping on Hamlet is absolutely straightforward and unadorned. Ophelia is quickly disposed of as merely a tool in affairs of state:

> How now, Ophelia?
> You need not tell us what Lord Hamlet said;
> We heard it all. (3.1.181-83)

This is, of course, a point of which Ophelia is already painfully aware. Polonius' final words to the king before the closet scene are also simple and businesslike:

> Fare you well, my liege.
> I'll call upon you ere you go to bed
> And tell you what I know.
>
> (3.3.33-35)

This is terse and almost entirely monosyllabic, a style in keeping with its expository purpose. It should seem clear by now that Polonius' figurative adornment is a self-conscious style rather than his normal speaking voice. Like a well-trained statesman, he can embellish his speech when the need arises.

In his domestic setting, Polonius uses a good deal of colloquial phrasing and syntax that would have a certain charm were it not so overbearing. We have already noticed his "Affection pooh!" (1.3.101) to Ophelia, who answers all of his assaults with the literalness of a dutiful daughter. "My lord, he hath importuned me with love/ In honorable fashion" (110-11), she says, to which her father replies with scornful mockery: "Ay, fashion you may call it. Go to, go to" (112). This is a wonderfully natural line, whose speech emphases are likely to be overlooked by a reader. In paraphrase, "Go to, go to" means something like: "Are you kidding me with your high-mindedness?" Polonius seems genuinely shocked that the daughter of the lord chamberlain should be so unsophisticated.

His long aside in the fishmonger scene with Hamlet is also attractively colloquial: "How say you by that? Still harping on my daughter. Yet he knew me not at first. 'A said I was a fishmonger. 'A is far gone, far gone. And truly in my youth I suffered much extremity for love, very near this. I'll speak to him again" (2.2.188-92). One could never extrapolate Polonius' decorative style from these fragments of speech, which are in the abbreviated syntax of ordinary conversation. " 'A" is the familiar contraction for "he." Polonius' confession of his amorous youth endows him with a pleasant avuncular quality not unlike that of Justice Shallow and his memorable exploits with Jane Nightwork (2 *Henry IV* 3.2.193ff.).

"That he is old—the more the pity—his white hairs do witness it" (*1 Henry IV* 2.4.452-53), Falstaff says in his own behalf, but Polonius' more advanced age is attested to by an inexhaustible appetite for flattery and self-magnification. At a hint of coldness in the queen, he asks archly:

Hath there been such a time, I would fain know
    that,
That I have positively said " 'Tis so,"
When it proved otherwise? (2.2.153-55)

This is a textbook example of a rhetorical question, to which the king answers distantly, "Not that I know" (155), when nothing less than an encomiastic panegyric would suffice. There is an even more unctuous rhetorical question earlier in this scene, when Polonius announces the joyful return of the ambassadors from Norway:

> *King.* Thou still hast been the father of good
> news.
> *Polonius.* Have I, my lord?   (2.2.42-43)

Much depends on the proper intonation of this question, since Polonius is preening himself on the "good news" that he is so coyly withholding: "that I have found/ The very cause of Hamlet's lunacy" (48-49). Polonius also loves ceremonial usages of all sorts, a trait inherited, with fatal consequences, by his son.

Polonius is neither a comic nor a tragic figure in *Hamlet*, but he is caught up in the tragic circumstances of the play and becomes their first casualty; his death precipitates all the deaths to follow. As the king's chief counselor, he is in some sense a victim of the tragic plot, so that for all of his rhetorical brilliance and gravity of manner, he is fated to be one of "These tedious old fools" (2.2.221), a bearer of stale news and a teller of twice-told tales. When we consider all the possibilities for Polonius in another sort of play, it seems a terrible waste that he should die "a foolish prating knave" (3.4.216) mistaken for his "better" (33).

11. Hamlet: "How pregnant sometimes his replies are"

UNLIKE Laertes, Hamlet has no single, identifiable style, nor does he, like Claudius, have a pair of styles, ornate and simple, ready for all occasions. We may distinguish at least four different styles for Hamlet: 1. a self-conscious style expressed chiefly in parody; 2. a witty style associated with his madness; 3. a passionate style used primarily in the soliloquies; and 4. a simple style for narration and special effects. These are only four possibilities among many, but they should help to make the point that Hamlet's mode of expression varies widely in different contexts. Laertes follows with a murderous simplicity his father's advice, "to thine own self be true" (1.3.78), and if the defeat of Rosencrantz and Guildenstern "Does by their own insinuation grow" (5.2.59), they are insinuating from their first appearance in the play to their last—the only variations are in intensity. But Hamlet's strong awareness of his own "Words, words, words" (2.2.194) does not permit this kind of consistency. The range and versatility of his dramatic role is reflected in a corresponding inventiveness and variety of style.[1]

Hamlet as Artist and Critic

The warrant for considering Hamlet as artist and critic may be drawn from his own active concern with

[1] See Madeleine Doran, "The Language of *Hamlet*," *Huntington Library Quarterly*, XXVII (1964), 259-78, and Marvin Spevack, "Hamlet and Imagery: The Mind's Eye," *Die Neueren Sprachen*, V (1966), 203-12.

style throughout the play. He is artist and critic in a literal sense that is true of no other Shakespearean character. As an amateur dramatist, he will write "a speech of some dozen or sixteen lines" that he will "set down and insert" (2.2.551-52) in the next night's performance of *The Murder of Gonzago*. No one has yet been able precisely to identify Hamlet's speech, although Shakespeare could certainly have tagged it for us had he wanted us to know. In any case, the difficulty in distinguishing Hamlet's topical insertion shows that it is completely in keeping with the rest of the play. The very fact that Hamlet chooses a play to test Claudius' guilt is itself a sign of the literary bent of his mind. We learn from his advice to the players that he has been coaching them for their evening performance: "Speak the speech, I pray you, as I pronounced it to you, trippingly on the tongue" (3.2.1-2). Since the conversation with the players begins *in medias res*, we can assume that Hamlet has already given them other bits of practical advice, such as: "do not saw the air too much with your hand, thus" (4-5)—the final gesture is grossly propaedeutic.

We already know that Hamlet is a competent actor from the "taste" of his "quality" (2.2.441) in the Aeneas speech (popularly called the "Player's speech," although Hamlet speaks almost one-third as many lines as the First Player). We have Polonius' enthusiastic testimony to Hamlet's skill: "Fore God, my lord, well spoken, with good accent and good discretion" (477-78). After the unanticipated success of *The Mousetrap*, Hamlet amusingly considers becoming a professional actor: "Would not this, sir, and a forest of feathers—if the rest of my fortunes turn Turk with me—with two Provincial roses on my razed shoes, get me a fellowship in a cry of players?" (3.2.281-84). The skeptical and bantering Horatio will allow his princely friend only "Half a share" (285), but Hamlet will be satisfied with nothing less than "A whole one, I" (286). He is no journeyman or apprentice, but experienced in the "mystery." In Hamlet's question, "this" is ambiguous, and J. Q. Adams believes that he may be gesticulating with the manuscript of the scene.[2] He certainly thinks of himself as its producer, and perhaps as its director, too. It is Hamlet's show, and the audience are his invited guests. We remember that the players have "order/ This night to play before him" (3.1.20-21), and that Polonius, officially charged as lord chamberlain with royal entertainments, entreats "your Majesties," at Hamlet's request, "To hear and see the matter" (22-23).

Besides those "dozen or sixteen lines" (2.2.551) of *The Mousetrap*, we also have some samples of Hamlet's nondramatic writing. There is his pleasantly conceited Petrarchan poem in his love letter to Ophelia. The affected style of this poem and letter are redolent of Hamlet as he once was, "The glass of fashion, and the mold of form" (3.1.156), rather than someone who has now "lost all my mirth" (2.2.304). The close of the letter, "Thine evermore, most dear lady, whilst this machine is to him" (123-24), is distinctively in the manner of Osric, especially that odd word "machine," which is indeed "very dear to fancy" (5.2.152). We also know that Hamlet wrote a new "grand commission"

[2] Adams' edition of *Hamlet*, p. 268.

(5.2.18) ordering that Rosencrantz and Guildenstern be put to death in England. No one ever suspects it to be a forgery, so well is it prepared and so authentic an example is it of the scrivener's art. Another professional skill—"to write fair" (34) —does Hamlet "yeoman's service" (36) in this emergency.

Hamlet carries with him a pocket notebook, or table book, of the sort in which every thoughtful, or merely polished, gentleman recorded the "wise saws and modern instances" (*As You Like It* 2.7.156) of reading and daily life. In an extended passionate image, Hamlet's brain becomes the table book in which he will inscribe his vow to remember the Ghost:

> Yea, from the table of my memory
> I'll wipe away all trivial fond records,
> All saws of books, all forms, all pressures past
> That youth and observation copied there,
> And thy commandment all alone shall live
> Within the book and volume of my brain,
> Unmixed with baser matter. Yes, by heaven!
>
> (1.5.98-104)

By telling us what he will expunge, Hamlet gives us a vivid social portrait of the "baser matter" of a young Elizabethan gentleman's memoranda. In the sort of link only possible in a play, the image leads to the stage property,[3] as "the table of my memory" becomes "My tables" (107), the little notebook that Hamlet now has in his hands: "meet it is I set it down/ That

[3] See J. L. Styan, *Shakespeare's Stagecraft* (Cambridge, Eng.: Cambridge University Press, 1967), pp. 59-60.

one may smile, and smile, and be a villain" (107-8). He proceeds to enter this observation, true at least for Denmark, in his "tables," and the physical act of writing is completed with the covering line, "So, uncle, there you are" (110).

A characteristic stage direction marks Hamlet's entrance *"reading on a book"* (2.2.167 s.d., Folio), as Polonius prepares to accost him "in the lobby" (161). On the basis of the remarks of the "satirical rogue" (198), keen-sighted commentators have identified Hamlet's book as Juvenal's Tenth Satire.[4] In *Troilus and Cressida*, the wily Ulysses is also characterized as bookish, and Achilles is made to interrupt his reading. The passage that follows—"A strange fellow here/ Writes me that man" (3.3.95-96) —has many verbal similarities to Hamlet's talk with Polonius.

Hamlet is not only a practitioner of the arts, but also a keen critic. This is the very word that Ophelia uses— "You are keen, my lord, you are keen" (3.2.254) — although Hamlet chooses to interpret his "edge" (256) immodestly. After the introductory badinage with the players, Hamlet calls for "a passionate speech" (2.2.441-42) from a Dido and Aeneas play that was an almost instantaneous flop: "it was never acted, or if it was, not above once, for the play, I remember, pleased not the million; 'twas caviary to the general" (444-47). There may well be an allusion here to an actual Eliz-

[4] See *Variorum*, I, 151, and Hardin Craig, "Hamlet's Book," *Huntington Library Bulletin*, Number 6 (1934), 17-37.

abethan play.[5] But if it "pleased not the million," to Hamlet and his literary friends it was "an excellent play, well digested in the scenes, set down with as much modesty as cunning" (449-51). Hamlet is distinguishing between a debased popular taste and the expert judgment of a cultivated elite, a distinction that is also the basis for his advice to the players about acting: "Now, this overdone, or come tardy off, though it makes the unskillful laugh, cannot but make the judicious grieve, the censure of the which one must in your allowance o'erweigh a whole theater of others" (3.2.26-30). "The judicious" versus "the unskillful" is an unmistakably aristocratic pairing.

To return to the Dido and Aeneas play, Hamlet praises it for being "well digested in the scenes," which indicates a coherent, logical structure rather than an episodic, spectacular one. The author avoids all "affection" (2.2.454, Quarto 2), or "affectation" (Folio). The play was "set down" with "modesty," or moderation, a virtue stressed in the advice to the players. The central criterion there is "that you o'erstep not the modesty of nature" (3.2.19-20), which is another way of expressing the theory of mimesis: "to hold, as 'twere, the mirror up to nature" (22-23). "Temperance" and "discretion" are synonyms for this ideal of "modesty." In sum, the

[5] The allusion is probably not to Marlowe and Nashe's *Dido, Queen of Carthage* (1587), since the verbal parallels are not at all close. There is also an anonymous *Dido and Aeneas* recorded as acted by the Admiral's Men on January 8, 1598. See Alfred Harbage, *Annals of English Drama 975-1700* (rev. S. Schoenbaum; London, 1964), p. 68.

play uses "an honest method, as wholesome as sweet, and by very much more handsome than fine" (2.2.454-56). "Fine" suggests "affection," something overly delicate and mannered, as Osric's style is "fine" rather than "handsome," and as the lawyer in the graveyard has "his fine pate full of fine dirt" (5.1.108-9). "Wholesome," "sweet," "honest," and "handsome" are all homely words meant to describe solid and unimpeachable stylistic virtues.

Within its own mode of emotional declamation, the tale of Priam's slaughter is splendidly successful, and if critics find it overwrought, it is worth remembering that Elizabethan writers did not put such a high value on the simple style as we do. With classical indignation, Dryden considers the speech an example of "the blown puffy style," in which "the fury" of Shakespeare's "fancy often transported him beyond the bounds of judgment. . . ."[6] Coleridge also thinks it "too poetical, the language of lyric vehemence and epic pomp, not of the drama."[7] For better or for worse, these comments attest that this is indeed the "passionate speech" (2.2.441-42) that Hamlet requested.

Hamlet's easy and personal manner with the players suggests a tiring-house familiarity, such as we might expect from a frequenter of rehearsals (cf. 2.2.444-45). He is the connoisseur of plays, the gifted amateur coun-

[6] John Dryden, "The Grounds of Criticism in Tragedy" (The Preface to *Troilus and Cressida*, 1679), in *Of Dramatic Poesy and Other Critical Essays*, ed. George Watson (London, 1962), p. 257.

[7] Samuel Taylor Coleridge, *Shakespearean Criticism*, ed. Thomas Middleton Raysor (2 edn.; London, 1960), I, 37.

seling limited professionals and attempting to raise their
standards by an appeal to fundamental principles. Hamlet insists on a rational mean between tearing "a passion
to tatters, to very rags" (3.2.10) and being "too tame"
(17). Speeches are to be "pronounced . . . trippingly
on the tongue" (1-2), not mouthed as if by the "town
crier" (3-4) thundering his proclamations in the mar-
ketplace. Gesture is to be used "gently" (5), a word
which carries a built-in pun on its social sense, "like a
gentleman." Decorum and naturalness are the principal
criteria: one should "Suit the action to the word, the
word to the action" (18-19), since the purpose of acting
is imitation, mimesis. Bad actors are monsters fashioned
by "some of Nature's journeymen" (35) rather than by
God, because "they imitated humanity so abominably"
(36-37). "They" is deliberately vague, so that it can
refer either to the players themselves botching their
imitation of "humanity" on stage, or to the journeymen,
whose product is an abominable imitation of an authentic human being.[8] Part of the wit in the passage comes
from the Elizabethan pun on "abominably" in its popular (and false) etymology: *ab+homine*.

Hamlet adds a special caveat against the ad-libbing of
clowns, whose "one suit/ Of jests" are conveniently recorded for us at this point in Quarto 1, including the
mysterious barb: "Cannot you stay till I eat my
porridge?" To Hamlet, the "necessary question of the
play" must always take precedence over the clown's
barren improvisation. This advice to the players pro-

---

[8] See Tilley, M162: "He is (is not) a Man of God's making."

vides a touchstone for Hamlet's own rhetoric and acting style, since he is occasionally guilty of the excesses he inveighs against. The whole passage, along with the discussion in theatrical affairs in Act II, Scene ii, also has interesting moral overtones. Horatio, for example, seems to have just those qualities of "temperance" (3.2. 7-8) that characterize the good actor, and, structurally, the advice to the players leads directly into Hamlet's praise of Horatio.

We see Hamlet at work as a drama critic during *The Murder of Gonzago.* His explications and stylistic observations are, as Ophelia says, "as good as a chorus" (3.2.251). He insists that it is only a foolish and crude old play; therefore, *honi soit qui mal y pense.* As producer of the entertainment, Hamlet takes the liberty of doing a little hasty prompting of Lucianus: "Begin, murderer. Leave thy damnable faces and begin" (258-59). He is apparently "mugging" his part beyond the limits of Hamlet's endurance, so that "damnable" serves for both the role and the actor. It is worth noting that Hamlet's own anticipations of the plot do not allow us to place too much weight on his comment: "The players cannot keep counsel; they'll tell all" (146-47); Hamlet himself has been telling us much more than the players. The point of *The Mousetrap* is not to create a sense of reality, but rather one of artifice. The trap is to be sprung unawares.

While Lucianus is pouring poison into the ears of the Player King, Hamlet is busily summarizing what remains of the plot, as if he were the official presenter called upon to explain "inexplicable dumb shows"

(3.2.12-13): " 'A poisons him i' th' garden for his estate. His name's Gonzago. The story is extant, and written in very choice Italian. You shall see anon how the murderer gets the love of Gonzago's wife" (267-70). It is at this point, precisely, that the king rises and breaks up the play. *The Murder of Gonzago* proves to be a kind of history play, "the image of a murder done in Vienna" (244), even then associated with international intrigue and dark deeds. Hamlet seems to be ironically suggesting that Claudius may wish to pursue this play to its "extant" sources, which are "written in very choice Italian." How characteristic is Hamlet's insistence on "choice" style at this moment, as if Claudius were interrupting the play only to rush to the royal library to read more about this "knavish piece of work" (246).

The Self-Conscious Style

Hamlet seems always to be conscious of himself as a user of words, and we often have the impression that he is trying out different styles to see what their effect on himself will be. This is particularly true of his experiments with the role of stage revenger, a part for which Laertes is much better suited. After Hamlet has been reminded of Pyrrhus' bloody deeds, he feels the impulse, in a long soliloquy, to make his own thoughts properly bloody. He begins this sequence with a series of irritating short questions:

> Am I a coward?
> Who calls me villain? Breaks my pate across?
> Plucks off my beard and blows it in my face?

> Tweaks me by the nose? Gives me the lie i' th'
>   throat
> As deep as to the lungs? Who does me this?
>
> (2.2.582-86)

These are all formal insults, deliberate provocations to a duel.

But Hamlet fears he may be a coward, and this fear leads him to use a swaggering style to reassure himself of his manliness:

> Ha, 'swounds, I should take it, for it cannot be
> But I am pigeon-livered and lack gall
> To make oppression bitter, or ere this
> I should ha' fatted all the region kites
> With this slave's offal.   (2.2.587-91)

Hamlet is cheering himself up, the strong words asserting a corresponding strength in their user. Once started, he continues with bolder exclamations to a breathless, polysyllabic climax:

> Bloody, bawdy villain!
> Remorseless, treacherous, lecherous, kindless villain!
> O, vengeance!   (2.2.591-93)

This is expressive rhetoric, since the meaning of the passage is conveyed as much by its sound as by the denotations of the words. In the theater, one could probably understand its intent without knowing a word of English.

So far Hamlet has not distinguished himself in this soliloquy from many another Elizabethan revenger, but once he has vented his passion, he suddenly becomes critical and self-conscious:

> Why, what an ass am I! This is most brave,
> That I, the son of a dear father murdered,
> Prompted to my revenge by heaven and hell,
> Must, like a whore, unpack my heart with words
> And fall a-cursing like a very drab,
> A scullion![9] Fie upon't, foh!   (2.2.594-99)

Hamlet confirms our feeling that the earlier part of the soliloquy was all self-indulgent rant, the meretricious billingsgate of whores, drabs, scullions, and other base, menial creatures. If the death of Polonius will later set Hamlet "packing" (3.4.212), the thoughts of his revenge have here set him to unpacking, as if his heart were loaded with deceptive words, the protestations of love that a whore reserves for her clients. The words are false wares and, like Claudius, Hamlet is conscious of a gap between his deed and his "most painted word" (3.1.53).

There is a quibble on "brave" in its positive sense of valiant and in its stronger negative sense of the bravado of mere words. Hamlet's own self-disgust is concluded with those strong interjections, "Fie upon't, foh!" "Foh" is uncommon in Shakespeare, and all of

---

[9] Wilson's attempt to justify the Quarto 2 reading, "stallion," in the sense of courtesan or male whore, seems farfetched; see p. 188 of his edition and *The Manuscript of Shakespeare's Hamlet,* I, 71. See also Parrott and Craig, p. 137. Hubler reads "stallion." Until we can believe that "stallion" was a word in common usage in this sense at the time of *Hamlet,* we must follow Folio's more workaday "scullion."

the examples indicate contempt or abhorrence, as in Iago's false accusation of Desdemona: "Foh! one may smell in such a will most rank" (*Othello* 3.3.236). The soliloquy form conventionally provides for an honest self-expression not possible in one's public utterances, but in this scene Hamlet uses soliloquy both for verbal pretense and for the deflation of that pretense. This doubleness is what I mean by a self-conscious style.

We can see the same effect at work in Hamlet's praise of Horatio, which is perhaps his most laudatory speech in the play. Horatio is the paragon of the just and non-heroic man, who has overcome those "slings and arrows of outrageous fortune" (3.1.58) that trouble Hamlet:

> Dost thou hear?
> Since my dear soul was mistress of her choice
> And could of men distinguish her election,
> S' hath sealed thee for herself, for thou hast been
> As one, in suff'ring all, that suffers nothing,
> A man that Fortune's buffets and rewards
> Hast ta'en with equal thanks. . . .   (3.2.64-70)

Hamlet's uncomfortably colloquial question—"Dost thou hear?"—prepares us for the unusual frankness of what is to follow. The whole speech comes dangerously close to being a personal confession of the strength of Hamlet's feelings for Horatio:

> Give me that man
> That is not passion's slave, and I will wear him
> In my heart's core, ay, in my heart of heart,
> As I do thee.   (3.2.73-76)

Hamlet is thinking of his own potential self outside the toils of tragedy, and in the triple repetition of "heart" (with a fourth use implied in "core"—Latin *cor*) , there is an attempt to establish the intensity of his attachment to his friend. But suddenly there occurs one of those abrupt shifts that we have just noticed in the "rogue and peasant slave" soliloquy. Hamlet breaks off his panegyric, which is beginning to sound fulsome and rhetorical: "Something too much of this—" (76) . It is as if language is a false and inadequate medium for conveying true emotion. He seems to feel that any commendation put into words is bound to appear overdone and hollow, and this is the last we hear of Horatio's sterling qualities.

Hamlet's self-conscious style achieves its most brilliant and most characteristic effects in parody, which, as the art of ironic imitation, shows at once a subtle mastery of style and a total abandonment of any individual style. By mimicking the rhetorical absurdities of others, Hamlet, like Ben Jonson, is endeavoring to put them out of their humors—and it is remarkable how strongly Hamlet's aristocratic canons and reformer's gusto seal him as one of the tribe of Ben. But the objects of the parody are usually beyond recovery, so that, like Osric, they applaud their own excesses when delivered by another: "Your lordship speaks most infallibly of him" (5.2.122) . This absence of effect turns Hamlet's parodies into demonstrations of satirical insight, whose chief target is the malevolent circumlocution of the court style. By holding this style up to scorn, Hamlet attempts to strip away the false appearances by which Denmark and the world are

"Rankly abused" (1.5.38). Much more than in any other play of Shakespeare, the pretensions and deceits of style in *Hamlet* are used to express the hidden evil, the "Something" that "is rotten in the state of Denmark" (1.4.90).

Hamlet's scene with Osric is the most extensive parody in the play. It is also the most exuberant, since Osric is so invincibly impervious to ridicule. His love of refinement in diction, as in dress and manners, is expressed in a series of new-minted, inkhorn terms, "never clapperclawed with the palms of the vulgar," as "A Never Writer, to an Ever Reader" puts it in his preface to *Troilus and Cressida*.[10] Osric consistently replaces vulgar monosyllables by nobler polysyllables, euphemizes all low and base words, subjunctivates and conditionalizes the indicative mood, and turns direct phrases into polite and meaningless circumlocutions. To sum up in the pleasant phraseology of Sister Miriam Joseph, "Cacozelia is Osric's characteristic vice."[11]

Osric is indeed, to dally with Milton's phrase, "Fancy's child." "There was good sport at his making" (*King Lear* 1.1.22-23), into which went a generous measure of Don Armado, who has been "at a great feast of languages and stol'n the scraps," and of Holofernes, too, who admires Ovidius Naso "for smelling out the odor-

[10] Quoted from the Signet edition of *Troilus and Cressida*, ed. Daniel Seltzer (New York, 1963), p. xli. The passage is not in Alexander.

[11] Sister Miriam Joseph, *Shakespeare's Use of the Arts of Language* (New York: Columbia University Press, 1947), p. 73. "Affected diction, especially the coining of fine words out of Latin, is a form of the vice cacozelia. Through it Shakespeare satirizes inkhornism" (p. 72).

iferous flowers of fancy, the jerks of invention" (*Love's Labour's Lost* 5.1.33-34; 4.2.118-19). Osric is also like the "popinjay" lord, "Fresh as a bridegroom," who comes to demand Hotspur's prisoners, "With many holiday and lady terms" (*1 Henry IV* 1.3.34, 46). In *Hamlet*, there is a preliminary sketch of Osric in the imagined courtier of the graveyard scene, who could say, " 'Good morrow, sweet lord! How dost thou, sweet lord?' This might be my Lord Such-a-one, that praised my Lord Such-a-one's horse when 'a meant[12] to beg it, might it not?" (5.1.83-87).

It is not difficult for Hamlet to parody Osric's style, and once he gets the feel of it, he is quickly out-Osricking his model. He answers Osric's high-flown praise of Laertes in an equally elevated style: "I know, to divide him inventorially would dozy th' arithmetic of memory" (5.2.114-15). The image is based on the inventory of goods in Laertes' huge warehouse of qualities, an amount that would "dozy" (an old form of "dizzy"),[13] or stagger, any systematic attempt to recollect them. One

[12] "Meant" is the Folio reading, which most modern editors prefer; Hubler reads "went," as in Quarto 2.

[13] All three extant copies of the 1604 printing of Quarto 2 read "dosie," a variant spelling of "dozy," which is a rare but correct form of the verb "to dizzy." The press corrector, however, did not seem to know this, and changed "dosie" to "dazzie," a nonsense word, in the printing of Quarto 2 dated 1605 (of which there are also three extant copies). See Parrott and Craig, p. 231. The Osric scene is one place where we might literally follow the textual principle of *durior lectio*, since Hamlet and Osric are vying with each other to produce a more esoteric and recherché style. The textual problem is complicated by the fact that Folio omits about thirty-eight lines from what must have seemed a very "literary" and dispensable passage (the cut extends from "here is" in line 107 through "unfellowed" in line 144).

can hardly use words for Laertes at all, since he is "a soul of great article, and his infusion of such dearth and rareness as, to make true diction of him, his semblable is his mirror" (117-20). An "article" is an item in an inventory, or any stipulation or clause in a legal document, such as the "carriage of the article designed" (1.1.94) in the "sealed compact" (86) between old Hamlet and old Fortinbras. Laertes' "dearth" or dearness in price, like that of other commodities in the market, is determined by his "rareness." When Osric suddenly slips into direct and vulgar speech, "Of Laertes?" (5.2.130), Horatio thinks it a sign of verbal insolvency: "His purse is empty already. All's golden words are spent" (131-32). Osric's aureate diction may be a purse with gold coins, but it is not overfull.

In announcing the king's wager against Laertes', Osric dwells lovingly on the ornamental details: "The King, sir, hath wagered with him six Barbary horses, against the which he has impawned, as I take it, six French rapiers and poniards, with their assigns, as girdle, hangers, and so. Three of the carriages, in faith, are very dear to fancy, very responsive to the hilts, most delicate carriages, and of very liberal conceit" (148-54). These are terms normally used for poetry, but "carriages" are the farthest extent of Osric's aesthetic capabilities. Hamlet is ruffled by that affected word "carriages," as he was earlier by the Player's "mobled queen" (2.2.514), and he demands a stricter lexicography from Osric: "The phrase would be more germane to the matter if we could carry a cannon by our sides. I would it might be hangers till then" (5.2.159-61).

But Hamlet soon abandons his verbal purism for a more gratifying self-indulgence in Osric's own element: "But on! Six Barbary horses against six French swords, their assigns, and three liberal-conceited carriages— that's the French bet against the Danish. Why is this all impawned, as you call it?" (161-65) . There is Osric's precious word "impawned" for honest English "bet," and Hamlet means to call attention to it—"as you call it"—to match Osric's own emphasis in "as I take it" (149-50) . In this direct borrowing by Hamlet of Osric's words, we have parody according to its textbook criterion: the imitation of another's speech with intent to burlesque. Osric is the "Courtier" of Quarto 2, the "Braggart Gentleman" of Quarto 1, and Phantasmo of *Der Bestrafte Brudermord*—a man "the drossy age dotes on" (5.2.191) . He has "much land, and fertile" and is a "lord of beasts" (86-87) , but when blown to his "trial" (196) , poor Osric proves to be only a "yeasty" (193) bubble.

Hamlet's parody of Laertes in the graveyard scene is also meant to explode, by ridicule, the inflated style of its object, but this parody is much more aggressive and lacerating than that of Osric. One has the impression that Hamlet is attacking Claudius through his minions, and even though Hamlet cannot know that the king and Laertes have sealed their triple plot against his life, he seems already to have that fateful feeling of "how ill all's here about my heart" (5.2.213-14) .

Hamlet and Horatio observe the funeral of Ophelia "apart," or concealed (conventionally) at one side of the stage, because it is not yet safe for the recently escaped Hamlet to reveal himself. He maintains his concealment even after he learns that they are burying "the fair Ophelia" (5.1.244), but when Laertes launches into his hyperbolical exclamations, Hamlet can no longer contain himself. His first speech is entirely devoted to his outraged sense of style rather than to any lamentations for his lost loved one:

> What is he whose grief
> Bears such an emphasis, whose phrase of sorrow
> Conjures the wand'ring stars, and makes them stand
> Like wonder-wounded hearers? This is I,
> Hamlet the Dane.   (5.1.256-60)

The terms are all specifically rhetorical and theatrical: "emphasis," "phrase of sorrow," "wonder-wounded hearers." Laertes is guilty of the same excesses that Hamlet complains of in his advice to the players, and the "wand'ring stars," or planets, seem to react like those ear-split "groundlings, who for the most part are capable of nothing but inexplicable dumb shows and noise" (3.2.11-13).

There is another link with the advice to the players in Hamlet's scornful comment to Laertes: "Nay, an thoul't mouth,/ I'll rant as well as thou" (5.1.285-86), which recalls: "But if you mouth it, as many of our players do, I had as lief the town crier spoke my lines" (3.2.2-4). The same criteria apply in both cases, and Laertes is made to illustrate the type of the bad actor. Ranting is the quality of "o'erdoing Termagant. It outherods Herod" (14-15), just as Laertes is now attempting to "outface" (5.1.280) Hamlet at Ophelia's grave. This is, by the way, the only occurrence of the word "rant" in Shakespeare (although we have "ranting" in *The Merry Wives of Windsor* 2.1.170). Another word expressing contempt for Laertes' style is "prate": "And if thou prate of mountains, let them throw/ Millions of acres on us" (5.1.282-83). The word means to prattle, to chatter, to talk idly; we remember that the dead Polonius was "a foolish prating knave" (3.4.216). Significantly, Laertes and Polonius are the only "praters" in the play. Later Hamlet is to regret "That to Laertes I forgot myself" (5.2.76), but he pleads strong provocation: "sure the bravery of his grief did put me/ Into a tow'ring passion" (79-80). "Bravery" and "tow'ring passion" both indicate flamboyant and overwrought emotional effects that lend themselves to ridicule.

Hamlet's parody of Laertes is set in the context of a strong self-consciousness of style. To answer Laertes' grandiloquence, Hamlet proposes a series of absurd, mock-heroic love trials:

> 'Swounds, show me what thou't do.
> Woo't weep? Woo't fight? Woo't fast? Woo't tear
>   thyself?
> Woo't drink up eisel? Eat a crocodile?
> I'll do't.   (5.1.276-79)

The abrupt colloquial questions and staccato rhythms are in themselves grotesque, apart from the content of the images. The burlesque crocodile seems to connect with "Woo't weep?", since it was best known for its trick of hypocritical or malicious tears, like Gertrude's "salt of most unrighteous tears" (1.2.154) and Laertes' own "tears seven times salt" (4.5.154) —another rhetorical absurdity in the spirit of the crocodile passage. Hamlet will match Laertes hyperbole for hyperbole and give him odds, too:

> Dost thou come here to whine?
> To outface me with leaping in her grave?
> Be buried quick with her, and so will I.
> And if thou prate of mountains, let them throw
> Millions of acres on us, till our ground,
> Singeing his pate against the burning zone,
> Make Ossa like a wart! Nay, an thou'lt mouth,
> I'll rant as well as thou.   (5.1.279-86)

There is an exaggerated oratorical delivery of that long period calling for "Millions of acres," but at "Nay" an abrupt shift in tone marks Hamlet's return to his normal style. He tells us directly that he has been ranting, but he will "outface" Laertes in all respects.

If we think of "whine" as a comment on Laertes' style, it should be placed with Hamlet's other vocal terms: "Let Hercules himself do what he may,/ The cat will mew, and dog will have his day" (293-94). All of these images seem to me to refer to Laertes: let this bombastic Hercules go through his *miles gloriosus* routines; we must allow cats and dogs to express their serio-comic, bellicose natures. Hercules is Antony's tutelary deity, and, to the accompaniment of *"hautboys . . . under the stage,"* "Now leaves him" (*Antony and Cleopatra* 4.3.12 s.d., 17). But Hamlet has forcefully rejected any resemblance to Hercules: Claudius is his father's brother, "but no more like my father/ Than I to Hercules" (1.2.152-53). I think the point of the allusion is that

"Ercles' vein" is "a tyrant's vein," as Bottom informs us, and he defines the role in a way that could apply to the ranting Laertes in the graveyard (and to Hamlet's parody of him) : "I could play Ercles rarely, or a part to tear a cat in, to make all split" (*A Midsummer Night's Dream* 1.2.33-34, 23-24).

Hamlet's desire to "outface" his rival would also include, it seems to me, his leaping into Ophelia's grave after Laertes. The parody is extended follow-the-leader fashion from words to stage action. If Quarto 1 is a memorial reconstruction of what was actually seen and heard during a performance, then its directions have a special value. Right after *"Laertes leaps into the grave"* (at 5.1.253), Quarto 1 notes in the margin: *"Hamlet leaps in after Laertes"* (at about 5.1.255). We would like to disavow this explicit direction, but it is clear from "A Funerall Elegye on ye Death of the famous Actor Richard Burbedg" (1618) that this was one of his remembered histrionic exploits:

> Oft haue I seene him, leap into the Graue
> Suiting the person, which he seem'd to haue
> Of a sadd Louer, with soe true an Eye
> That theer I would haue sworne, he meant to
> dye. . . .[14]

The stage action of jumping into the grave and scuffling there supports the verbal aggression of Hamlet's parody; it is also a preparation for the lethal fencing match of

[14] Quoted from Edwin Nungezer, *A Dictionary of Actors* (Ithaca, N.Y.: Cornell University Press, 1929), p. 74. See Granville-Barker's objection to this staging in his *Prefaces*, I, 139, note 19.

the next scene. In the Elizabethan staging of this un-
seemly brawl, Ophelia's coffin would be quickly removed
from the stage-trap grave to make it ready for Laertes
and Hamlet.

Parody is part of Hamlet's counterattack on Claudius
and his minions. There is little direct burlesque of the
king, a dangerous topic on the Elizabethan stage, but
there are at least two places where Claudius is the object of Hamlet's verbal assault. First, Hamlet's unexpected letter to the king mocks the polite circumlocutions of the court style. Since the writer of the letter has
just escaped the death plot of the addressee, the porten-
tously respectful tone is meant to be taunting: " 'High
and mighty, you shall know I am set naked on your
kingdom. Tomorrow shall I beg leave to see your kingly
eyes; when I shall (first asking your pardon thereunto)
recount the occasion of my sudden and more strange
return' " (4.7.43-47). The begging of leave and the
"first asking your pardon thereunto" are fine strokes of
ironic subservience. "Thereunto" alone should identify
this letter as a parody—we might, in fact, separate all
of the characters in *Hamlet* into potential users or non-
users of the word "thereunto."

The other parody of Claudius is in Hamlet's spirited
account to Horatio of the wording of his forged "grand
commission":

An earnest conjuration from the King,
As England was his faithful tributary,
As love between them like the palm might flourish,
As peace should still her wheaten garland wear

And stand a comma 'tween their amities,
And many suchlike as's of great charge,
That on the view and knowing of these contents,
Without debatement further, more or less,
He should those bearers put to sudden death,
Not shriving time allowed.   (5.2.38-47)

The imagery is of the ornamental sort one might expect in a public proclamation, and each of the conditional particles marks another meaningless stipulation. The phrasing throughout is mock-legal, a series of empty formulas distilled from official documents. With the repetition of "as," Hamlet is at once parodying a recognizable feature of the king's style[15] and giving his forged commission an air of authenticity.

The two "bearers" of this "conjuration" "of great charge" are, of course, those serviceable "asses" Rosencrantz and Guildenstern, and Hamlet takes special delight in having overreached their shallow wits. They are much more workaday courtiers than the fantastic Osric, whose court rhetoric they echo, but stripped of all its entertaining flourishes. Hamlet never tires of twitting this ignoble pair of witlings. He is not just parodying their style; he is also mystifying them, since it is apparent that they have no comprehension either of wordplay or metaphor. "A knavish speech sleeps in a foolish ear"

---

[15] In Act IV, Scene vii, for example, Claudius uses "as" eight times: "as the star moves not but in his sphere" (15), "As how should it be so?" (58), "As checking at his voyage" (62), "As did that one" (75), "As had he been incorpsed" (87), "as many / As" (120-21), and "As make your bouts more violent to that end" (158).

(4.2.23-24), and "to be demanded of a sponge, what replication should be made by the son of a king?" (12-13). "Replication" is an exception of the second degree made by the plaintiff upon the answer of the defendant, being the third step in common pleadings.[16] This impressive legal word is much more likely to gain respect for "the son of a king" than the homely "reply" that it replaces.

It is difficult to make a complete survey of Hamlet's parodies, since he slips in and out of parody so quickly and so naturally. In the closet scene, for example, when Gertrude begins to "lay home" to her son and "be round with him" (3.4.1, 5), he defends himself and begins his attack on her by mimicking her lines. The effect is one of stilted, stichomythic echoing:

> *Queen.* Hamlet, thou hast thy father much offended.
> *Hamlet.* Mother, you have my father much offended.
> *Queen.* Come, come, you answer with an idle tongue.
> *Hamlet.* Go, go, you question with a wicked tongue.
>
> (3.4.10-13)

"Come, come" and "Go, go" are exactly parallel, but Hamlet answers his mother's familiar "thou" with the more formal "you."

In the swearing ceremony after the scene with the Ghost, Hamlet projects the response of his friends to his "antic disposition":

> That you, at such times seeing me, never shall
> With arms encumb'red thus, or this headshake,
> Or by pronouncing of some doubtful phrase,

[16] See *Variorum*, I, 315.

As "Well, well, we know," or "We could, an
    if we would,"
Or "If we list to speak," or "There be, an if they
    might,"
Or such ambiguous giving out, to note
That you know aught of me. . . .   (1.5.173-79)

The parody proceeds both by gesture ("With arms encumb'red thus, or this headshake") and by words, and
those cryptic, oracular phrases, pronounced with suitable
innuendo, show that Hamlet is also a master of the colloquial style.[17] The aftermath of the Ghost scene in
Hamlet is much more solemnly funny than is usually
thought, particularly "old mole" (162) crying "in the
cellarage" (151). Hamlet's "wild and whirling words"
(133) are neither so wild nor so whirling as we would
like to believe. He is outraged, hysterical, stirred to the
depths of his being by what the Ghost has said, but his
ability to parody it all is surely a sign of control rather
than of madness.

    There is probably much more parody of other works,
especially of other plays, in *Hamlet* and in all of Shakespeare than critics recognize. Along with the proponents

[17] The collection of speech fragments—"hard fractions"—in
this passage seems to be brilliantly echoed in Flavius' report of
the senators in *Timon of Athens*:

They answer, in a joint and corporate voice,
That now they are at fall, want treasure, cannot
Do what they would, are sorry—you are honourable—
But yet they could have wish'd—they know not—
Something hath been amiss—a noble nature
May catch a wrench—would all were well!—'tis pity—
                (2.2.204-9)

of dramatic collaboration, the topical allusionists have so discredited their field of investigation by their own excesses that we no longer think of these as respectable topics. Yet we know that *Hamlet* contains a good deal of local discussion of theatrical affairs at the turn of the century, and the Gravedigger's reference to Yaughan's tavern (5.1.61, Folio) is almost certainly to a familiar place on the Bankside near the Globe theater. The archaic style and manner of *The Murder of Gonzago* imitate old plays, so that it is just another step to identify these plays, as some commentators have done.[18] In the larger sense of the term, the play within the play is entirely a parody, as is also Aeneas' speech to Dido.

There are at least two examples of literary parody in Hamlet's part. His little song-poem after the play is a takeoff on *The Spanish Tragedy* (1587), which was one of the most parodied works of its time:

> For if the King like not the comedy,
> Why then, belike he likes it not, perdy.
>   (3.2.299-300)

> And if the world like not this tragedy,
> Hard is the hap of old Hieronimo.
>   (*The Spanish Tragedy* 4.1.197-98)[19]

Hamlet is amusing himself by calling *The Mousetrap* a comedy and by creating a nonsense line to fill out a rhymed couplet. Hieronimo's speech comes at the end

---

[18] See, for example, Kittredge, p. 224.

[19] Thomas Kyd, *The Spanish Tragedy*, ed. Philip Edwards, The Revels Plays (London, 1959), p. 108.

of a scene, in a place where we might expect a couplet. Since Hamlet refused to rhyme in his preceding poem (3.2.290), he can now gratuitously make his couplet contribution to Kyd's play.

There is another example of parody also provoked by *The Mousetrap*. While Lucianus is conscientiously "mugging" his part, Hamlet pricks him on to his proper duties: "Begin, murderer. Leave thy damnable faces and begin. Come, the croaking raven doth bellow for revenge" (3.2.258-60). The last line sounds like a prompter's cue, which R. Simpson has identified as a "satirical condensation" of two lines from *The True Tragedy of Richard III* (1591): "The screeking Rauen sits croking for reuenge./ Whole heards of beasts comes bellowing for reuenge."[20] We remember that Hamlet will not forgive the bad actor who "strutted and bellowed" (3.2.34), like Macbeth's "poor player,/ That struts and frets his hour upon the stage" (*Macbeth* 5.5. 24-25), or like Hamlet's own "outstretched heroes" (2. 2.268). We seem to discern echoes of the mysterious *Ur-Hamlet* that preceded Shakespeare's play, whose Ghost, according to Thomas Lodge, "cried so miserably at yᵉ Theator, like an oister wife, Hamlet, revenge."[21] In *Hamlet* proper the Ghost does not bellow at all, but only urges, with what might be taken as polite circumlocution, "Remember me" (1.5.91).

[20] Quoted from Wilson, p. 204; see also p. 205, and *What Happens in Hamlet*, pp. 161-62. The original text reads "heads."

[21] Quoted from Chambers, *William Shakespeare*, I, 411.

The Witty Style

Like parody, Hamlet's witty style is also exuberant and inventive, and its function is only partly pragmatic. Our assumptions about the rational quality of a play tend to exaggerate the purposiveness of dramatic speech. True, Hamlet puts "an antic disposition on" (1.5.172), as one might put on the fool's costume in order to claim the license and immunities of the role, but he is not always at work pursuing his ends. The Hamlet of the source story seems an altogether more enterprising and businesslike young man than Shakespeare's prince, who sometimes engages in free association, broken syntax, veiled innuendo, double-entendre, lyric extravagance, and nonstop wordplay for their own sake, as exercises of wit and recreations of the spirit. It need hardly be said that, rhetorically, Hamlet is not always acting in his own best interest.

Punning is the most direct expression of Hamlet's witty style;[22] it assumes that language is full of "springes to catch woodcocks" (1.3.115) and that "a knavish speech" may sleep "in a foolish ear" (4.2.23-24). Part of Hamlet's wordplay is playful self-expression, but the more significant part is biting and satirical. Among many possible examples, we may consider the extensive quibbling on "common" in Act I, Scene ii, which should also help us to distinguish Hamlet's sense of words from that of the king and queen.

When Gertrude provides "a back or second" (4.7.

[22] See Mahood, *Shakespeare's Wordplay*, whose perceptive comments are not limited to the discussion of puns.

153) to the cold comfort of Claudius, she offers her mourning son a well-meaning couplet platitude:

> Thou know'st 'tis common; all that lives must die,
> Passing through nature to eternity.   (1.2.72-73)

Surprisingly, Hamlet seems to assent: "Ay, madam, it is common" (74) —at least Gertrude's answer shows no awareness of wordplay: "If it be,/ Why seems it so particular with thee?" (74-75). We now have three distinct senses of "common": 1. death is the "common fate," the expected end of all men, in which 2. they share jointly as in a common stock corporation, but to Hamlet these religious commonplaces are 3. low, base, mean, vulgar, ordinary, and therefore disgusting. "Common" becomes a key word in Act I, Scene ii. Claudius is unaware of, or refuses to acknowledge, his stepson's pun, but he seems magnetically attracted to "common" in his next speech:

> For what we know must be and is as common
> As any the most vulgar thing to sense,
> Why should we in our peevish opposition
> Take it to heart?   (1.2.98-101)

Claudius is conveniently making the link for us between "common" and "vulgar," and he goes on to repeat Gertrude's truisms about mortality: nature's "common theme/ Is death of fathers" (103-4). The king is not a man to be overwhelmed by the death of those near and dear to him.

In the context of Act I, Scene ii, Hamlet would probably interpret the king's first words to him in a punning sense: "But now, my cousin Hamlet, and my son—"

(64). "Cousin" and "cozen" (to cheat, to conycatch) are homophones,[23] and we remember how disgusted Hamlet is by his uncle's "coz'nage" (5.2.67). In *Richard III*, Queen Elizabeth quibbles bitterly on Richard's murder of her children:

> King Richard. You speak as if that I had slain my
>   cousins.
> Queen Elizabeth. Cousins, indeed; and by their uncle
>   cozen'd
>   Of comfort, kingdom, kindred,
>   freedom, life.
>
>   (4.4.221-23)

Unlike "cousin" in its modern usage, the Elizabethan word is a general term for a family relationship more distant than brother or sister. If the "cousin-cozen" pun in *Hamlet* seems farfetched to us, we ought to keep in mind that Elizabethan playgoers were more sensitive to wordplay than we are and placed a much higher value on it as an expression of wit. The highly sophisticated spectator might test his verbal skill on Hamlet's "Seems, madam? Nay, it is. I know not 'seems.' " (1.2.76). Hamlet can distinguish between appearance and reality, the "seamy side" (*Othello* 4.2.147) from the fair outward garment; and "seam" also means hog's lard, as in the "rank sweat of an enseamèd bed" (3.4.93). I would not want to argue Shakespeare's intention in these two ex-

---

[23] See Walter W. Skeat, *A Concise Etymological Dictionary of the English Language* (New York, 1963), first published, 1882; Robert Nares, *A Glossary*, rev. J. O. Halliwell and Thomas Wright (London, 1905); and Eric Partridge, *A Dictionary of the Underworld* (New York, 1950), under "cousin."

amples, but punning is a reflex, and once the possibility of puns is acknowledged, the English language has so many multiple meanings that it is difficult to avoid wordplay.

"The pretended madness of Hamlet causes much mirth,"[24] observed Samuel Johnson, who was always on the lookout for amusement in Shakespeare. Hamlet's witty style is chiefly, but not exclusively, connected with his "mad" scenes. The obtuse objects of his satirical wit are sometimes dimly aware that they are being ridiculed. In the fishmonger dialogue, for example, Polonius knows that "Though this be madness, yet there is method in't" (2.2.207-8), and we are assured from other scenes that the lord chamberlain is a good judge of "method." He sums up Hamlet's witty style in an admiring aside: "How pregnant sometimes his replies are! A happiness that often madness hits on, which reason and sanity could not so prosperously be delivered of" (210-13). Hamlet's *répliques* are "pregnant" with significances beyond those of simple denotation, which he is "delivered of"—to complete the image—"prosperously" and with an intuitive rightness or "happiness." Polonius seems to be confessing that madness has some stylistic advantages over reason and sanity.

There is ample justification for Polonius' feeling of inadequacy in the fishmonger scene, where he becomes the "straight man" for Hamlet's wit, the one who feeds him the proper naïve and literal lines. Even so neutral a verbal formula as "My lord, I will take my leave of you" (215-16) stimulates one of Hamlet's most unfor-

[24] *Johnson's Notes to Shakespeare*, ed. Arthur Sherbo, p. 181.

gettable rejoinders: "You cannot take from me anything that I will more willingly part withal" (217-18). Hamlet's chief trick with Polonius is "like French falconers" to "fly at anything we see" (439-40), and his punning is relentless and unremitting. "Conception is a blessing, but as your daughter may conceive, friend, look to't" (185-87). The father is a "fishmonger" (174) for "a good kissing carrion" (182) as well as a fisher in Hamlet's own troubled waters. Hamlet's "matter" (195) may be either a legal dispute or "Words, words, words" (194) that reveal the physical decrepitude of old men, who cannot "like a crab . . . go backward" (205-6).

Besides Hamlet's own word for it, there is good evidence in the play that his "antic disposition" is deliberately "put on" (1.5.172). At a number of points, Hamlet changes suddenly from his normal to his "mad" style. Like Malevole in *The Malcontent* (1604), he *"shifteth his speech"* (1.4.43 s.d.),[25] a quick movement from verse to prose by which Marston marks the return to the malcontent's role. The verse-prose distinction is not so consistently maintained in *Hamlet*, but the shifts from mad to reasonable style are quite clear and were probably indicated on stage by a change of voice. At the entrance of Polonius, for example, Hamlet adopts a different tone from the one he has been using with Rosencrantz and Guildenstern, and he even takes the trouble to explain to them what he is doing: "I will prophesy he comes to tell me of the players. Mark it.—You say right, sir; a Monday morning, 'twas then indeed" (2.2.395-97).

[25] Marston, *The Malcontent*, ed. M. L. Wine, p. 26. See Levin, *The Question of Hamlet*, pp. 117-18.

"Prophesy" is an amusingly portentous word that seems to carry Hamlet right into his mantic vaticination about Monday morning.

In the play scene he warns Horatio of an imminent change in his discourse: "They are coming to the play: I must be idle;/ Get you a place" (3.2.92-93). "Idle" means foolish, vain, frivolous, thoughtless, and absurd, qualities bred by inactivity and lack of employment. Like Touchstone and other professional fools, Hamlet "uses his folly like a stalking-horse, and under the presentation of that he shoots his wit" (*As You Like It* 5.4. 100-1). From his pretended madness he gains the satirical license of the allowed fool, so that he can goad the king and queen freely with his barbs.

Hamlet's frantic gaiety before and during the play is a kind of entertainment in its own right, a calculated exacerbation. He is "merry" (3.2.125), as Ophelia says, since he must counteract the pompous formalities of the tragedy now playing. Hamlet has a more difficult role than any of the professional actors, but he carries it off with wonderful aplomb. In Francis Fergusson's description, Hamlet acts "as showman, as master of ceremonies, as clown, as night-club entertainer who lewdly jokes with the embarrassed patrons."[26] The improvisation belongs to a prepared part, but it is never more invincibly right than in this scene. He is also, of course, amusing himself and Horatio with his stylistic virtuosity, as in his alliterative line that anticipates the style of the old play: "Marry, this is miching mallecho; it means mischief" (142-43). In this context, Hamlet's auditors were

[26] Fergusson, *The Idea of a Theater*, p. 134.

as likely to be mystified by the foreign word "mallecho"
as we are.

Hamlet's witty style runs throughout the play, and it
is associated not only with his supposed madness, but
also with scenes of heightened emotion, as in his "wild
and whirling words" (1.5.133) after the revelations of
the Ghost, and in his lyric exclamatory speeches and
songs after the success of *The Mousetrap*. The most neglected witty sequence is Scenes ii and iii of Act IV,
where there is an ironic contrast between Hamlet's present status—"Without, my lord; guarded, to know your
pleasure" (4.3.14), as Rosencrantz puts it—and his absolute self-assurance. With colloquial mockery, he taunts
the king and his court, whose only defense is to pretend
not to understand. In Hamlet's talk with Rosencrantz
and Guildenstern, he steadfastly refuses to answer their
questions with anything except "pregnant" nonsense.
Rosencrantz begins: "What have you done, my lord,
with the dead body?" (4.2.5), to which Hamlet replies
as the pharmacist-preacher: "Compounded it with dust,
whereto 'tis kin" (6). It is, in fact, "A little more than
kin" to dust, being dead, "and less than kind" (1.2.65),
no longer being in the natural state of the living.

Hamlet seems to be energetically devoting himself in
these scenes to making "the galled jade winch" (3.2.
248), while brazenly asserting how "unwrung" (249)
his own withers are. He taunts Rosencrantz with a doggerel riddle: "The body is with the King, but the King
is not with the body. The King is a thing—" (4.2.27-28).
Does Hamlet mean that Polonius' body is with the
King of Kings rather than with the king of Denmark? Or

that the king of Denmark is not yet with the body of Polonius, but will shortly be? If the "King is a thing," he cannot also be a person, and therefore is already kin to dusty matter. These portentous little truisms may have whatever meaning we may choose to give them; Hamlet merely wants to twit Rosencrantz and Guildenstern for their stupid questions. Guildenstern's only contribution to this scene is his shock at Hamlet's treasonous words: "A thing, my lord?" (29), which Hamlet undercuts with another paradox: "Of nothing. Bring me to him" (30). As Laertes says of his mad sister's songs: "This nothing's more than matter" (4.5.173).[27]

With Claudius, Hamlet is so much at his ease that he can enjoy the perturbation into which he has thrown the court by killing Polonius. To undermine the official interrogation, Hamlet makes jokes at Claudius' expense. At the king's second demand, "Where is Polonius?" (4.3.32), Hamlet seems to be delivering a factual answer: "In heaven. Send thither to see. If your messenger find him not there, seek him i' th' other place yourself" (33-35). There is an implication that the king's messenger service is as extensive as his spy system. To cap it off, Hamlet mocks the king's officious haste in dispatching his attendants: "'A will stay till you come" (39). Hamlet has presented the king with

[27] See Rosalie L. Colie, *Paradoxia Epidemica* (Princeton: Princeton University Press, 1966), esp. Chap. 7: "'Nothing is but what is not': Solutions to the Problem of Nothing." Miss Colie explores the sexual implications of "thing," "nothing," and "something." There is possible wordplay on "nothing-noting," which were homophones in Shakespeare's time; see Kökeritz, *Shakespeare's Pronunciation*, pp. 132, 233, and 320.

his own little graveyard scene, with some menacing hints about his imminent arrival there. In a final thrust, Hamlet bids farewell to him as "dear Mother" (49), since "man and wife is one flesh" (52), another satirical reminder of Claudius' method of usurpation. It would be wrong to call Hamlet bitter in this scene. He is clownish, antic, grotesque, in high spirits, and very unconstrained, even though he is now under guard and about to be shipped to his death in England. It is this self-possession of Hamlet's witty style that makes Claudius so powerfully uneasy, even in a moment of seeming victory: "Till I know 'tis done,/ Howe'er my haps, my joys were ne'er begun" (67-68).

Hamlet's witty style is put directly to the test only once, in the scene with the Clown-gravedigger, and we have the impression that the prince cannot stand up to the Clown's intransigent punning and logic-chopping, so reminiscent of Shakespeare's earliest comedies. The Clown must always have the final word in each of his quid pro quos, but he is slow and plodding about it and does not mean to rush the triumph of his mother wit over a gentleman. With amused exasperation, Hamlet acknowledges his defeat: "How absolute the knave is! We must speak by the card, or equivocation will undo us" (5.1.139-40). Hamlet's words have strong moral connotations, especially "equivocation," so important a term for the "juggling fiends" of *Macbeth* (5.8.19). The "card" is the compass card, by whose thirty-two points sailors steer, but Hamlet has never been one to speak so mathematically.

The Clown, however, has been putting him on his

mettle, completing the prince's education as a wit. The representative hero of this scene is Yorick, old Hamlet's fool, "a fellow of infinite jest, of most excellent fancy," who was "wont to set the table on a roar" (5.1.186-87, 192-93). It is Yorick's skull that Hamlet holds in his hand and contemplates, as if to absorb some part of that "infinite jest" in order to prepare himself for the final encounter with his enemies.

The Passionate Style

"Passion" and "passionate" are complex words in Elizabethan English, and *Hamlet* makes more significant use of them than does any other play of Shakespeare. When Hamlet asks the First Player for a "taste of your quality," he specifies "a passionate speech" (2.2.441-42). Here passion is the strong emotion aroused by Pyrrhus' relentless revenge, Priam's pitiful slaughter, and Hecuba's withering grief. In the Player's speech, the death of old Priam "Would have made milch the burning eyes of heaven/ And passion in the gods" (528-29). "The burning eyes of heaven" are presumably the stars, now weeping tears in a conceited analogy with the Milky Way, but the normally calm and dispassionate gods would themselves be moved to compassion as the First Player is, with "tears in's eyes" (531), for what Hamlet calls merely "a fiction" and "a dream of passion" (562). "Passion" in its general sense is any vehement, commanding, or overpowering emotion; in its more restricted sense it means violent sorrow. Thus, the Player Queen *"makes passionate action"* when she *"finds the King dead"* (3.2.140 s.d.).

According to Renaissance psychology, the passions are a basic human faculty, subordinate but necessary to the reason, which provides the motive force for human actions.[28] This doctrine is neatly summarized in the Player King's couplet:

What to ourselves in passion we propose,
The passion ending, doth the purpose lose.

(3.2.200-1)

Hamlet's apology to the Ghost for being "lapsed in time and passion" (3.4.108) is based on the same notion, because revenge is not possible without a motivating "passion." This is the vital human quality that the Stoics were mistakenly trying to dispense with, since the efficient cause for all acts of the will, even virtuous ones, is the prior perturbation of the passions. We may conclude that passion is an ambivalent quality that, depending upon the degree of rational control, may produce either emotionally powerful expression or self-indulgent and histrionic rant.

Hamlet's passionate style is chiefly associated with his soliloquies, which are the most misunderstood stylistic feature of the play. According to the traditional view, as stated by Dowden, they are "the utterance of thought in solitude,"[29] but it seems to me that neither thought nor solitude—with all their connotations of Romantic

[28] See Lily B. Campbell, *Shakespeare's Tragic Heroes: Slaves of Passion* (New York, 1959), esp. Chap. 6. First published by Cambridge University Press, 1930.

[29] Edward Dowden, *Shakspere: A Critical Study of His Mind and Art* (New York, 1881), p. 111. See also the passage from Lamb on page xxi of the Introduction.

lyric poetry—are properly relevant to the dramatic soliloquy.[30] It is admittedly a private as opposed to a public expression, and it is spoken by a character on stage,
as if to himself, but we must remember that it is intended to be overheard by the audience and is a form
of direct address to that audience. This is hardly "solitude." Rather than expressing "thought" in our modern
sense of discursive reasoning, the soliloquy in *Hamlet*
is used primarily to give free vent to emotions that must
otherwise be suppressed. It is this passionate, emotional
quality that makes the soliloquy so different in kind
from other speeches.

Stylistically, soliloquy represents a radical departure
from the norm of dramatic dialogue, so that there is
special need to make a smooth transition from one to
the other. Shakespeare usually takes pains to create a
credible situation for the soliloquy, especially in Act I,
Scene ii, where the context is carefully developed in
relation to the speech that will follow. Although this is
Hamlet's first appearance in the play, he speaks only
fifteen lines before his soliloquy. He must listen with
ill-concealed disgust to the new king's platitudes about
mourning, while the gay court, including his mother,
takes up its business again as if the elder Hamlet had
never existed. Four of Hamlet's speeches in this scene
are "one-liners": "A little more than kin, and less than
kind!" (65), spoken aside; "Not so, my lord. I am too

[30] See the perceptive comments on the Romantic interpretation
of soliloquy in Robert Langbaum, *The Poetry of Experience*
(New York, 1963), Chap. 5: "Character versus Action in Shakespeare." First published, 1957.

much in the sun" (67); "Ay, madam, it is common"
(74); and "I shall in all my best obey you, madam"
(120). Hamlet also speaks eleven lines on the theme of
appearance and reality: "Seems, madam? Nay, it is . . ."
(76-86), which Claudius tactfully ignores. Hamlet's
brooding passivity in this scene provides the context for
his first soliloquy.[31] Like Cordelia, he understands how
to be an outcast from fashionable pieties: "Love, and be
silent" (*King Lear* 1.1.61). By the time the king and
queen and their followers exit with a flourish at line 128,
Hamlet is ready to burst into a torrent of passionate
words.

Hamlet's soliloquy is entirely different from the artful oration of Claudius at the beginning of this scene,
with its complex syntax, epigrammatic wit, and calculated antitheses. Hamlet is not artless, but his speech
avoids any effects of the polished style. There is a good
deal of variety in the rhythms and irregularity in the
meter, and Hamlet tries to give the impression of a natural, emotional utterance that follows the winding turns
of thought. There is a passionate insistence on the brief
interval of time, "A little month" (1.2.147), between
the death of Hamlet's father and the remarriage of his
mother. This is the leitmotif of the soliloquy, the gross
reality that dominates Hamlet's disgust and also dominates the syntax by a series of parenthetical reminders:

[31] Ophelia is in a similarly constrained situation in Act I,
Scene iii, as she listens to the homilies of her brother and father.
Of the 136 lines in the scene, she speaks only 13 full lines and 8
part-lines; up to line 45 she says only, "Do you doubt that?" (4)
and "No more but so?" (10). Unlike Hamlet in the previous
scene, she has no soliloquy to release her pent-up emotions.

Why, she would hang on him
As if increase of appetite had grown
By what it fed on; and yet within a month—
Let me not think on't; frailty, thy name is woman—
A little month, or ere those shoes were old
With which she followed my poor father's body
Like Niobe, all tears, why she, even she—
O God, a beast that wants discourse of reason
Would have mourned longer—married with my uncle,
My father's brother, but no more like my father
Than I to Hercules. Within a month,
Ere yet the salt of most unrighteous tears
Had left the flushing in her gallèd eyes,
She married. (1.2.143-56)

The modern dashes indicate breaks in the syntax that would be expressed by the actor's changes of voice, tone, and tempo. Hamlet's passion develops in this soliloquy through these repetitions, emphasized by the abrupt shifts in the rhythm.

It is interesting to note that in the "very torrent, tempest, and . . . whirlwind" (3.2.6) of Hamlet's soliloquy, his disgust turns fetishistically to his mother's shoes —"A little month, or ere those shoes were old" (1.2. 147). We can imagine him brooding on those shoes during his long silence in this scene, as his "vailèd lids" seek for his "noble father in the dust" (70-71).

Hamlet's trick of doubling and tripling his words,[32] a

[32] Hamlet's repetition of words is probably not so distinctive a feature of his style as Bradley thought (*Shakespearean Tragedy*, pp. 148-49). See also Levin, *The Question of Hamlet*, p. 49, and Wilson, *The Manuscript of Shakespeare's Hamlet*, I, 79-82. Many

rhetorical device that encourages the feeling of insistent stress, is evident in this soliloquy. He begins with a wish for his "too too solid flesh" to "melt,/ Thaw, and resolve itself into a dew" (1.2.129-30), as if he lacked words to express his longing for nothingness, like Dr. Faustus' ardent desire for his soul to "be chang'd into little water drops,/ And fall into the ocean, ne'er be found."[33] Hamlet exclaims "O God, God" (132) and "Fie on't, ah, fie" (135) to double the effect of his disgust. "That it should come to this" (137) is paralleled in form by the briefer "that was to this" (139). There is nagging colloquial energy in the line: "But two months dead, nay, not so much, not two" (138), that turns on its negative axis. A similarly nervous and rhythmically harsh line is: "Like Niobe, all tears, why she, even she—" (149). This uses the familiar figure of incredulous repetition, but Hamlet manages to make it convincing by the emotional pressure behind it.

The soliloquy proper ends at that decisive line: "It is

---

of Hamlet's most familiar doublets and triplets occur only in the Folio text and are quite possibly playhouse interpolations. See Harold Jenkins, "Playhouse Interpolations in the Folio Text of *Hamlet*," *Studies in Bibliography*, XIII (1960), 31-47. There seems to be a consistent pattern in Folio of the expansion of words and the economizing of actors. The difficult question of "*how* additions and deviations of the players came to be incorporated" in the Folio text still remains to be answered, as Jenkins acknowledges (p. 47). As an addendum to this topic, it is worth noting that the Ghost has a striking number of triplets in its speech in Act I, Scene v, as this speech appears in the Quarto 2 text.

[33] Christopher Marlowe, *Doctor Faustus*, ed. John D. Jump, The Revels Plays (London, 1962), Scene xix, 185-86.

not, nor it cannot come to good" (158). By the next line, "But break my heart, for I must hold my tongue" (159), Hamlet already sees Horatio, Marcellus, and Barnardo approaching. It is a warning to himself to put on the mask of silence or falsely ceremonial speech; he needs to guard himself lest he utter the passionate truths of his first soliloquy, and it is this constraint that he fears will cause his heart to "break."

We may also see Hamlet's passionate style at work in what is acknowledged to be his most meditative speech in the play: "To be, or not to be" (3.1.56ff.).[34] One of the difficulties in diagramming the argument of this soliloquy arises from its sinuous, emotional logic, which proceeds by verbal association rather than by a formal, preconceived plan. In the first ten lines, for example, the infinitives perpetuate themselves in an orderly sequence: "To be, or not to be" (56); "to suffer" (57) "Or to take arms" (59); "To die, to sleep—" (60) and "to say we end" (61); "Devoutly to be wished.[35] To die, to sleep—" (64); "To sleep—perchance to dream" (65). After these dozen infinitives, there is only one more ("To grunt and sweat") in the next twenty-five lines.

[34] See the full commentary on this soliloquy in Irving T. Richards, "The Meaning of Hamlet's Soliloquy," *PMLA*, XLVIII (1933), 741-66. See also C. C. Clarke, "A Note on 'To be or not to be,'" *Essays in Criticism*, X (1960), 18-23, and Alex Newell, "The Dramatic Context and Meaning of Hamlet's 'To be or not to be' Soliloquy," *PMLA*, LXXX (1965), 38-50.

[35] There is much to be said for the lighter punctuation of Quarto 2 that Wilson follows here and elsewhere in this speech. Quarto 2 runs together "wished" and "To die" without any punctuation at all, which does better justice than Folio to the soliloquy's improvisational quality.

The form is discarded for other methods of organization. One of the effects of all the infinitives is to suspend both the syntax and rhythm in a way not possible in the indicative mood. This is what gives the beginning of the soliloquy its unforgettably slow and lingering quality.

Two long questions of exactly six and a half lines each make up the central section. These are questions with a set of vivid examples to illustrate what it means to "bear the whips and scorns of time" (70), those avenging lashes of Hieronimo's speech in *The Spanish Tragedy*:

> Well, heaven is heaven still,
> And there is Nemesis and Furies,
> And things call'd whips. . . .   (3.11.40-42) [36]

But in Hamlet's speech the "fardels" one must "bear" (3.1.76) are all unjustly laid on; they are "the spurns/ That patient merit of th' unworthy takes" (73-74),

> Th' oppressor's wrong, the proud man's contumely,
> The pangs of despised love, the law's delay,
> The insolence of office. . . .   (3.1.71-73)

The examples draw their eloquence from the realities of the play.

Hamlet is setting the known evils of this life against the unknown "dread of something after death" (78), just as Ophelia says mysteriously: "Lord, we know what we are, but know not what we may be" (4.5.43-44), and the Player King traces a process in which

[36] Kyd, *The Spanish Tragedy*, ed. Philip Edwards, p. 126 (The Third Addition).

Our wills and fates do so contrary run
That our devices still are overthrown;
Our thoughts are ours, their ends none of our own.

(3.2.217-19)

Hamlet is here "thinking too precisely on th' event"
(4.4.41), or, as Horatio tells him: " 'Twere to consider
too curiously, to consider so" (5.1.207-8). He is trying
to understand why he will not make "his quietus . . ./
With a bare bodkin" (3.1.75-76). In a practical sense
the soliloquy is about suicide, or the rejection of suicide,
although this is only part of a larger discourse.

The consideration of "something after death" "puzzles the will" (3.1.78,80), so that one's passionate arguments cannot lead to any clear-cut decision. "Puzzles"
was a much stronger and rarer word in Shakespeare's
time than it is today. It meant perplexes, confounds, be-
wilders, puts in a maze, as Enobarbus tells Cleopatra
that her presence in battle "needs must puzzle Antony"
(*Antony and Cleopatra* 3.7.10) and thereby destroy
him, and as Feste the clown mystifies the supposedly
mad Malvolio by informing him that "there is no darkness but ignorance; in which thou art more puzzled than
the Egyptians in their fog" (*Twelfth Night* 4.2.41-43).

The end of Hamlet's soliloquy is deliberately anticlimactic and unsatisfactory:

> Thus conscience does make cowards of us all,
> And thus the native hue of resolution
> Is sicklied o'er with the pale cast of thought,
> And enterprises of great pitch and moment,
> With this regard their currents turn awry,
> And lose the name of action.   (3.1.83-88)

"Thus," "And thus," and "With this regard" are all terms of a logical conclusion in which nothing can be concluded. The resolution of this soliloquy does not occur until the last scene of the play, in which Hamlet has come to understand the wisdom of "rashness" (5. 2.7) : "Our indiscretion sometime serves us well / When our deep plots do pall" (8-9) . Once he has arrived at this point, he no longer needs to soliloquize.

The crucial fact of the soliloquy is that the dramatic character is alone on stage, or believes himself to be, so that he can take stock of his situation, appraise his own motives, release his pent-up feelings, or even—despite the assumption that all soliloquies are sincere—indulge in wish-fulfillment roles. Hamlet does all of these things in different soliloquies, and Wolfgang Clemen has recently called our attention to the "new kind of dramatic speech" evident in them, "which by its rapid transitions, its dissolution of syntax, its extraordinary economy and its fusion of several emotions and ideas can follow the quickly changing reactions of a sensitive mind better than speech in dialogue ever could."[37] If there is thought in the sense of reflection, especially the weighing of alternative courses of action, it is the sort of passionate thought that attempts to follow the psychological turns of an argument as it presents itself in the mind, with all of its inconsequentiality, repetition, intrusive irrelevance, lack of sequence, hesitation, and broken syntax. In other words, Hamlet's soliloquies are

[37] Wolfgang Clemen, "Shakespeare's Soliloquies," The Presidential Address of the Modern Humanities Research Association (Cambridge, Eng.: Cambridge University Press, 1964), p. 22.

dramatically conceived. They are by no means the direct expression of Shakespeare's own views, and their importance as the soul of the play has been grossly exaggerated.

The Simple Style

Hamlet's simple style is not very extensive, and Shakespeare is following good precedent in using simplicity not as a general style, but for certain special effects. A lucid and unadorned style was not, in the Renaissance, thought to have the virtues it has since acquired, especially because it conflicted with the wit and eloquence expected from persons trained in classical rhetoric. Some of the characteristics of this style are a strongly monosyllabic diction without wordplay, a natural syntax of the subject-verb-object kind that avoids subordination, and a literal, nonfigurative discourse. Not all of these qualities are always present, but the purpose of the style is to speak perspicuously and to make all clear.

It lends itself especially to heroic assertion, as in Hamlet's resolution to accompany the Ghost that "beckons" (1.4.58) to him: "It will not speak. Then I will follow it" (63). The Ghost continues its beckoning, and Hamlet repeats his intention: "It waves me forth again. I'll follow it" (68). At the next repetition, Hamlet addresses the Ghost directly: "It waves me still./ Go on; I'll follow thee" (78-79), and just before he exits, after breaking away from his friends, he asserts yet once more: "I say, away! Go on. I'll follow thee" (86). The style is unusual for Hamlet because it is so straightforward and literal, but Shakespeare wants to impress us in a very early scene with his hero's incontrovertible will.

Another effect of the simple style in these early scenes is to create an atmosphere of uncertainty and anxious anticipation. This is most brilliantly accomplished at the opening of the play. The abrupt part-lines set the mood for the first appearance of the Ghost, whose stylistic effect in Act I is to make everyone speak with exceptional brevity, if not curtness. We may see this truncated style at its best when Hamlet questions Horatio (and Marcellus and Barnardo) about the Ghost. His series of short questions, mixed with a few equally brief assertions, conveys an uncanny sense of foreboding: "Saw? Who?" (1.2.190); "The King my father?" (191); "For God's love let me hear!" (195); "But where was this?" (212); "Did you not speak to it?" (214); "'Tis very strange" (220). I am giving all of Hamlet's words in order not to falsify the impression his speech makes, which is radically different from that of his usual stylistic invention.

Hamlet continues: "Indeed, indeed, sirs, but this troubles me./ Hold you the watch tonight?" (224-25); "Armed, say you?" (226); "From top to toe?" (228); "Then saw you not his face" (229); "What, looked he frowningly?" (231); "Pale or red?" (233); "And fixed his eyes upon you?" (234); "I would I had been there" (235); "Very like, very like. Stayed it long?" (237); "His beard was grizzled, no?" (240); "I will watch tonight./ Perchance 'twill walk again" (242-43). This kind of dialogue has no intrinsic eloquence, but develops its persuasiveness from the dramatic context. The colloquial skill of these part-lines is also worth remarking, especially in line 240: "His beard was grizzled, no?"

The role of narration in Shakespearean tragedy has never been fully studied, although Francis Berry has recently presented some original speculations about narrative "insets."[38] The simple style lends itself admirably to narration. It can convey a large body of factual material quickly and lucidly, and it can also create the impression of actual speech and thus encourage a sense of credibility in what is being said. These effects are very different from those of the rhetorically heightened style of Senecan tragedy, in which the formality of the presentation works against any feeling of verisimilitude. The use of narration may, in fact, offer a meaningful comparison between Shakespeare and Seneca, since the tragedies of Seneca rely so significantly on reports of action, usually violent, that has already taken place offstage. Elizabethan audiences, however, liked to savor their violence directly, so that there is not the same need in Shakespeare as there is in Seneca for highly colored, emotional narratives. The Player's speech about the death of Priam is, of course, an exception, but Shakespeare is successfully imitating Seneca's trick of combining frantic sensationalism in the subject matter with the almost excessive control of a highly wrought style.

One of the most effective narrations in *Hamlet* is the hero's account of the exciting events of his sea voyage to England. In the swift prose of Hamlet's letter to

[38] See Francis Berry, *The Shakespeare Inset*, esp. Chap. 8 on *Hamlet*.

Horatio, he tells his friend enough both to satisfy his immediate curiosity and to whet his appetite for more details: "Ere we were two days old at sea, a pirate of very warlike appointment gave us chase. Finding ourselves too slow of sail, we put on a compelled valor, and in the grapple I boarded them. On the instant they got clear of our ship; so I alone became their prisoner" (4.6.15-21). This is free of wordplay, except possibly in the first clause, and it has the breezy and businesslike pace of prose narratives in the voyage literature. We see Hamlet in an entirely new light, as a romantic adventurer at sea, who appeals to us, like Othello, to love him "for the dangers" he "had pass'd" (*Othello* 1.3.167). The urgency of Hamlet's return does not allow for leisurely expatiation; Horatio is to "repair" to him in his hiding place "with as much speed as thou wouldest fly death" (4.6.24-25). The letter ends with another triumphant piece of information: "Rosencrantz and Guildenstern hold their course for England. Of them I have much to tell thee. Farewell" (28-30). As we can see in the phrase "hold their course," the simple style also offers possibilities for ironic understatement: the king's agents pursue their doom with tenacity and unshakable determination!

Hamlet's exuberance has fuller scope for its expression in the scene with Horatio, which, like Act IV, Scene vii, begins vigorously in the midst of a conversation: "So much for this, sir; now shall you see the other" (5.2.1). By the laws of dramatic grammar, "this" has a nonexistent, offstage referent. There is a fine sense of actual speech:

Hamlet. You do remember all the circumstance?
Horatio. Remember it, my lord!   (5.2.2-3)

Horatio's answer is the equivalent either of "How could I forget it?" or "How could you ask me such a question?".

Hamlet's narration in this scene is more self-consciously ironic than that of his letter, but it is still primarily in the simple style. Like many another adventure story, it begins with the inability to sleep: "Sir, in my heart there was a kind of fighting/ That would not let me sleep" (4-5). The steps in Hamlet's counter-conspiracy are marked by active verbs:

> Up from my cabin,
> My sea gown scarfed about me, in the dark
> Groped I to find out them, had my desire,
> Fingered their packet, and in fine withdrew
> To mine own room again, making so bold,
> My fears forgetting manners, to unseal
> Their grand commission. . . .   (5.2.12-18)

This is all one breathless sentence that begins at line 12 and continues through line 25, for which we need to recreate the actor's suspension of the parts in telling the story. Although the words themselves convey a tactile impression—"Groped," "Fingered"—there are no rhetorical embellishments to slow down the pace of the narrative.

Hamlet takes a good deal of satisfaction in his own resourceful cleverness, which is proof to him that he can act decisively as well as cunningly. In his enthusiasm to give Horatio all the details—and to preserve the illusion of dramatic dialogue in the midst of narration—he asks his friend two very teasing questions: "But wilt thou hear now how I did proceed?" (27) and "Wilt thou know/ Th' effect of what I wrote?" (36-37). Horatio, of course, says what is expected of him: "I beseech you" (28) and "Ay, good my lord" (37), but at the next natural pause, it is he who provides the continuity: "How was this sealed?" (47).

One of the effects of the simple style in this scene is to create a sense of colloquial verisimilitude, as in Hamlet's statement: "I sat me down,/ Devised a new commission, wrote it fair" (31-32). The abbreviated speech syntax can dispense with grammatical connectives. In fact, some of Hamlet's periods in this scene are anacolutha, which don't make sense grammatically, but which raise no difficulties at all in their spoken form. The sentence beginning "Rashly" (6) is never completed, but seems to be continued in the verbs of Hamlet's next speech. Later on, Hamlet begins a question which is suddenly broken and then begun again:

> Does it not, think thee, stand me now upon—
> He that hath killed my king, and whored my mother,
> Popped in between th' election and my hopes,
> Thrown out his angle for my proper life,
> And with such coz'nage—is't not perfect conscience
> To quit him with this arm?   (5.2.63-68)

This passage also uses a series of strong monosyllabic verbs—"killed," "whored," "Popped"—to emphasize direct action, and the breaks in syntax give the impression that certain things must be said that override the requirements of formal grammar.

The most significant use of the simple style in *Hamlet*, and in all of Shakespeare's tragedies, is to create a sense of tragic calm, a kind of tranquil self-assurance, at climactic moments in the action. Where another dramatist might be inclined to heighten the crises of his play, Shakespeare deliberately frustrates our natural expectations of grandeur. He seems to be working toward a feeling of quiet that will transcend mere pity for the inevitable tragic doom. I find this effect most powerfully achieved in *King Lear*, in a series of monosyllabic lines toward the end of the play: "You do me wrong to take me out o' th' grave" (4.7.45) ; "Be your tears wet? Yes, faith. I pray weep not" (4.7.71) ; "Why should a dog, a horse, a rat have life,/ And thou no breath at all? Thou'lt come no more" (5.3.306-7). There is an extraordinary defiance of the art of rhetoric in these monosyllables, as if Shakespeare could no longer rely on the truthfulness of anything except the simplest expressions. "Pray you undo this button" (5.3.309) is one of the most moving lines in the play, just because Shakespeare is so deliberately scorning eloquence in Lear's death speech. The gesture that accompanies the line helps to insure its poignancy.

There are no simple effects in *Hamlet* of the same intensity as those in *Lear*, yet there is one passage that comes very close. It occurs just before the catastrophe of the play and right after the stylistic extravaganza with Osric. Hamlet has now agreed to the fencing match with Laertes, but he has a sense of fateful "gaingiving" (5.

2.217) that Horatio confirms: "You will lose this wager, my lord" (210). The rational Horatio offers to make excuses for him, but if Hamlet wishes to "defy augury" (220), he must refuse Horatio's sensible intervention and, like Caesar, "go forth" (*Julius Caesar* 2.2.28). Hamlet answers Horatio with an amusing jingle, "Not a whit" (5.2.220), that completes "you are not fit," but his prose apologia is absolutely straightforward and simple: "There is special providence in the fall of a sparrow. If it be now, 'tis not to come; if it be not to come, it will be now; if it be not now, yet it will come. The readiness is all. Since no man of aught he leaves knows, what is't to leave betimes? Let be" (220-25). "The readiness is all" matches Edgar's "Ripeness is all" in *King Lear* (5.2.11) in both sound and sense, as many commentators have pointed out, but Hamlet's series of twenty-seven monosyllables is unique. The eloquence of these vatic phrases grows out of a new sense of tranquillity in Hamlet. Ever since his "rashness" (5.2.7) on the sea voyage proved to him that heaven is "ordinant" (48), he has ceased to struggle against his fate. If "The readiness is all," then time present and time "to come" —"now or whensoever" (204)—are both equally significant, and the only wisdom is, as Florio translates Montaigne, "to learne how to die." The final two monosyllables, "Let be," are among Hamlet's most memorable words. They are meant to tell Horatio that all persuasion is vain, and they are also a farewell to Hamlet's tumultuous past.

The next line in the play is the king's: "Come, Hamlet, come, and take this hand from me" (226), while he treacherously reconciles the swordsman with his victim. "Let be" echoes in Hamlet's speech after he has been mortally wounded. Had he but time now and could forestall "this fell sergeant, Death" (337), he could a tale unfold—"But let it be" (339). That, too, can no longer be a part of any mortal concern. Hamlet's simple style has a clairvoyance in it in this final scene. He is moving away from complexities and perturbations of thought as well as of language, so that his very last words—if we exclude the "O, o, o, o" of Folio[39]—have an ironic appropriateness for a discussion of style: "the rest is silence" (359).

[39] Editors agree unanimously in rejecting these quadruple "O" groans as a playhouse interpolation, although they are generally skeptical about most of the other items on Jenkins' list (see note 32, above). In the Pied Bull Quarto (1608) of *King Lear*, the next to the last speech of Lear concludes: "O thou wilt come no more, never, never, never, pray you undo this button, thank you sir, O, o, o, o" (Shakespeare Quarto Facsimiles, Number 1, ed. W. W. Greg [London: Oxford University Press, 1939]). The dying O's seem to be a characteristic flourish of Richard Burbage that somehow found its way into the copy used by the printer. See Wilson, *The Manuscript of Shakespeare's Hamlet*, I, 77-82.

Conclusion

SOME APOLOGY is due to the reader for presenting what might appear to be a fragmented, analytic approach to *Hamlet*. I am conscious of the fact that I seem to be taking the play apart, under various pretexts, and never putting it together again. I am not trying to demonstrate a new nominalist approach to Shakespeare, but only attempting to work out rigorously and in detail the style of *Hamlet*.

The vast pyramid of literature on the play is directed to "what happens in *Hamlet*" and what the characters are like. It is essentially concerned with what I would call subject matter. Hamlet's delay in taking revenge, for example, is a favorite topic, and, in good exegetical fashion, passages are quoted from the play either to support or to deny the validity of this interpretation. If, however, we look at *Hamlet* stylistically (that is, not in terms of its subject matter, but in the way that subject matter is represented or symbolized), then delay does not seem to be a significant topic. Even with good will, one cannot find a meaningful expression of delay embodied either in the imagery or in any other recognizable imaginative form.[1] Thus, my commitment to the style of *Hamlet* is a consciously restricted point of view, which may offer some justification for excluding any talk about general "issues" of the play.

[1] But see Robert Hapgood, *"Hamlet* Nearly Absurd: The Dramaturgy of Delay," *Tulane Drama Review*, IX (1965), 132-45. It seems to me that Hapgood's speculations do not have a distinctive application to *Hamlet*.

I am convinced that there is now a pressing need to restore *Hamlet* criticism to the play *Hamlet,* and to dispel the feeling among cultivated persons that it is a convenient exercise book for intellectual divagations. *Style in "Hamlet"* insists not only that we read the play closely, but also that we try to place it in its theatrical context. In this sense, the section on staging and structure makes the strongest demands on the reader to think of the play as a performance both in Shakespeare's Globe and in the modern theater. Some readers are likely to be alarmed by this strenuous insistence that *Hamlet* is a play, which would immediately preclude certain kinds of psychological and lyric criticism. All genres impose limitations within which an author must work, but these limitations may also offer characteristic excellences—it is the old paradox of difficulty overcome. One of the functions of a critic of Shakespeare, it seems to me, is to pursue the distinctively dramatic means of expression in his plays. This is the subject of Part Two, in which I attempt to relate gesture and stage action, sound effects and music, costumes, stage properties, and the technique of scenic construction to the style of *Hamlet.*

Although I have not tried to draw conclusions about *Hamlet,* my own point of view is strongly implied by the emphasis on certain topics rather than others. In the section on imagery, for example, I have chosen to begin with war, weapons, and explosives because I believe that *Hamlet* is a much more active and energetic play than do those critics who stress disease. I do not recoil from the notion that *Hamlet* may be, in part at least, unpleasant and disturbing, full of secrecy, poison, exploding weapons, and lacerating aggression. If there is a strong sense of disease, as is generally acknowledged, it is a hidden disease, craftily concealed, that "inward breaks, and shows no cause without/ Why the man dies" (4.4.28-29). When restored to its context, the Romantic corruption that has been attributed to *Hamlet* is found to be much more a part of the traditional warfare between good and evil than a special property of the protagonist. We should remember that "Something is rotten in the state of Denmark" (1.4.90), not just in Hamlet, who, after all, has not killed his father himself, despite the malicious promptings of Freudian critics. It is difficult to preserve a "sweet Prince" (5.2.360) in a rotten world, and the Ghost's injunction to his son, "Taint not thy mind" (1.5.85), is an impossible restraint. In terms of my emphasis, then—as emphasis implies conclusions—it should be clear that, like Kitto, I am actively convinced of the presence of evil in *Hamlet*, and that I feel no weakness, as Eliot did, in the "objective correlative."

To pursue this line of inquiry, I would like to evaluate briefly some of the implications of *Style in "Hamlet"* for an interpretation of the play. My reading of the imagery insists on a much more significant role for Claudius than has usually been accorded him, so that the structure of the play is seen as a conflict between "mighty opposites" (5.2.62), antagonist set against protagonist. We should not forget the adventure story on which *Hamlet* is based, in which we see how overwhelming are the forces against which Hamlet must struggle in order to achieve his revenge.

The imagery of animals, food, and gardens, like the imagery of disease, reveals something important about the world of the play, which is as much Claudius' world as Hamlet's. This imagery conveys a sense of a more gracious existence before the play began: Hamlet was "Th' expectancy and rose of the fair state" (3.1.155), Hamlet's father had "A station like the herald Mercury/New lighted on a heaven-kissing hill" (3.4.59-60), and he was "so loving" to Gertrude "That he might not beteem the winds of heaven/ Visit her face too roughly" (1.2.140-42). These are possibilities that are irretrievably lost—certainly never to be revived by the regime of Fortinbras anticipated at the end of the play. The imagery of limits helps to define this sense of restriction by claiming that man is like a god only "in apprehension" (2.2.315); in actuality, man is a "quintessence of dust" (317), horridly shaken with "thoughts beyond the reaches of our souls" (1.4.56).

The relation of style to dramatic character draws more directly on traditional notions of style as an individual form of expression. Style is the man, and in a play the writer must conscientiously provide the details that will differentiate one character from another. This is easiest to do according to the "humors" principle of Ben Jonson, in which caricature of a few leading traits and mannerisms replaces any extensive characterization. Hamlet is at an opposite pole from Morose in Jonson's *Epicene* (1609), whose insane aversion to noise provides the spring for his character. There is no such easy principle by which to grasp Hamlet; in fact, he has no single distinctive style, but is self-conscious, witty, passionate, and simple as the occasion demands. He uses these various styles to attack, explore, evaluate, and even play with the reality around him, and one of the conclusions we may draw from Hamlet's stylistic virtuosity is that he thinks of experience as a work of art that can only be mastered by aesthetic means. This interpretation works against any purely ethical understanding of what Hamlet is doing in the play. He refuses to kill Claudius in the act of praying, for example, in order to wait for a "more horrid hent" (3.3.88), and in the graveyard scene he comes out of hiding only to protest against Laertes' insufferable rant: "What is he whose grief/ Bears such an emphasis" (5.1.256-57). There is an overpowering aesthetic revulsion in that question.

I don't mean to claim Hamlet as an aesthete, but the customary moral analysis of his character fails to take account of his commitment to excellence of style. He praises an old Dido and Aeneas play that was "caviary to the general" (2.2.447), and he is constantly registering his disgust with the new tone and atmosphere of Claudius' Denmark. But there is a thin line that separates style from morality, and there are ethical implications in all of Hamlet's aesthetic judgments. The observation he sets down in his tables, "That one may smile, and smile, and be a villain" (1.5.108), applies equally well to Claudius' radiant platitudes as to his unctuous geniality. The contrast in Claudius and in Polonius between their fair outward show and their inner ruthlessness is made by identifiable aspects of style.

One moral-aesthetic postulate in this play, as in most of Shakespeare, is that the arts of rhetoric are associated with hypocrisy and disguise—Claudius' "most painted word" (3.1.53)—whereas simplicity of expression may be strong and willful, but it is also, conventionally, honest and sincere. The polished antitheses of the king's first speech in the play, offering a specious consolation to the grieving Hamlet—"With an auspicious and a dropping eye,/ With mirth in funeral, and with dirge in marriage" (1.2.11-12)—immediately identifies his shallow morality. Hamlet certainly uses "art," too, but his most eloquent speech in the play is the almost monosyllabic declaration just before the catastrophe: "If it be now, 'tis not to come; if it be not to come, it will be now; if it be not now, yet it will come. The readiness is all" (5.2.221-24). There is a consistent feeling in Shakespeare that this sort of bare and lucid style is most suitable to moments of the highest tragic intensity, as if any hint of embellishment would create a false tone in what the characters are saying.

Shakespeare places a special emphasis on the notion that a character may use different styles for different purposes. This involves more than the classical doctrine of decorum, since the changes in style seem to derive not from the playwright, but from the characters' own awareness of themselves as dramatis personae. This is particularly true of Hamlet himself, although both Claudius and Polonius seem to be able to switch quickly from a figurative and "witty" style to a direct and businesslike one. The self-conscious style of the play may be seen most literally in the allusions to art, acting, and the theater—what we may call Shakespeare's "professional" imagery. We are not allowed to forget that the

play itself is only "a fiction" and "a dream of passion"
(2.2.562), just as

> This wide and universal theatre
> Presents more woeful pageants than the scene
> Wherein we play in.
>
> (As You Like It 2.7.137-39)

Ultimately, a strong sense of style works against any
convincing sense of illusion. As audience, we are never
forced to surrender our own insistent awareness of the
play as a work of art. The self-consciousness of style
that pervades *Hamlet* serves both to suggest and to justify a critic's own self-conscious discussion of that style.

Index

actors and acting, 68, 137-50, 158, 159, 161, 166-68, 182, 216-20, 244-46, 250, 259-60, 263, 264-66, 276, 283, 285, 286, 290-91, 299, 309
Adams, Joseph Quincy, 183n, 188, 260
Aeneas speech, *see* Player's speech
Alexander, Peter, xi, 92n, 272n
Altick, Richard D., 54, 57n
Antony and Cleopatra, 61, 79, 83, 89-90, 104n, 123, 128, 132, 151-52, 168, 174, 183, 278, 303
Arden of Feversham, 9
Aristotle, 243, 244
Armstrong, Edward A., 57n
As You Like It, 56, 104n, 132, 186, 261, 291, 320
aside, 233-37

Babcock, Weston, 73n
Bacon, Francis, 45
Barnardo, 117, 165, 166-67, 180
Bartlett, John, xi, 133n
Beckerman, Bernard, 197n, 234n
Beckett, Samuel, 80
Belleforest, F. de, 51
Berry, Francis, 188n, 307
Bestrafte Brudermord, Der, 153, 275
Bethell, S. L., 152
Betti, Ugo, 194
Booth, Edwin, 192
Bowers, Fredson, 60n
Bradley, A. C., 27n, 73n, 215, 219, 299n
Brecht, Bertolt, 137
Burbage, Richard, 87, 168, 246n, 279, 313n
Burton, Robert, 82

Campbell, Lily B., 296n
Capell, Edward, 22n, 199
Chambers, E. K., 17n, 25n, 285n
characterization, xx, 13, 215-20, 317-18; nonpsychological, 40, 135, 152, 218-19, 236-37; by costume, 186-87; character analysis, 215-16, 219; by figures of speech, 231; by soliloquy, 304-5
Charney, Maurice, xix, 90n
Christian doctrine, 44, 88, 102, 108, 110n, 119, 120, 287, 292, 302-3; Doomsday, 10n, 83; Old Testament, 28, 57, 102, 105, 118, 131, 132, 185; sin, 34, 54, 102, 104-5, 123, 129-30, 238-39; heaven as "ordinant," 43, 50, 52, 84, 113, 122, 189, 217, 312-13; man's place in nature, 53, 54, 64, 74, 89, 112-13; devil, 83, 146; New Testament, 84, 241; atheism and blasphemy, 103, 228; "churlish priest," 110; infinite-finite, 114-15; Anglican catechism, 169
Clarke, C. C., 301n
Claudio (in *Hamlet*), 40, 52
Claudius, 10, 29, 121-23, 153, 186, 193-94, 200, 267, 316-17; sound effects, xx, 17-19; and Hamlet, 6, 11-12, 15, 16, 22-23, 31, 33, 37-38, 42-43, 47, 51-52, 64, 65, 67, 77-78, 87, 101, 115-17, 174, 218, 224, 225, 228, 230-31, 232, 236, 287, 312-13; and Laertes, 12-13, 42-43, 44, 48, 72, 74, 119, 131, 144-45, 180, 208, 223-24, 225-33, 234n, 236-37; and Iago, 13, 50, 58, 144, 232;

drinking, 17-18, 99-102; concern for appearances, 21-22, 56, 116-17, 193-94; poisoner, 23, 31, 34-37, 42-44; and brother, 24, 40, 82, 120; and Henry IV, 33; and *The Mousetrap*, 39-42; and Macbeth, 41, 43, 58, 102, 239-40, 241; plotter, 46, 47-48, 48n, 50-52, 144-45, 218; subtle and tough villain, 66, 69, 84-85, 120, 225, 239; physical description, 73-74, 91, 100, 115, 225; emphasis on action, 86, 122-23, 221-23, 227, 233; and Ophelia, 119-20; and Gertrude, 120, 194, 202, 230

style: 221-41, 254, 258, 286-87; embellished, 33, 221, 223, 224, 230-31, 238, 241, 298, 319; monosyllables, 42, 222, 231, 237, 241; soliloquies, 49-50, 57-58, 84-85, 118, 129-30, 233-34, 237-41, 294; lyric expatiation, 73, 233; antitheses, 86, 99, 222, 238-39, 319; images on parts of the body, 115, 120; similes, 177, 221, 228-29, 230-31, 238; colloquial, 221, 223-24, 231; simple, 221, 223, 227, 231-32, 237, 241; orations, 222, 224; in style of Polonius, 222-24; questions, 226-27, 233; broken discourse, 232-33; aside, 233-35, 237-38; in style of Hamlet, 240
Clemen, W. H., 4-6, 35-36, 102n, 304
Clown-gravedigger, 62-63, 78, 95, 127, 135-36, 146-47, 164, 185, 284, 294-95

Clutton-Brock, A., 10n
Coghill, Nevill, 151n
Coleridge, Hartley, 215
Coleridge, Samuel Taylor, xv, 264
Colie, Rosalie L., 293n
Collier, John Payne, 252n
Comedy of Errors, The, 148, 175-76
Comito, Terry Allen, 102n
Coriolanus, 21, 139
costume, 139, 157, 164, 172, 186-90, 193, 194, 197, 198; military uniform, 20; armor, 24-27; "nightgown," 26; "sea gown," 52, 189; "stockings fouled," 58; imagery, 143-46; "inky cloak," 145, 187; Osric's hat, 173, 190; pirate sailor, 218; shoes, 299
Cotgrave, Randle, 37, 120n, 189
couplets, 44, 134, 186, 187, 202, 203-6, 206-7n, 235, 240, 284-85, 287, 292, 296, 312
Craig, Hardin, 262n. *See also* Parrott, Thomas Marc
Crashaw, Richard, 97

Danby, John F., 112n
Davies, Tom, 192n
De Witt, Johannes, 121
Dekker, Thomas, xvii
delay as theme, xv-xvi, 314
Delius, Nicolaus, 94
Dido and Aeneas play, *see* Player's speech
Donne, John, 185
Doran, Madeleine, 258n
Dorius, R. J., 88n
Dowden, Edward, 296
drama as a genre, xx-xxi, 143, 159-60, 176, 177, 180n, 243-

44, 261, 308; transfer of roles, 33; calculation of characters' ages, 136; villain as actor, 144-45, 147, 232; cartharsis, 152-53; moral utility, 153; poetic drama, 158; narration, 163, 188, 307-10; relation to film art, 219; purposiveness, 286; departures from dialogue form, 297, 304-5
Dryden, John, 264
dumb show or pantomime, 39-41, 111, 147, 148, 157, 158, 162, 182-83, 183n, 194, 201, 245, 266
Dunn, Waldo H., 88n
Dymling, Carl Anders, 135n

Edwards, Philip, 284n
Eliot, T. S., 32, 316
Ellis-Fermor, Una, 221, 230n
Empson, William, 195n
Euripides, *Medea*, 180n

Fairchild, Arthur H. R., 137-38n, 138, 192n
Farmer, J. S., 25n, 92n
Fechter, Charles Albert, 192
Fergusson, Francis, 31-32n, 195n, 291
First Player, 28, 97, 142-43, 152, 166, 217, 243, 244-45, 259, 274, 295
Fitzgerald, F. Scott, 130
Florio, John, 120, 312
Foakes, F. A., 6n, 47, 54, 111n, 146n
Forker, Charles R., 150n
Fortinbras, 19-21, 28-29, 32, 37, 65, 75, 92, 125, 136, 177, 205, 222, 317
Fortinbras' Captain, 123

Frame, Donald M., 120n
Francisco, 84
Franklin, Benjamin, 99
Freiligrath, Ferdinand, xv
Frye, Roland Mushat, 110n
Furness, Horace Howard, 215. See also *Variorum Hamlet*

Garrick, David, 61, 168
Gascoigne, George, 194
Gellert, Bridget J., 82n
Gertrude, 10, 47, 168-69, 177-78, 186, 193-94, 202, 217, 225, 227, 277; conscience, 8, 59-60, 83, 105, 235-36; imperceptivity, 27-28, 36-37, 79-81, 146, 164; death, 43-44, 101; lust, 55-56, 59, 60, 79-80, 89-91; style, 80, 109, 206n, 236, 286-87; and Hamlet, 87-88, 107, 147, 167, 246, 282; and Cleopatra, 89-90; and Ophelia, 101, 108, 109-11, 180, 235, 235-36n; aside, 235-36, 237
gesture and stage action, 84, 115, 121, 145, 150, 157, 159-60, 161-76, 239, 265, 279-80, 282-83, 312-13
Ghost (in *Hamlet*), 59, 88, 91, 98, 126, 146, 194, 198, 203, 208-10; and Hamlet, 7, 15, 32, 53, 59, 104, 118-19, 126, 167-68, 169-70, 285, 305-7, 316; context for its entrances and exits, 18, 159-60, 164, 165-66, 180, 181, 200; in cellarage, 24, 117, 130, 165, 171-72; military figure, 24-27, 28, 29, 169; murder, 33-36, 39-40, 58, 76-77, 96, 97, 103, 130-31, 209; style, 33-34, 300n, 306; and Claudius, 73; otherworldly

associations, 82, 96, 113, 146; and Gertrude, 90, 105, 146, 164; purgatory, 98, 110n, 117-18, 168; sense of sin, 104-5; ubiquity, 170-72
Gielgud, John, 186
Globe theater, 17n, 121, 150-51, 157, 160, 195, 246n, 284, 315
Gold, J., 211n
Granville-Barker, Harley, 189, 196-97n, 201n, 223n, 234, 236n, 279n
Gravedigger, see Clown-grave-digger
Greg, W. W., 313n
Guildenstern, see Rosencrantz and Guildenstern

Hamlet, in its historical context, xvi, 186, 195; closet scene (3.4), 8, 26-28, 32n, 36-37, 56, 69, 79-81, 82, 85, 90-91, 104, 107, 120, 124, 138, 147, 149, 164, 166, 167-68, 179, 191-92, 202, 205, 235, 246, 282; prayer scene (3.3), 9-10, 14, 100, 104-5, 130-31, 240, 318; fencing match (5.2), 11-13, 18-19, 39, 48, 86-88, 172-73, 229, 236, 239, 279-80, 311; graveyard scene (5.1), 12, 16, 61-63, 95-96, 127-28, 163-64, 189, 203, 210-11; 273, 275-80, 294-95, 318; nunnery scene (3.1), 105-6, 128, 145-46; "without words," 158-60, 195; Danish allusions, 183
Hamlet, Folio (1623), xi, 33n, 178-79, 195, 273n, 299-300n; stage directions, 19, 20-21, 48, 112, 147, 157, 160n, 169, 178n, 178-79, 181, 182, 183, 184n, 187, 191, 202, 210, 217,

233-34n, 262; spellings, 27n; speech prefixes, 41n, 110n; act-scene divisions, 201; lineation, 218n; punctuation, 301n
readings: "affection," 263; "bitter business," 10n; "Fellow," 39; "handsaw," 66; "How, sweet queen," 180; "Lamound," 72n; "like an ape," 93n; "meant," 273n; "O, o, o, o," 313; "O, vengeance," 143; "paiocke," 68n; "politician," 161-62n; "rites," 110; "rots," 104n; "scullion," 269n; "solid," 60; "three thousand," 125; "tragical-historical, tragical-comical-historical-pastoral," 243; "winking," 45; "Yaughan," 95n, 284
Hamlet, Quarto 1 (1603), xi, 184, 195, 265, 275; stage directions, 26, 112, 158, 184, 279; speech prefixes, 41n; spellings, 66
readings: "godly Ballet," 185; "Tend'ring," 252n
Hamlet, Quarto 2 (1604), xi, 33n, 195, 273n, 275, 300n; stage directions, 18, 19, 112, 157, 159-60, 178n, 181, 182, 182n, 183, 184, 187, 202, 217, 233n; spellings, 21, 27n; speech prefixes, 41n, 69n, 110n; lineation, 218n; punctuation, 301n
readings: "affection," 263; "another man," 39; "bitter day," 10n; "But stay, what noise?" 180; "crants," 110; "dosie, dazzie," 273n; "handsaw," 66; "Hum," 218n;

"Lamord," 72n; "Ostricke," 69; "paiock," 68n; "pelican," 161-62n; "roots," 104n; "sallied," 60; "stallion," 269n; "threescore thousand," 125; "went," 273n

Hamlet, Quarto of 1676, 160n, 201

Hamlet, 29-30, 32, 191, 202, 215-16, 246n, 316-18; Romantic criticism of, xv-xvi, xx-xxii, 3, 30, 82-83, 296-97, 305, 316; swordsman, 7-12, 14, 87-88, 166; revenger, 8-11, 53, 58-59, 100-1, 267-70; aesthetic revulsion, 15-16, 62, 131, 274, 276, 318; death and military funeral, 19-21, 147, 313; magnanimity and honor, 19, 47-48, 124; madness, 44, 51, 66, 162, 187-89, 246-47, 282-83, 286, 289-92; melancholy, 53, 55, 75, 82-83, 136, 150-51, 159; moral questioning, 74, 79-80; tragic foreboding, 83-84, 275, 311-12; physical description, 87-88, 167-68; constraint, 115-17; regeneration, 122, 189; dramatic chronology, 135-36, 210-11; costume, 145, 187-89

relation to other characters: Claudius, 6, 11-12, 16, 23, 31, 33, 38-39, 42-43, 48n, 51-52, 55, 66, 67, 68-69, 73-74, 77-78, 90, 93-94, 99, 101, 104-5, 121, 130-31, 147, 187, 218, 225, 240, 259, 267, 275, 278, 280-81, 287-88, 291, 292-94, 297-98, 318; Laertes, 11, 47, 127, 258, 275-80, 318; Ophelia, 15, 105-6, 108, 131, 145-46, 148-49, 199, 260; Gertrude, 16, 27n, 36, 79-81, 90-91, 104, 105, 132, 164, 179, 282; Rosencrantz and Guildenstern, 23-24, 66, 92-93, 114, 124, 125, 140, 150-51, 169, 174-75, 183-84, 281-82, 290, 292-93, 308; Ghost, 33, 45, 67, 81, 85, 118-19, 130, 142, 146, 150, 162, 164, 167-68, 169-70, 171-72, 261, 282-83, 292, 296, 305-7; Polonius, 42, 70, 94-95, 123, 127, 142, 149-50, 150-51, 166, 262, 289-90, 290-91, 292-93; Clown-gravedigger, 62-63, 127, 294-95; Horatio, 70, 86-87, 93, 99, 119, 170, 175, 200, 266, 270-71, 291, 306, 308-10, 312; Osric, 173, 260, 271, 272-75

style: 221, 258-313, 317-18; theatrical and artistic interests, 40-41, 128, 134n, 142, 149, 153, 162, 218, 244-45, 258-67, 291-92; songs, 68, 184-86, 284, 292; monosyllables, 84, 305, 310, 312, 319; poetic artifice, 84, 260; ranting, 127-28, 268, 269, 276-79; puns and wordplay, 149, 251-52, 265, 286-89; parody, 169, 186, 271-85, 286, 291-92; couplets, 204-6; in style of Claudius, 240, 269; Polonius as critic of, 242-43, 244; self-conscious, 258, 267-85, 309, 319; passionate, 264, 295-305; colloquial, 270, 277, 283, 292, 300, 307, 308-9, 310-11; repetition, 271, 299-300, 305; witty, 286-95; breaks in syntax, 299, 310-11; simple, 305-13, 319

soliloquies: 8-9, 21, 237, 270, 296-305; "rogue and peasant slave" (2.2), 34, 142-

43, 152-53, 166, 267-70, 295;
"To be, or not to be" (3.1),
49, 67, 83, 88, 126-27, 131,
234, 301-4; "too too solid
flesh" (1.2), 56, 60, 84, 103,
297-301; "How all occasions"
(4.4), 124, 199
Hapgood, Robert, 314n
Harbage, Alfred, xi-xii, 263n
Hardy, Thomas, 4
Hart, Alfred, xviii
Hazlitt, William, xv, xxi, xxii
Heilman, Robert Bechtold, xix
1 Henry IV, 72, 78, 92, 256, 273
2 Henry IV, 33, 56, 87, 126,
249, 256
Henry V, 59n, 149, 159, 174,
193, 196
2 Henry VI, 133
Henry VIII, 56
Henslowe, Philip, 111
heraldry, 14, 97
Herrick, Robert, 143
Heywood, Thomas, 153
Hilliard, Nicholas, 192
Hodges, C. Walter, 151n
Holmes, Martin, 157, 192n
Horatio, 20, 69, 113, 181, 235,
274; and Hamlet, 7, 84, 86-
87, 93, 119, 136, 147-48, 170,
179, 260, 266, 270-71, 275,
280, 303, 309-10, 312; and
Ghost, 24, 82, 160, 166-67,
169, 170-71, 181; and pirate
sailor, 217-18
Hosley, Richard, 121n
Hubler, Edward, xi, 10n, 60n,
68n, 93n, 95n, 218n, 252n,
269n, 273n

imagery, in criticism of Shakespeare, xviii-xix, 3, 31; em-

blematic, 28, 41, 122, 253;
multiple subjects, 35-36; reversibility, 37, 38-39, 77-78;
literal versus symbolic uses,
75-76; associative links, 92,
261; properties as a presentational imagery, 190-91
  subjects: animals, 18, 43,
45, 51, 54, 55, 63-74, 89, 90-
95, 106, 113, 161, 161-62n,
181, 185-86, 190, 253, 277-78,
278-79, 290, 292; armor, 24-
28; art, acting, and the theater, 137-53, 319-20; breath,
85-87; card-playing, 48, 61;
confinement, 115-23; corruption, 3, 53-113, 317; death, 60-
63, 65, 71, 84, 94-95; disease,
3-5, 35-39, 54, 55, 59, 63, 75-
88, 89, 100, 103, 315-16;
drinking, 95, 96, 99-102;
falconry, 66-68; food and eating, 35, 54, 65, 70, 89-99, 288;
foulness, 58-59; gardens, 34,
54, 56, 57, 102-13; heart, 83-
85; hunting and angling, 33,
64-66; limits, 114-36, 317;
milk, 96-97, 295; money and
numbers, 123-36, 252, 273-74;
poison, 12-13, 22, 23, 32, 34-
36, 39-44, 73, 76-77, 82, 87, 96,
97, 121; prison, 115, 117-18;
rankness, 55-58, 105; secrecy
and concealment, 31-34, 36-
39, 41, 44-47, 51-52, 58; smells,
33, 53-54, 57-58, 62, 71, 95-96;
soiling and tainting, 53, 59-
60, 108; sword, 7-15, 47-48,
166; violet, 106-8, 109; war,
weapons, and explosives, 6-
30, 81, 171, 177-78, 315-16
Ingegnieri, Angelo, 146n

Jacquot, Jean, 121n
Jenkins, Harold, 178-79n, 300n, 313n
Johnson, S. F., 189n, 246n
Johnson, Samuel, 10, 33n, 69, 100, 201-2, 230n, 247-48, 289
Jonson, Ben, xvii, 149, 207, 271, 317
Jorgensen, Paul A., 37n
Joseph, B. L., 162n
Joseph, Sister Miriam, 272
Julius Caesar, xvii-xviii, 18, 20, 26, 64, 65, 178, 246, 312
Jump, John D., 300n
justice as theme, 41, 50-51, 131-32
Juvenal, 262

King James I and Queen Anne of Denmark, 183
King John, 138, 183
King Lear, xix, 54, 71, 73, 74, 89, 103, 107, 110, 112-13, 272, 298, 311, 312, 312n, 313n
Kitto, H.D.F., 31n, 84, 316
Kittredge, George Lyman, xii, 33n, 88n, 107n, 134n, 153n, 169n, 284n
Knight, G. Wilson, 54
Knights, L. C., 32n, 53n, 215-16
Kökeritz, Helge, xi, 60n, 94n, 104n, 293n
Kott, Jan, 157
Kyd, Thomas, *The Spanish Tragedy*, 112, 186, 284-85, 302

Laertes, xvi, 70, 190, 232, 273-74, 277; revenger, 9, 29, 59, 267; and Hamlet, 11-12, 64, 127-28, 132, 136, 236-37, 275-80; swordsman, 12-13, 35, 72, 76-77; and Ophelia, 16-17, 72,

81, 106-7, 131-33, 185, 293; and Claudius, 22, 42-43, 48, 50, 72, 133, 161-62, 225-33; style, 81, 128, 131-33, 161, 258, 276, 318; rebellion, 116, 121, 133, 177-79, 208, 225-29; and Polonius, 129, 162n, 248, 257; aside, 235, 236-37
Lamb, Charles, xxi, xxii
Langbaum, Robert, 297n
Lawrence, William J., 25n, 170n, 180n, 181n, 192n
Levin, Harry, vii, 13n, 185n, 206n, 226, 290n, 299n
Lodge, Thomas, 285
Love's Labour's Lost, 123, 144, 149-50, 238, 243, 272-73
Lucianus, 34, 40-41, 82, 266, 285

Macbeth, xix, 30, 41, 43, 58, 81, 92n, 96, 101, 102, 112-13, 114, 122, 129, 140-41, 146n, 181, 183, 193, 215, 239-40, 241, 285, 294
McManaway, James G., 181n
Macquoid, Percy, 190n
Mahood, M. M., 49n, 78n, 286n
Manley, Frank, 185n
Marcellus, 7, 66, 113, 117, 169, 170-71, 175, 179
Marlowe, Christopher, 14, 134n, 144, 263n, 300
Marston, John, 190, 290
Maxwell, J. C., 88n
Measure for Measure, 34, 40, 70-71
Mehl, Dieter, 183n
Merchant of Venice, The, 15, 55, 109, 111-12, 138, 139-40
Merry Wives of Windsor, The, xvii, 55, 277
Midsummer Night's Dream, A,

111, 140, 147, 216-17, 279
Milton, John, 272
Montaigne, Michel Eyquem de, 120n, 312
Morozov, Mikhail M., 219n
Muir, Kenneth, xviii-xix, 4-7, 36n
Murder of Gonzago, The, or The Mousetrap, 8, 15, 38, 39-42, 65-66, 71, 126, 134-35, 141, 149, 182, 183n, 185-86, 194, 206n, 235, 237, 259, 266-67, 284, 285, 292
music, xx, 157, 181-86; Claudius' rouse, 17-18, 183; "soldiers' music," 20-21; songs, 68, 184-86; trumpets, 157, 182-83, 198; oboes, 182-83; recorders, 183-84; jig, 245
mythology, Greek and Roman, Centaurs, 73, 100; Corybantes, 100; Dido, 109; Fortuna, 25, 115, 126; Hercules, 278-79; Jupiter, Jove, 18, 68, 69; Mars, 69; Mercury, 69; Odysseus, 210; river Lethe, 104; satyrs, 100; Vulcan, 59. *See also* Player's speech

Nares, Robert, 288n
Nashe, Thomas, 9-10, 263n
nature, *see* Christian doctrine
Newell, Alex, 301n
Nicoll, Allardyce, 146n
Norton, Thomas, and Thomas Sackville, *Gorboduc*, 182-83, 201
Nungezer, Edwin, 279n

Ophelia, 7, 100, 199-200, 251-52, 255-56; and Hamlet, 15, 29-30, 44-46, 81-82, 86, 93, 126, 162-63, 185, 187-88, 206n, 262; military imagery, 16-17; flowers, 57, 83, 106-11; death and funeral, 70-71, 101, 107-9, 180, 203, 275-76, 279-80; style, 93, 108, 126, 206n, 298n; madness, 107-10, 119-20, 158, 167, 178-79, 184, 185, 227, 235-36n, 302; constraint, 119-20, 298n
Osric, 19; bird imagery, 69; social ceremony, 173, 174; costume, 190; style, 243, 252, 260, 264, 271, 272-75, 281, 311
Østerberg, V., 135n
Othello, xix, 13, 20, 48, 50, 57-58, 103-4, 109, 113, 144, 147, 232, 270, 288, 308

painting, 137-40, 191-92
Papp, Joseph, 21
Parrott, Thomas Marc (ed. *Hamlet*, Quarto 2, with Hardin Craig), xii, 10n, 34n, 92n, 104n, 110n, 162n, 244n, 269n, 273n
Partridge, Eric, 288n
Pearn, B. R., 183n
Pericles, 196
Phialas, Peter G., 189n
Pirandello, Luigi, 194
pirate sailors (in *Hamlet*), 52, 189, 217-18
Plato, 138
Plautus, 148, 244
Player King, 23, 34, 39-41, 43, 51, 88, 111, 112, 134, 135, 149, 194, 296, 302-3
Player Queen, 40, 99, 134-35, 136, 158, 194, 206n, 236, 295
Player's speech, 13-15, 28, 34,

97-98, 128, 141, 152-53, 217, 244-45, 259, 262-64, 284, 295, 307; Pyrrhus, 13-15, 97-98, 135, 267; Hecuba, 14-15, 97, 98, 217; Priam, 14-15, 96-97, 295

Poel, William, 109n, 189

Polonius, 41n, 142, 166, 184, 186, 199-200, 203, 246n, 256, 260; death, 7, 10, 42, 46, 60-61, 71, 80, 94-95, 142, 149-50, 166, 277, 292-93; precepts, 13, 16, 119, 128-29, 190, 200, 248-49; and Ophelia, 16, 251-53, 254-56; and Claudius and Gertrude, 41, 163, 200, 234, 256-57; eavesdropping, 44-46; and Laertes, 59, 65, 277; and Hamlet, 64-65, 80, 151, 159, 256, 259, 262, 289-90; *style*: 221, 242-57, 318; complex syntax, 44, 204-5; orator and rhetorician, 45, 163, 246-48, 255, 257; imagery, 124, 128-29, 253; theatrical interests, 149-50, 244-46; literary and dramatic criticism, 242-44; in relation to Hamlet, 242-43, 251, 289-90; self-awareness of his art, 246-48, 255; excessive fullness, 247-51; simple and brief, 247, 253-55; colloquial, 248, 251, 255-57; Polonius as *senex*, 248-51, 256-57, 290

Prosser, Eleanor, 10n, 101n, 189n

proverbs, 50n, 53, 54, 56, 64, 66, 70, 71, 77-78, 126, 127

puns and wordplay: "abominably," 265; "act, action," 144, 145, 146-47, 158, 200; "*afar*," 210-11; "affront," 46; "air-heir," 94; "antic-antique," 14; "arms," 11, 13-14; "art," 246-47; "as-ass," 281; "beautified," 242-43; "blast," 81-82; "blown," 82, 105; "bound," 118-19; "brave, bravery," 143, 269, 277; "brute-Brutus," 149; "cannon-canon," 21; "capital-Capitol," 149; "close," 44, 46; "coil," 49; "common," 286-87; "comply," 173, 175; "contracted," 120; "core," 271; "counterfeit," 138-39; "country," 245; "cousin-cozen," 287-88; "crafts," 33; "crammed," 94; "cunning," 153; "damnable," 266; "dearly," 252; "diet of worms," 94; "disclosed," 106; "dismantled," 68-69; "double," 129, 238; "draw toward an end," 60-61; "ear," 82; "edge," 262; "enactures," 149; "encounter," 45-46; "enginer," 23; "fares," 93; "fine," 264; "fool-Fool," 142; "free," 125, 238; "gently," 265; "giantlike," 226; "gilded," 130; "globe-Globe," 150; "hoist," 23-24; "idle," 291; "lets," 7; "lively," 139; "loose," 45-46; "modesty," 263; "moor-Moor," 91; "mute," 147; "naked," 52; "nothing-noting," 293n; "numbers," 131; "offense," 39, 57; "opened," 38; "packing," 61, 269; "part," 147, 149-50; "passion, passionate," 264, 277, 295-96; "perform, performance," 145; "petar," 24; "physic," 55;

"play," 145; "plot," 147-48; "plurisy-pleurisy," 22, 85-86; "politic," 94; "practice," 47-48; "privates," 126; "put on," 143; "questionable," 146; "quietus," 131; "rank," 55-58; "relief," 84; "remembrance," 125-26; "render," 98; "root, rot, rut," 104n; "secure," 119; "seems-seams," 288; "shadow," 114, 139-41, 151; "shape," 144-46; "show," 145, 147, 148-49, 187; "shuffling," 47, 48-50; "sized-o'ersizèd," 135; "tender," 251-53; "topped," 72; "touch," 77; "tropically-trapically," 65-66; "union," 43-44; "virgin crants-Rosencrantz," 110-11; "where," 235-36n; "Wittenberg," 94; "word," 126. *See also* words

Rann, Joseph, 33n
Ratsey, Gamaliel, 9
Raysor, Thomas Middleton, 264n
revenge conventions, xviii, 9-15, 53, 88, 267-69, 285, 296
Reynaldo, 200, 249-51
Reynolds, George Fullmer, 111n
rhetorical figures and devices, 232, 243-44, 246-48, 272-75, 299-300, 305, 309, 311, 318-19; metaphor, xix, 27, 54, 80, 85, 87, 115; invidious comparison, 14, 134n; conceit, 16, 97, 101, 222, 295; oration, 45, 222, 224, 246-48; oxymoron, 99; "pathetic fallacy," 110; hyperbole, 132-33, 133-34n, 276-79; paradox, 140, 222,

238, 241, 293; heightening, 224, 307, 311; interrogation, 226-27, 233; simile, 228-29, 230-31; cacozelia, 272; incredulous repetition, 300
Ribner, Irving, 189n
Richard II, 8, 54, 67, 97-98, 102-3, 108, 110, 173-74, 183, 223
Richard III, 40, 73, 139, 158, 288
Richards, Irving T., 301n
Rickert, R. T., 111n
Righter, Anne, 137n
Robinson, Clement, 107
Romeo and Juliet, 11, 77, 109, 196, 207, 242, 251
Rosencrantz and Guildenstern, 24-25, 110-11, 114, 130, 136, 140, 200, 258, 281-82; deaths, 12; agents of Claudius, 15, 23, 38, 48, 64, 92-93, 100, 115, 117, 125-26, 127, 174-75, 179, 203, 308
Rossi, Ernesto, 192
Rowe, Nicholas, 26, 192n, 199, 201

Sade, Marquis de, 241
Sartre, Jean-Paul, 121
Saxo Grammaticus, 51
Schmidt, Alexander, xii, 79, 80
Schoenbaum, S., xi-xii, 263n
Scoloker, Anthony, 188
Second Clown (in *Hamlet*), 127
self-consciousness, 39, 50, 137, 141-53, 258, 319-20
Seltzer, Daniel, 272n
Seneca, 97, 244, 307
Seng, Peter J., 182n, 184n
Sewell, Arthur, 197n
Shakespeare, William, Roman

plays, xix; actor, 25; English history plays, 30, 193; early comedies, 203, 294; and Seneca, 307

Shepard, Warren V., 50n

Sherbo, Arthur, 10n

Shirley, Frances Ann, 17n, 180n

Sieveking, A. Forbes, 72n

Simpson, Percy, 111n

Simpson, Richard, 285

Sisson, C. J., 104n, 244n, 252n

Skeat, Walter W., 288n

soliloquy, xxi, 233-34, 235, 237-41, 270, 296-305

Sonnets (of Shakespeare): XV, 148; XVI, 138; LXXIII, 122; CXI, 53

Sophocles, *Oedipus*, 31-32

sound effects, xx, 157, 177-81; cannonading and firing of weapons, 17-21; offstage, 18, 19, 170, 178-79; under the stage, 171-72; bells, 179-80; crowing of the cock, 181

Southern, Richard, 197n

Spencer, Hazleton, 192n

Spencer, T.J.B., xv n, 124n

Spevack, Marvin, xi, 258n

Sprague, Arthur Colby, 168

Spurgeon, Caroline F. E., 3-6, 36, 53-54, 69-70, 91n

stage properties, xix, 157, 163, 190-95; sword, 7-15; "tables," 45, 191, 261-62; skulls, 62, 295; portraits, 80, 124, 138, 191-92; "napkin," 87; flowers, 108-11; flower bank, 111-12; arbor, 112; gifts, 126, 194-95; books and writings, 191, 245, 262; royal properties, 193-94; throne, 193, 198

staging, xvi, 157-60, 172-73, 202, 207; under the stage, 7, 165,

171-72; arras, 11, 44, 45-46, 192n; "chambers" or cannon, 17-19; "stage" or dais, 20; traps, 25, 157, 165-66, 170, 280; torches, 41-42; doors, 121, 164, 165, 169, 178, 198; "Swan drawing," 121; masques, 141, 171; private theaters, 141; supernumeraries, 147, 233-34n; "shadow," 151; stage directions, 157-61, 210-11; editorial staging, 161, 197; "fright wig," 168; blood, 173

scenes and uses: military procession, 20-21; metaphorical uses, 41-42; representation of time, 41-42, 95, 175, 181, 198, 207-11, 244; eavesdropping, 44-47, 246; fencing match, 48, 101, 172-73; removal of corpses, 60, 157-58; social ceremony, 101, 173-76, 187; Ghost, 146, 170-72; royal scenes, 157, 183, 192-94, 198; representation of place, 163-64, 165, 171, 196-99, 244; "covering" lines, 164-66, 171, 172, 262; Laertes' rebellion, 177-78; relation to art of movie, 197-98; interior and exterior scenes, 198-99; prayer scene (3.3), 240; "apart" convention, 275; Hamlet and Laertes in Ophelia's grave, 279-80

Steevens, George, 10n, 19n

Sternfeld, F. W., 182n

Stone, George Winchester, Jr., 61n

structure, 42, 196-211, 236-37, 263; symmetry of beginning, middle, and end, 39, 75, 193;

ironic reversal, 43, 50-51, 101, 240; five acts, 200-3; scene-ending couplets, 203-6, 206-7n; "bridge" scenes, 207-9

Styan, J. L., 261n

style, 311, 317-18; as approach to Shakespeare, xvi-xvii, 176, 177; "Roman," xvii-xviii; archaic, 134, 206n, 284; moral implications, 271-72, 318

Taming of the Shrew, The, 182

Tempest, The, 216

Theobald, Lewis, 159, 161, 199, 244

Thiselton-Dyer, William T., 34n

Thorp, Margaret Farrand, 138n

Tilley, Morris Palmer, xii, 50n, 53, 56, 71, 72n, 88n, 126n, 127, 194, 265n

Timon of Athens, 85, 124n, 138-39, 158-59, 283n

topical allusions, 67-68, 150, 183, 246n, 259, 262-63, 283-84

tragic effect, 30, 31-33, 42, 47-48, 50-51, 56, 75, 84, 101-2, 113, 122-23, 132, 148, 152-53, 173, 232, 239-40, 257, 271, 307, 311-13, 319

Travers, R., xii, 24, 68n, 183n, 190n

Traversi, D. A., 32n

Troilus and Cressida, 28-29, 69, 91, 130, 141, 158, 184, 196, 249, 262, 272

True Tragedy of Richard III, The, 285

Twelfth Night, 303

Two Gentlemen of Verona, The, 163, 194-95, 242

Ur-Hamlet, 25, 285

Van Buchell, Arend, 121n

Van Laan, Thomas F., 50n

Variorum Hamlet, xii, 10n, 23n, 27n, 37n, 86n, 94n, 100n, 109n, 120n, 135n, 153n, 183n, 189n, 192n, 199n, 262n, 282n

Warhaft, Sidney, 60n

Warning for Faire Women, A, 25

Webster, John, 190

Weiss, Samuel A., 60n

Whetstone, George, 71

Whitman, Walt, 135

Wilson, John Dover, xii, 10n, 11, 27n, 34n, 49n, 60n, 62, 69n, 78, 86n, 92, 110n, 125n, 172-73, 182, 188n, 244n, 269n, 285n, 299n, 301n, 313n

Wine, M. L., 190n

words, xi, xvi, xviii; Latinate diction, 14, 224; technical versus general senses, 23-24, 141-50; "policy" words, 47-50; "o'er" prefix, 133, 133-34n; terms of art, 137-41; ink-hornism, 272-75

   demonstratives: "thus," 161-63; "this-that, these-those," 163; "here-there," 163-64; "look, look you," 164

   discussed in text: "appe-tite," 89-90; "blister," 79; "blood," 80; "brazed," 27n; "canker," 78; "cap-a-pe," 24-25; "card," 294; "carriages," 274; "chanson," 185; "closet," 27; "discretion," 244; "dozy," 273; "equivocation," 294;

"fat," 85, 87-88; "foh," 269-70; "foul," 58-59; "gorge," 95-96; "gross," 56-57; "heartache," 83; "hebona," 34; "impawned," 252, 275; "imposthume," 37; "liberty," 244; "long purples," 57n, 110; "machine," 260; "mallecho," 291-92; "mobled," 243; "pith," 99-100; "posset," 96;

"prate," 277; "puzzles," 303; "rant," 276-77; "readiness," 122; "reechy," 59; "replication," 282; "rhapsody," 120; "scene," 196-97; "stuck," 42; "taint," 59-60; "tetter," 76; "thereunto," 280; "thrift," 70, 98-99, 129; "upspring," 100. *See also* puns and wordplay